Best Food Writing
2001

Best Food Writing 2001

EDITED BY

Holly Hughes

Marlowe & Company
New York

BEST FOOD WRITING 2001

Compilation and introductions copyright © 2001 by Holly Hughes
and Avalon Publishing Group Incorporated

Published by
Marlowe & Company
A Division of Avalon Publishing Group Incorporated
161 William Street
16th floor
New York, NY 10038

A Balliett & Fitzgerald book

Book Design: Susan Canavan

Photography: Tessa Traeger

Library of Congress Cataloging-in-Publication Data is available.

ISBN: 1-56924-577-0

9 8 7 6 5 4 3

Printed in the United States of America
Distributed by Publishers Group West

Contents

Stocking the Larder

Home Cooking

Someone's in the Kitchen

Food Fights

Personal Tastes

Introduction
by Holly Hughes

There have been days when I could swear that the publication of our debut anthology, *Best Food Writing 2000,* marked a turning point for the profession of writing about food. Look at the signs: A glossy scholarly journal, *Gastronomica: The Journal of Food and Culture,* commenced publication this year. The Modern Library Food series was launched to reprint culinary classics by masters such as Henri Charpentier, Laura Shapiro, and Eduoard De Pomiane. And several food books skipped onto the best-seller lists—Anthony Bourdain's *Kitchen Confidential* (which made it into last year's edition), Eric Schlosser's searing exposé *Fast Food,* Ruth Reichl's fascinating *Comfort Me with Apples,* Michael Pollan's *The Botany of Desire,* and Peter Mayles' *French Lessons*—all of which proved that you don't have to write a cookbook or a diet book to sell truckloads of copies to the food-obsessed American public.

Was it just my imagination, or was the news media obsessed with food this year, too? Our meat supply appeared threatened by mad cow disease and hoof-and-mouth disease, with E. coli and salmonella fears still haunting the background. The Slow Food movement gained ground, while the fast food industry came under attack (devout Hindi were scandalized to learn that they had been eating McDonald's french fries that had had beef flavorings added). While some consumer advocates raised a red flag over genetically modified crops, others protested government proposals to block U.S. imports of raw milk products (including some of our favorite foreign cheeses). Even organic food began to fall under scrutiny: Is, for example, milk from organically fed cows really safer than commercial dairy milk if it has been subjected to ultra-pasteurization for longer shelf life?

In the "foodie" world, the running conversation centered on this year's food fashions. Comfort food countered fussy fusion cooking, architectural plate presentations peaked with foam concoctions, each fad succeeding another in bewildering rapidity. Chefs in quest of the new new thing experimented with raw food, tobacco, and organ meats. Foie gras accompanied everything. The idea of "heirloom" fruits and vegetables took root like kudzu.

All in all, however, it has been a pleasure to spend the past twelve months poring over food magazines, web sites, local newspaper's food sections, dining columns in weekly and monthly magazines, and what used to be called the cookbook section of the bookstore (I am particularly grateful for the excellent Kitchen Arts and Letters in Manhattan, where you can find just about every book about food you ever wanted). What seemed like a profusion of fine prose in 2000 turned into a positive deluge in 2001, e-mailed, messengered, and snail-mailed to me from skilled practitioners of the craft all over the country. My only regret is that there wasn't room for all the delightful pieces I found when it came time to making the final selection. This field is packed with writers who, like poets, make you taste the food they're describing, feel its texture and smell its fragrance; like the best travel writers, they really put you into the settings where they've eaten; like novelists, they tell the story of a kitchen session or a night of dining out with all its dramatic ramifications. Indeed, a number of the writers in this year's collection are also well-known novelists, playwrights, or non-fiction writers (notably Michael Lewis, Jeffrey Eugenides, and David Sedaris). Renowned as these authors may be, however, they certainly have to be at the top of their game to win a place alongside full-time food writers like John Thorne, Amanda Hesser, Colman Andrews, Jeffrey Steingarten, or Ruth Reichl. The ones I most marvel at, however, are that curious little club of folks who manage to be gifted writers as well as chefs—Patric Kuh, Greg Atkinson, and Gabrielle Hamilton being this year's class. To do not one but two things better than the rest of us rank amateurs—it's just not fair.

As I've worked on this book, dining out has become a much more intensely colored experience for me. It's true that reading *Kitchen Confidential* made me pause before ordering seafood on a Saturday night or risking the hollandaise sauce on my eggs Benedict at Sunday brunch, but I also now appreciate the workmanship in a perfectly assembled meal on a plate, knowing what frenzy goes on behind those swinging kitchen doors. Luckily, since nearly every top-drawer food writer had to write up Alain Ducasse's breathlessly awaited new Manhattan restaurant, I now feel as if I have already eaten there, without having to spend a penny. It isn't all a question of high-end dining, though, by any means. Plenty of the food writers whose work I enjoyed most this year weren't reviewing gourmet establishments, but cruising diners and coffee shops and storefront ethnic restaurants— even, as in the case of Robb Walsh in his piece "The Inkblot Test," finding a key to one's own psyche in a preference for a certain kind of restaurant.

Shopping for produce seems more like an adventure now, as I pay increased attention to where each food was grown and what the season is. Why buy California strawberries when I live in New York, it's late June, and New Jersey blueberries are at their sweet peak? My reading this year has widened my appreciation of radishes, beet greens, and pears, just to name three things. It wouldn't be fair to say that my interest in asparagus was reawakened—it's always been one of my favorite foods—but after reading David Nussbaum's "Hadley Grass," I ate steamed asparagus every night for a week (I didn't even urge my children to try some—I wanted it all for myself).

And as for cooking—well, there were days when I'd just been reading about some master chef's triumphs and I didn't feel worthy to lift a spatula, but there were also days when something I'd read made me long to bring the aroma of baking bread or the comforting burble of a simmering soup kettle to my own kitchen. In fact, what I'm going to do right now is make myself a tuna-salad sandwich, inspired equally by James Villas' "Ode on a Can of Tuna" and Alan Brown's "The White Album." And if I'm lucky, I'll find a couple stalks of celery to go with it (inspired by Dorothy Kalins's "Crunch"). And afterward, start reading for next year's collection.

Stocking
the
Larder

Toro, Toro, Toro

by Jeffrey Steingarten
from *Vogue*

It's worth subscribing to *Vogue* just to read Jeffrey Steingarten's monthly food articles—hearty appreciations of the art of eating well. In this installment, he takes us on a wild ride in search of fresh tuna.

A**ft here, drive 'em aft," I shouted. "Call all hands! Man the capstan! Lower away . . . and after him!"

I stood before the mirror in my bedroom, admiring my new outfit and rehearsing the handful of nautical phrases I had collected from my dog-eared copy of *Moby Dick*. Soon I would be jetting toward Ensenada on the Pacific Coast of Baja California, where I would set out upon an epic hunt for . . . the giant bluefin!

Why the bluefin? Simply because the raw meat from its belly is one of the most delicious things on Earth. Isn't that enough?

Bluefin are tunas, one of about thirteen species, depending on who is doing the counting. They are among nature's most perfectly designed creatures. They are among the largest (1,800 pounds appears to be the record) and the fastest (capable of bursts as high as 56 miles an hour) fish in the sea. Bluefin are able to navigate from Japan to California and back, from the Caribbean to Norway—they have binocular vision, acute hearing, sensors in their skin for pressure and temperature, and magnetic particles in their body that are thought to act as compasses. They are astonishingly streamlined, with hollows into which their fins retract and flatten at high speeds. Their bodies are 75 percent muscle. From birth until death, bluefin can never stop moving forward. If they did, they would die of suffocation. Bluefin are hungry predators, consuming up to 25 percent of their weight each day in sardines, squid, herring, and other living treats. They hunt like wolves, in deadly packs, which we call "schools" to make them seem cuter.

Bluefin are also the most valuable wild animals on Earth.

I have read that the world record for one giant bluefin is $83,500, set in 1992 at Tsukiji, the world's largest central wholesale market in Tokyo. This comes to nearly $120 a pound. I've read higher numbers since 1992. More typical auction prices these days at Tsukiji (pronounced "skee gee") range from $15 to $40 a pound, a weakness ascribed to Japan's current economic problems. The daily auctions at Tsukiji set the world prices for bluefin, because the Japanese are prepared to pay more than anybody else for its flesh. Go to www.fis-net.com/fis/species, choose Tuna as the species, click on Market Prices, scroll down to Bluefin, and you can follow bluefin prices throughout Japan whenever you're curious. I am always curious.

The price of a bluefin depends on its size, freshness, and shape (it should be roughly football-shaped, with a swelling underside). Most important is the quality of its flesh, especially the amount and grade of toro—the meat from its tender, fatty belly. Bluefin experts at Tsukiji carry a sashibo, a long, thin, hollow metal rod that can be plunged under the gills and right through the fish to extract a sample of its meat, layer by layer, like a geological core.

The upper half of the body consists of rich, shiny red meat called akami, of which the middle section, the naka, is of the highest quality. Between the upper body and the belly is a dark, bloody muscle called the chiai, which many people will not eat, though my dog, Sky King, has no compunctions. Nearly all the toro is found in the belly, which gets fattier, more delicate, and more sought after the nearer it is to the head. The middle and tail sections of the belly are medium-grade toro, chu-toro. Right behind the gills is the kama, perhaps the choicest cut on the entire bluefin, although among some connoisseurs, just the masticatory muscle is an object of profound gastronomic worship. I had some the other day and found it a bit sinewy. Some bluefin also have a rare and valuable form of toro near the bones on their dorsal side, the upper body, called se-toro. I may have tasted se-toro at a little dump of a sushi place in Santa Monica, but I'm not sure.

Two thin little rectangles of o-toro at a top sushi place in this country will cost you $20, in Tokyo much more. That is why I have never been able to eat enough toro for complete satisfaction.

The Japanese are not alone in their love of tuna belly. I have an Italian bluefin map from 1919. It shows the vetresca or sorra bianca, the fatty belly, and above it, where the Japanese chutoro lies, is the Italian tarantello. And the part of the belly just behind the head—the fattiest and most valuable— appears to be called pendini or spuntatore. Things have not changed much since Pliny the Elder wrote in his *Natural History*, in the first century: "The choicest parts are the neck and the white flesh of the belly, and the throat, provided they are fresh. . . . ; the parts from near the jaw are the most sought after."(Ahi, which you see

listed with pride on most American menus these days, is yellowfin tuna, which the Japanese consider inferior not only to
bluefin but also to southern bluefin, bigeye, and albacore, and
just ahead of skipjack.)

Where were you when you first tasted o-toro? I was in Los
Angeles, ten years ago, sitting at the counter of Ginza Sushiko, a
very fine sushi restaurant then in a little strip mall on Wilshire.
The chef, Mass Takayama, placed two smooth pink rectangles of
fish on my plate, and I took one into my mouth, unaware that
this, at last, was toro. At first it was like having a second tongue
in my mouth, a cooler one, and then the taste asserted itself, rich
and delicately meaty, not fishy at all. The texture is easier to
describe—so meltingly tender as to be nearly insubstantial,
moist and cool, not buttery or velvety as people sometimes say.
Have you ever tasted a piece of velvet?

I knew this was one of those peak gastronomic moments you
never forget, like the last time you ate a perfect peach, or the first
time you tasted raw milk Camembert or sautéed foie gras, or
every time you have white truffles or pizza bianca. I immediately
formulated a theory that moments like these draw on the genetic
memory of the human race, reaching across national and racial
lines, superseding all questions of taste.

I can vaguely appreciate the romance of fishing. As a boy, I
was able to read the first half of Ernest Hemingway's *The Old
Man and the Sea* before losing interest. I have shared a charter or
two out of Montauk at the end of Long Island to catch striped
bass and bluefish (no relation). And one of my oldest friends,
usually well-balanced, has become a fly fisherman. He jets to
Tierra del Fuego (no joke) to catch river trout and then throw
them all back. The idea is to outwit these intelligent creatures—
and more generally to subdue the primordial forces of nature.

That is not my goal. My goal is not to subdue Nature. My goal
is to eat Nature.

Preparations for my trip to Ensenada had gone smoothly. The

only snag was in finding the right outfit. It was December. The weather could be balmy and dry, balmy and wet, cold yet dry, or cold and wet. I knew what I needed: a light but not flimsy shell crafted from a space-age fabric that was breathable yet waterproof. My closet was littered with 20 years' worth of allegedly breathable yet waterproof shells that either admitted water like cheesecloth or hermetically held in one's body heat and moisture like a terrarium. At last I found the ideal balance in a vastly overpriced shell from Patagonia in chic and slimming black, not the perfect color if you need to be rescued from the angry sea. But since when was high fashion supposed to be practical?

Gloria Steinem once told me that she avoids any occasion for which you have to buy new clothes. That's where we part ways. To pursue and eat the giant bluefin, I would gladly buy any number of superfluous new outfits. Ms. Steinem's scruples would leave her languishing on the dock.

My plan was to drive down to Ensenada and visit one of the few bluefin farms in the eastern Pacific. Then I would go in search of a tuna boat—commercial or sports—that would take me out in search of the giant bluefin. Ensenada is an hour and a half down the coast of Baja California from the U.S.-Mexico border crossing. The last half hour of coastline is spectacularly beautiful in any weather, and that day the air and ocean were crystalline and pure. I was driven down by Philippe Charat, a principal owner of Maricultura del Norte and its bluefin farm off the coast, who had offered to show me his operation and help me find a tuna fishing boat. Somewhere in between we would have a lunch of abalone and perhaps a little raw bluefin. Only the thought of lunch could alleviate the mild depression brought on by the weather, which was too warm and clear for my brand-new outfit.

The water was too choppy for us to take a small company boat from a rocky beach conveniently opposite the floating farm, and so we traveled farther down the coast, clambered into a company truck, and drove for a nauseating eternity on one of the most perilous dirt-and-rock roads I have ever known. Driving high above the sea, we occasionally glimpsed a magical sight—eight delicate, perfect circles on the glittering ocean. These were the bluefin holding pens, in fact not small at all, 130 feet in diameter. At long last we reached another beach. Disoriented and, I feared, permanently damaged, I clumsily boarded a small motorboat, and we threaded our way among the tiny pastel boats of sea-urchin divers and out onto the open water.

The international trade in fresh bluefin developed in the 1970s, when methods of refrigeration and air-cargo handling became sophisticated enough that a giant bluefin could be caught or harpooned off the coast of New England on a Monday and be auctioned fresh in Tokyo on Wednesday. Until then, bluefin were a popular game fish but a complete nuisance to Northeast commercial fishermen, worth pennies a pound, and then only when the cat-food business was brisk. Americans did not enjoy eating oily, dark bluefin. Tuna here was a light, canned sandwich spread. James Beard once wrote (or so I've been told— I can't find the reference) that tuna is the only food better canned than fresh.

Once the heady prices at Tsukiji became available to nearly every bluefin boat in the world a fishing frenzy followed. Purseseine technology involving vast nets that could be drawn closed around entire schools of giant bluefin meant that more fish could be caught by one boat in one year than by all the other fishermen in the world combined! By the 1990s the world bluefin population had been reduced by 80 to 90 percent. Quotas have been enacted and poorly enforced.

These issues are the subject of bloody battles among conservationists, commercial fishermen, and sports fishermen. Satellite-tagging studies may help us to understand the life cycle and migration patterns of the bluefin, about which we know next to nothing. Bluefin farms—established years ago in Japan and later developed with Japanese help in Port Lincoln, Australia, Spain, Ensenada, and elsewhere—may someday help to alleviate this potential disaster.

In ten minutes we arrived at the busy farming operation and its eight pens, each one a huge ring of pipes and floats from which hung a cylindrical net going 30 feet deep and anchored to the ocean floor another 20 feet below. Six months earlier thousands of young bluefin had been caught using the purse-seine method, towed back very slowly, and distributed among the eight holding pens. Here they were fattened up on a diet of fresh sardines.

We climbed onto a thankfully stable, flat-bottomed barge tied up to one of the holding pens, were briefly amused by sea lions and pelicans, then turned our attention to the bloody business taking place on the barge next to ours. It was harvesting time. Two hundred of the bluefin were confined in one small section of the pen. They were all about four feet long, and weighed between 50 and 60 pounds. (Only bluefin farms in the waters off Spain produce 300- to 400-pound fish, just large enough to qualify as giants.) In all bluefin farms, the fish are kept for no more than six months, just long enough to fatten them and enhance the quality of their toro.

Divers swam among the bluefin and took hold of them, one at a time, by thrusting a gloved hand and forearm into its gills and lifting it onto the open edge of the barge, which was completely padded with what looked like a gigantic sky-blue mattress. (Without the padding, and maybe even with it, the side of the bluefin that lies against the deck, called shitami in Japanese, will bring a lower price at the Tsukiji market than the upper side, uwami.) As each bluefin was slid onto the barge, one of several workers wearing blood-splashed yellow slickers and pants killed it nearly instantly, in the Japanese manner, with a spike to the head and a wire down the spinal column, which not only is humane but prevents continuing muscle spasms that can damage the meat, "burning" it with lactic acid, which is also released when a bluefin struggles for too long in a net or at the end of a sportsman's line. A good judge of tuna at Tsukiji, they say, can taste how a fish died.

Now the bluefin was immediately bled, gutted, hosed down, and dropped into a slurry of water and ice to bring down its body temperature and prevent spoilage. (Tuna are warm-blooded.) Tomorrow, it would be cleaned again, packed for shipment, and driven to the Los Angeles airport for its last run—probably to Tokyo but possibly to New York City, certainly one of the largest sushi markets outside Japan. Sometimes I feel like a giant bluefin, my powerful musculature propelling me about the world in search of food. If we stop, we die.

By now, after long conversations with many tuna men, I had concluded that I was not going to find my tuna boat in Ensenada. The season was over. There were no sports fishermen in sight. Bluefin were being caught, but only as an incidental catch, by very large commercial fishing vessels that stay hundreds of miles out for three weeks or more, at least 20 times the number of days I had allocated for my boat ride, o-toro or no o-toro.

Though I was inconsolable, I kept it bottled up. I was even able to simulate voracious hunger at our very late abalone lunch. Then I gathered up my new outfit, still unused. We bade good-bye to our companions and crossed the gestapo-like U.S. border just after dark.

The next day Philippe generously brought me a quarter of one of the harvested bluefin, about ten pounds of solid muscle in one long piece. It was a lower quarter, the part with the toro. I immediately got out my Japanese diagrams and began slicing and eating, eating and slicing. But my joy was tinged with foreboding. For I knew that my fated meeting with a giant bluefin lay ahead.

My mouth still full of toro, I got on the phone, searched the

Internet, and after several hours ascertained that the only bluefin fishing in the entire world had just begun off Cape Hatteras on the Outer Banks of North Carolina. My new outfit and I would be ready.

My friend Joe, an avid game fisherman, and I chose Captain Jeffrey Ross and his 55-foot boat, *The Obsession,* on the basis of very little information; chartered the boat for $1,000 (plus a 20 percent tip for the mate); figured out how to get to Hatteras, a town at the remote southern end of Cape Hatteras; and counted the days. I bought a practical book about fishing for giant bluefin. It was called *Fish the Chair if You Dare.* (This refers to the revolving chair bolted to the deck, into which the angler is strapped to keep him or her from being dragged off the boat by his or her prey.) I judged this book only by its cover and concluded that the last thing I wanted to do was go fishing in the open sea in the middle of winter. What arbitrary and destructive force was pulling me ineluctably toward my star-crossed encounter with this monstrous ruler of the frozen deep? I believe it was the editor of *Vogue.*

Two weeks later I flew to Norfolk alone—Joe's wife had just given birth—and drove nearly three hours in the dark to an ocean-front motel in Nags Head, North Carolina, near the northern end of Cape Hatteras. I booked a wake-up call for 4:45 a.m. the last time, I hope, that this will ever prove necessary. I was sharing tomorrow's charter with several anglers from Richmond, Virginia. They would pick me up at 5:30 for the 75-minute drive to Hatteras, to Teach's Lair Marina, to *The Obsession.*

We arrived as the sun was rising, and were soon speeding past the harbor buoys and into the open sea. The air was warming—my new outfit was perfect—and the sky was clear. But the water was painfully choppy. One of us became very sick. Two others, including me (wearing a scopolamine patch behind my ear), barely held our own until we reached the place where the bluefin were supposed to be. 34 miles out, an hour and a half from land, where the ocean was suddenly calm.

The bluefin fishery off Hatteras was discovered by chance in December 1992, in the waters over a shipwreck about fourteen miles from shore. Cape Hatteras vaguely parallels the coast of North Carolina in a sweeping curve, where a cold stream from the north and a warm stream from the south meet, a confluence that for some reason attracts the migrating bluefin. The National Marine Fisheries Service allowed us to keep one bluefin per boat per day, if we caught any at all, but we were not allowed to sell it. No commercial bluefin fishing is allowed here. If Neptune smiled on us that day, we would have to eat all the kama, o-toro, and chu-toro ourselves.

Here is how you catch a bluefin: The mate plants three or four short, thick fishing rods in receptacles on both sides of the deck. Then he takes three or four dead fish from a cooler and baits the hooks with them. He pulls out several yards of line from each reel—big, brass reels—and throws the baited hooks into the water. Meanwhile the boat is moving slowly forward. The mate cuts up fish from another cooler and throws the pieces into the water, which is called chumming and is intended to attract a school of bluefin. Which is exactly what it did.

First one reel and then another started whizzing and whirring as bluefin went for the bait, were hooked in the sides of their mouths, and sped away from the boat, drawing out yards and yards of line. You sit in the fighting chair; a rod is thrust between your legs into a gimbal attached to the seat; another man stands behind the chair to turn it as the direction of the fish changes. You begin reeling in the bluefin, sometimes allowing it to make another run and pull out more line. Turning the reel against the pull of the bluefin is impossible. Instead, you repeatedly pull the rod back toward you by pushing off with your feet and then, as you lower it again, you furiously wind the reel to take up the slack.

Neptune did smile that morning. One bluefin after another hooked itself onto our rods. Each time, as soon as the bluefin was pulled to the side of the boat, the mate cut the line and set it free. We caught fifteen, I think, and kept one, which later, on the docks, weighed in at 145 pounds and 65 inches.

After watching nearly all morning, I took the fighting chair and caught an eighteen-pound blackfin tuna, not very good eating. I could not decide whether to be happy or embarrassed. Then, in the afternoon, there was a 180-pound bluefin on the other end of my line, the largest of the day. Several times in our struggle, I had to let it run free before reeling in the line once again. Getting it next to the boat took two of us. I have some photos. People have been extremely impressed.

We returned to shore just before dusk. The sky was beyond spectacular. For 30 cents a pound, $40 in all, a man would butcher our bluefin. I was put in charge of seeing that the meat was properly divided six ways and that I was given whatever cuts I required. Good thing, too. Not only is it customary in this part of the world not to separate the o-toro and the chu-toro from the loin, but the fattiest part of the belly, five pounds of priceless kama, two thick triangles joined at an angle, is—strap yourself in for this one—thrown into the trash!

I washed off the blood and cut one edge of the fatty meat into several slices of sashimi. After eating two myself to make sure they were truly top toro, I offered the rest to my former shipmates. They refused even the smallest taste. "Keep it all," they said to a man. And so I did. If I lived near Hatteras, I could have my fill of o-toro every day of the week.

In the light of day, I examined those two triangles of fatty kama. The flesh itself was pale pink, shot throughout with the forest veins of fat, arranged in an infinitely branching pattern— close to the ultimate bluefin experience. I cannot describe how delicious it was.

Yet I felt only small satisfaction in having nearly landed a large, handsome, dumb, pitiable bluefin, and now that I have done it once, I will feel zero satisfaction if I do it again. I do not feel stronger or nobler for having triumphed over a fish. If I can do it, how hard can it be? I did feel physically, spiritually, and intellectually satisfied at landing, then sharing and consuming— nearly to the point of surfeit, but not quite—a vast quantity of a food of which I had previously only dreamed.

My theory about the universal DNA of gastronomic pleasure soon came crashing down. I asked my friend Nafumi Tamura to translate several Japanese books about sushi. It came as a shock to learn that though the Japanese have eaten tuna for thousands of years, in recent centuries tuna had been considered a poor man's food, and became popular only during the food shortages after World War II. But the fatty belly of the bluefin was rarely eaten—it was considered too oily—until the 1960s!

Ernest Hemingway wrote to Bernard Berenson the year he published *The Old Man and the Sea*, "There isn't any symbolism. The sea is the sea. The old man is an old man. The boy is a boy and the fish is a fish. The sharks are all sharks no better and no worse. All the symbolism that people say is shit. What goes beyond is what you see beyond when you know." Now I know. Now I see beyond the symbolism of the primordial bluefin. Fatty tuna belly is fatty tuna belly, and I can't get enough of it.

The Secret Garden

by Geoffrey Tomb
from *The San Jose Mercury News*

"Heirloom" fruits may be this year's buzzword, but reporter Geoffrey Tomb's profile of a small northern California grower shows us what really makes an heirloom a treasure—the care with which it is nurtured.

D own at the dead end of Carter Avenue in South San Jose is a freeway sound wall. Over the wall is Highway 85 and now: noisy, polluted, speeding, anonymous. On this side of the wall is a two-acre sliver of then: secluded, slow, ripe, of character.

Squeezed against the high wall is an honor-system fruit stand and an orchard of 508 trees. Incredibly, 100 varieties of fruit grow here, much of it the heirloom kind thought to be as lost as Shangri-La.

There are an astounding 27 kinds of peaches, peaches with

uppercase names such as this week's Indian Blood, September Snow or Summer Set. Their shapes aren't perfect. They have goiter-like seams called sutures or less-than-Kodak-moment looks. Fingerprints quickly turn to bruises, and they come with fuzz that feels like a teenage boy's cheeks.

To earn a place here, where trees are jammed as close as rush hour traffic, the fruit must pass a rigorous test imposed by the man who farms this bit of ground.

"It eats good," says Phil Cosentino, using his highest form of praise.

He has just cut into an Indian Blood, which has gray-beige skin and meat the color of a slaughterhouse. At its peak of ripeness, from high off the tree, the fruit is almost hot from the late summer sun. Sugary juice runs down our chins and sticks to our fingers.

"Like a piece of candy," smiles Cosentino.

"People today, they know all about fashion. They buy Gap or Gucci, Old Navy or Adidas. But when it comes to food, no. They just buy peaches. But peaches have names, and farmers used to put the names on their fruit because people knew the varieties and knew what they liked.

"Today, everything is aesthetics. It's all looks, looks, looks. Nobody cares about flavor. We grow fruit for flavor."

And he sells it by name. Each fruit stands by its variety name. He sells only what's in season now. He picks it himself, when it's ripe, visiting a tree over and over until it is bare. Nothing is shipped.

Cosentino is owner, grower, pruner and picker of J&P Farm. The J is for Jean, his wife. The P is for Phil. But this is really a one-man show, the daily work of a 69-year-old whose passion is farming.

"I love working here all day long. It helps keep my weight down. I love to prune. I love to smell the blossoms. I love to see it grow," he said. "And I love to eat it."

In the tiny fiefdom of Phil in the duchy of Cosentino, its last king walks to work, stepping into the back and side yard of his home and traveling in time. No universal bar codes. No cash registers. No cashier.

"Hi Neighbor. We are picking fruit or talking to our trees," says the J&P stand's hand-lettered sign. "Please help yourself and put money in the slot on window ledge. Thanks for your honesty."

Does he really talk to his trees like the sign says?

"Oh, I talk to them. But they don't listen."

This speck of land is the last portion of a 10-acre site bought in 1945 by his father, Dominic Cosentino. The father, originally a huckster in Youngstown, Ohio, came to the fertile Santa Clara Valley at the end of World War II and thought he saw his native Sicily.

He started a fruit stand in front of La Scola's Market on Bascom Avenue at Apricot Way, an operation that grew, first in the 1950s into Cosentino's Vegetable Haven, and then into what is today a three-store supermarket operation.

The supermarket side of the business began when a bakery truck driver talked Dominic Cosentino into stacking a dozen loaves of bread, according to Phil. Bread led to full service, Tide to toilet tissue, yet many consumers say the stores still feature the South Bay's best produce.

Dominic Cosentino had four sons, Sal, Phil, Marino and Dom. They are partners in the supermarkets but only one still farms.

Back in the 1970s, the sons were set to sell off the family farm and see it developed. The orchard was bulldozed. The land was cleared. Condos were planned. But at the last moment, Phil said "no" and eventually bought out his brothers' land. He replanted, using some root stock saved from his dad's trees and adding what he thought would eat good.

Later, the state took most of it, eight acres, for Highway 85.

So he is down to the last of the last, just two little acres, as much to honor his father's memory as anything. He grows five kinds of grapes and three kinds of prunes, even though there isn't much call for either.

"My father always did, so I do it," he says. "I'm glad he died before they tore out the orchard. Or it would have killed him on the spot."

The stand is open daily from mid-May to October, but the farmer is usually working, not talking. These days he is battling walnut husk fly, which attacked his entire nectarine crop, claiming nearly all of his Arctic Pride white nectarines. He doesn't use sprays except on the apple and pear trees.

He planted three apple trees named Smokehouse because he liked the name. He also has an eight-acre apple and pear orchard off Summit Road in the Santa Cruz Mountains.

On Carter Avenue, Cosentino does give occasional tours to school groups and organizations such as the Greenbelt Alliance. Why? An elementary school visitor once asked him why his apple trees were decorated for Christmas. The child didn't know apples grew on trees.

A visit is like an education. One discovers, for instance, that Moorpark is a variety of apricot, as well as the name of a San Jose street. J&P grows them. And prunes don't grow with wrinkled skin.

"Most people don't know about prunes. I tell them that's what made this valley famous. They used to delay school for three weeks in September so the kids could pick the prunes. We sell Imperials. There haven't been Imperials in this valley in 30 years. You've got to find an old-timer who's ever heard of an Imperial."

Besides fresh Imperial prunes, he grows Sugar and French prunes. Other names are just as wonderful: Blenheim and Sweet Heart apricots, Heavenly White and Flamkist nectarines, Fuyu persimmons, Kim Elberta and Belle of Georgia peaches, plus Elephant Heart and Satsuma plums.

"People used to wait for Satsumas," he said, cutting into a tiny fruit with blotchy skin that bursts open with meat the color of garnet. Wow, it does eat good.

"Like a million dollars," he said.

"The growers want to know why Americans don't eat fruit the

way Europeans do. It's because of the taste. Today's fruit just doesn't eat good. The commercial guys can't afford to lose anything. So they want to go through and pick once, pick it all, even if it isn't ripe. I go through five or six times. The growers do it to themselves.

"People ask me what's the best one. There isn't a best one. They are just all different. If I had more room, I'd have more varieties," he said.

It is late in the day but he wants you to sample his prickly pears, comparing the orange to the red.

Sitting in the shade, next to his 1947 John Deere tractor, you wonder what will happen when the keeper of the tiny kingdom of heirloom fruit is gone.

"Then it will be condos," he said. "And it will be just like L.A."

Hadley Grass

by David Nussbaum
from *Saveur*

In this piece, David Nussbaum not only makes us hunger for fresh asparagus, he celebrates how ineffably a delicious local crop can root itself in a community—in this case, his own corner of western Massachusetts.

There I was, at 5:30 on a chilly, damp morning last May, at Waskiewicz Farm in Hadley, Massachusetts—about 20 miles north of Springfield—staring at an asparagus spear. Should I cut it or let it grow another day? I looked pleadingly at Mark Waskiewicz, already an expert harvester at age 12. "Take it," he said confidently. I thrust the razor-sharp blade of a long asparagus knife into the ground at a 45-degree angle, praying that I wouldn't cut some hidden baby shoot beginning its journey to daylight. Voilá! The thick, pale green stalk, with licks of purple on its tight arrowhead tip and cold dirt clinging to its white butt, fell gently into my hand. A beauty.

Knife poised, I moved on to a slightly shorter spear, then hesitated again. "Leave it!" called Mark's cousin Jeff Kristek, also 12 years old, waving me on. There was no time to dither. The boys' grandfather, Barney Waskiewicz—a sturdy, squat-faced, no-nonsense man who has been growing asparagus in Hadley for most of his 74 years—was bouncing toward us on his old tractor to collect our baskets and assess our progress. In the misty morning light, I saw row upon row of pointy stalks stretching down the four-acre field. We had a lot of cutting to do before the boys left for school.

The asparagus harvest is a rite of spring in Hadley and a handful of other towns, including Hatfield, Sunderland, and Whately, along the Connecticut River in western Massachusetts. From the 1930s through the 1970s, this area, blessed with a deep layer of sandy loam—the sediment of a glacial lake that once covered the valley—was one of America's premier asparagus-growing regions. In this fertile soil, the vegetable—and especially the standard Mary Washington variety—thrived as it did nowhere else, sending down strong roots and often producing for 30 years or more. And the combination of the rich soil and cool New England climate yielded spears of incomparable sweetness.

Hadley "grass"—as the crop is still called in these parts (it's short for "sparrow grass," a corruption of *asparagus* popular in the 17th and 18th centuries)—was once a mainstay of the local economy and an important source of community spirit. (Hadley got top billing because most Massachusetts asparagus was grown here, and it was reputed to be the finest.) During the annual harvest in May and June, townsfolk young and old would join forces to help pick, sort, trim, and bunch a total of about 50 tons (that's a couple of million spears) of the vegetable by hand each day. The asparagus was then trucked to Boston and by the following morning was in markets and restaurants throughout the Northeast, sporting colorful labels proclaiming its origin. It was also said to be a prized export, served at restaurants in Paris and Germany and at Queen Elizabeth II's annual spring feast in England.

But where once several hundred small, family-owned farms in the valley grew asparagus, there are now only a handful, and the road signs that read WELCOME TO HADLEY—ASPARAGUS CAPITAL OF THE WORLD are long gone. In the mid-1970s, a soil-borne fungus known as *Fusarium* attacked and destroyed the seemingly inexhaustible Mary Washingtons. Production plummeted, and field after field was plowed under. Some determined growers, including Wally Hibbard of Hibbard Farm in North Hadley, kept the crop in production and eventually replanted newer, disease-resistant hybrids, but this investment proved too expensive and time-consuming for most. Many farmers focused on potatoes, corn, tobacco, or onions instead; others stopped farming altogether. Nowadays, total production is barely a tenth of what it used to be, and what little asparagus is still grown is sold almost exclusively in the area, at farm stands and small markets.

Seventy-nine-year-old Wally Hibbard has never known a springtime without an asparagus harvest. His father, Ernest, planted the first asparagus in North Hadley in 1910 and soon became one of the valley's biggest producers. The fungus shriveled the Hibbards' crop from 40 acres down to just six, but the family refused to give up. Late last March, Hibbard showed me his newest asparagus bed, a one-acre plot hiding 7,000 baby root crowns—Jersey King hybrids—grown from seed the summer before. It would take three more years of careful tending to yield a full harvest of asparagus, he explained, and with luck the crowns would produce for eight, maybe ten years. Hibbard, who now farms a total of 16 acres of grass, would be well into his 80s by the time this field was generating a profit, but this did not concern him. "My father lived until he was 98," he told me, "and was at the farm almost every day, so I think I have time left. Besides, someone's got to grow asparagus."

When the industry collapsed, the character of the valley changed, too, a fact that saddens those who remember when asparagus was king. "Even growing up in the '60s and '70s, grass was always on your mind," said Allan Zuchowski, a 43-year-old third-generation Hadley farmer who stopped growing asparagus in 1996 when production costs got too high. "You'd be in class and see someone nodding out; you knew they'd been up picking since before dawn." It was tedious work, he acknowledged, but doing it with friends made it easier. The button local kids wore said it all: "Asparagus Isn't a Vegetable, It's a Way of Life."

But on a few farms, this way of life persists. The only major difference between a bunching session on Waskiewicz Farm (which actually stopped growing asparagus for about two decades after the *Fusarium* struck) today and one 30 years ago is the amount of asparagus handled. When I arrived at the barn after a morning of picking, three generations of Waskiewiczes, along with a neighbor, Helen Rodak, herself a former asparagus grower, were sitting at a long table surrounded by baskets of the day's bounty. Each person had two wood-and-iron contraptions called bunching boxes in front of them, one of which they filled with the thickest spears, or #1s, the other with the "skinnies," or #2s. Wiry "shoestrings" (which Rodak uses for soup) and misshapen "crooks" were tossed into discard piles. Working quickly and chatting all the while, they set the tips of the asparagus flush against the top of each box and, when it was full, cut the ends off at a designated spot. Then they jostled the spears into a tight cylinder and slipped rubber bands over both ends.

Meanwhile, Barney Waskiewicz, who passed ownership of

the farm to his son, Tom, in 1992, gathered and stacked the bunches in wooden crates. At the end of the session, he happily counted three times as many #1s—which fetch the highest prices because they are the "meatiest" (and some say the most flavorful)—as #2s. "When Tom told me he was going to plant grass again, I told him he was crazy," Waskiewicz said. "After the fungus drove me out of the business, I said, 'Never again.' But this field is coming in beautiful, and the 'spargus tastes terrific, too."

For every farmer who is still passionate about growing Hadley grass, there are countless locals who are equally passionate about eating it. They wait patiently for the short season to begin—shunning trucked-in asparagus at the supermarket the rest of the year—and then indulge in the vegetable almost every day while it's available. In the process, they've become pretty creative in the kitchen with the spears, cooking up everything from asparagus casserole to asparagus on toast. Everyone seems to have a version of the last, but I discovered two standouts. Margaret Barstow, who used to own a produce-trucking business with her husband, Norman, piles boiled asparagus soaked in a good dose of cream over toasted home-made bread. Karen Smiarowski, who with her husband, Charlie, owns the Smiarowski Farmstand and Creamy in Sunderland, just north of Hadley, makes hers with a cream sauce so tasty that the dish sells out whenever she offers it at her shop. But Karen's "fried" asparagus was my greatest find. It's Charlie's favorite, and she makes it at home when she has time. Gently sauteed in a bit of vegetable oil until they're wrinkled and caramelized, the pieces are as intense as candy but much more interesting.

The big event of the asparagus season in Hadley is the asparagus supper at the First Congregational Church. Held on the third Saturday in May, it's part of a 70-year-old tradition, a reunion of sorts. It is also one of the church's biggest fund-raisers. Thus, I was pleased when Margaret Barstow, who has organized the event many times, invited me to help out last year.

Barstow had prepared me for what to expect. At exactly 5:15 p.m., 192 ticket holders would have 45 minutes to gobble up as much buttered asparagus, baked ham, potato salad, and strawberry shortcake as the waiters could rush to the tables. The makeshift dining room in the church hall would then be cleared and reset, and at 6:30 sharp another 192 diners would take their places.

About a dozen of us kitchen volunteers, led by Barstow's daughter Robin Bialecki, spent most of the day rinsing, trimming, and cooking 240 pounds of Hadley grass. It was another example of asparagus's bringing people together, but the real action started a couple of hours later, after the first set of guests had been seated. When we heard the Reverend Bill Cobb clearing his throat for the blessing, we began taking the pans of asparagus out of the warming oven, whipping off the foil covers, and spooning the steaming chunks into serving bowls as fast as we could. Then, at "Amen," 30 waiters plucked the bowls from the counter. I barely had time to get another pan from the oven when the first empty bowl came back for a refill, then another, and another. The frenzy ended only when the waiters brought out coffee and dessert.

During the short break, I managed to sneak a few pieces of asparagus. All that time in the warming oven had drastically changed Bialecki's perfectly cooked pieces: firmness had given way to flab, vivid green had faded toward olive. But to my surprise, the asparagus was still incredibly delicious—it melted in my mouth and bathed my tongue with that special sweetness. Its glory days may be past and its future uncertain, but Hadley grass is still one of the great blessings of spring in this corner of New England.

Crunch

by Dorothy Kalins

from *Saveur*

You may never think of celery as a homely vegetable again after reading this lyrical piece by Dorothy Kalins, who this year moved on after a long and successful reign as editor-in-chief of *Saveur.*

I come to celebrate celery, a vegetable so commonplace it's almost invisible. I ask that you reconsider those banal supermarket platoons of foot soldiers (not even officers) lined up for review in the combat uniforms of their tough-guy outer stalks. I ask that you strip a bunch, and gaze in awe at the surprise underneath: Behind that stringy ribbed exterior lives the most feminine of vegetables. Undress it down to its delicate, white thighs, and then marvel at its secret: A perfect, pale miniature of itself, a fully formed infant tree, lives inside.

I ask that you tolerate celery's slapstick antics—that hairy stalk wigging out a bloody mary—and its juvenile nursery jokes, as straight man for peanut butter (add raisins for Ants on a Log) or for Velveeta with pimientos. I ask even that you forget what you know of the French céleri au gratin, wherein a boiled hunk of the stuff lies airless under a cheesy blanket, in an indiscriminate preparation that would work just as well on the thinly sliced soles of Reeboks.

Picture celery, instead, thousands of years ago, at the source of its flavor, waving wild in the perfumed air of windswept Mediterranean hillsides, just waiting to be gathered.

Vibrant cousin to parsley and kin, too, to carrots, celery in its wild form was adored by the ancient Romans for its aromatic properties. A cookery book credited to Apicius, that Roman gourmand, in the first century, suggests this succulent preparation: A bunch of celery is steamed, seasoned with precious black pepper, lovage, coriander, and savory, then simmered in a bit of wine, stock, vinegar, and olive oil. A dash of flour thickens the sauce; then, a sprinkle of thyme. That the selfsame Romans were said to have dined wearing crowns of celery leaves (and we thought they were laurels) to ward off the hangovers inevitably acquired from washing down, say, a celery-stuffed suckling pig, is, in my book, even more tribute to the plant.

Celery (Apium graveolens var. dulce) is a vegetable with heart. Such a heart, in fact, that at the beginning of its domestic cultivation—either in Renaissance Italy or in France or both—a new variety emerged that was all heart: celeriac (as in céleri rémoulade, julienned celery root in a mustardy mayonnaise). It was these Renaissance growers, obsessed with the aforementioned whiteness of celery's thighs, who began the practice of whitening it still further by mounding protective dirt around the stems like so many sand castles.

Even without this blanching—which is no longer done, incidentally—celery was difficult to cultivate, because it takes a

very long time to grow. Indeed, for all its garden-variety familiarity, if you start seeds inside in, say, April, you won't be able
to set out the tender plants until June—and if you're truly lucky
and the temperature never strays from 40 to 65 degrees, you'd be
munching a stalk by October. Suddenly, supermarket celery
starts to look a whole lot better, since savvy growers now tend
to plant hybrids of the Pascal variety, whose pesky tendency to
stringiness has been bred out.

That celery's most famous characteristic is its texture is pretty
impressive for a plant that's 95 percent water. Think of it as water
erect, and understand for the first time the meaning of the word
toothsome. Once you discover celery in salad, you wonder what
you ever saw in lettuce.

And it becomes, miraculously, almost a different vegetable
depending on how you slice it. Italians, celery maestros once and
forever, set translucent slivers of it in a pool of fruity olive oil,
topped with salty filets of anchovy or baby octopus. In a
Barcelona restaurant, we found celery nestled under bright ser-
rano ham, peeled to the heart and shaved in vertical sheets so
wide that we weren't sure which part they came from. In Chinese
hands, celery sliced on the bias becomes the star of stir-frys. The
leaves alone are more pungent than the herb that celery's closest
to, lovage, and many's the soup that has been saved by the addition of an entire bunch of chopped leaves.

Celery is my onion; a rough dice with carrots is the way my
cooking starts. The aroma of celery softening in oil confirms for
me a kind of primal connection. But to what? The celery and
olives that were my childhood's only antipasto? The clean shot of
Cel-Ray soda that went with every deli sandwich? My first juice-
bar health drink? Or does it go back even further, to wandering
some Mediterranean slope in another life?

Ode on a Can of Tuna

by James Villas

from *Bon Appetit*

Author of *My Mother's Southern Kitchen*, among a host of other books and magazine articles, James Villas is a confirmed booster of the kind of day-to-day food Americans really eat.

I make absolutely no apologies for my lifelong and intense love affair with canned tuna. In fact, I find it utterly appalling that this delectable staple has been disparaged by food snobs who have somehow come to the fatuous conclusion that only the fresh fish is worthy of human consumption. Despite what the parvenus think, canned tuna is and always will be one of the world's great delicacies, and the very idea of using anything else to make a sumptuous tuna melt, a classic *salade niçoise*, an intelligent tuna and noodle casserole or, above all, a sublime tuna salad is absurd.

As for fresh tuna itself, which is probably the most wildly popular item on any trendy restaurant menu in America, I've been trying to analyze why I resolutely refuse to eat the stuff in this country. I suppose it could be because of the tiny, squiggling, repulsive white worm I noticed in a fashionably underseared piece of yellowfin served some time ago at a chic bistro in San Francisco.

Perhaps I'm convinced that most chefs simply don't know the first thing about preparing fresh tuna correctly (that is, slowly baked), as it's done around the Mediterranean. It might have something to do with the glitzy, status-conscious, gullible crowd that perceives the fish as a healthful, thinning substitute for meat. But the more I reflect, the more I'm apt to believe it's just because my fancy for canned tuna is so strong that I have a mental block against those dry, bland, grilled slabs and all the raw fish used in tartares and sushi. No doubt there are many who would classify me as a gastronomic philistine.

My devotion to canned tuna is rather wanton. At the moment, for instance, there are no less than 27 cans of various weights and grades of fish on my kitchen shelf. Each was acquired compulsively either at the supermarket (on sale, of course) or during my foreign travels, and each contains tuna packed in vegetable oil, canola oil, olive oil or brine (I wouldn't touch that flavorless product canned in water).

When I'm forced to fly, I never go without at least two 3-ounce flip-top tins of solid white albacore that's easy to eat with a plastic fork. Europeans (like the Japanese) take their tuna very seriously, and in central London I know exactly which Italian delis make the best tuna and corn salad. In Paris, I head for shops such as Hédiard that stock the exquisite white tunny (*le germon*) of Brittany and the firm, unctuous *thonine*, packed flat in olive oil like sardines, of the Riviera.

On trips to Italy, I search for cans of the highly prized, expensive, creamy-pink belly cut called *ventresca*. And when my primal instincts are turned loose in restaurants and cafés anywhere along the Mediterranean, I sniff out everything from Catalan *xató* (tuna and salt cod salad) to Greek tuna with chickpeas to fried Tunisian *briks* stuffed with tuna, capers and tomatoes to that glorious French tuna, onion and bell pepper sandwich known as *pan bagnat*—all prepared traditionally with the region's superior canned bluefin, albacore or yellowfin.

But after all is said and done, there's still nothing on earth that can equal a good all-American tuna-fish-salad sandwich made with the generally high-quality Pacific tuna readily available in any supermarket. All I can say about those pretentious phonies who think they're elevating the classic salad's pedigree by making it with grilled fresh tuna steaks instead of the full-flavored canned tuna fish is that they really should seek medical help.

I wish I could provide a definitive recipe, but since the distinctive fish lends itself to so many delectable interpretations, the best I can do is offer a few basic guidelines. While I do prefer any major brand of "solid white" albacore packed in oil, I don't object to the lower-grade (and less expensive) "chunklight" varieties. I do, however, avoid cheap supermarket house brands, which tend to be a flaky mush of the lowest grade of tuna.

Tuna salad almost demands a little finely chopped celery and sweet pickle, plus black pepper, but beyond those three essentials, additions might include discreet amounts of chopped stuffed olives, hard-boiled egg, bell pepper, red onion, chives, fresh dill, avocado or capers. The trick is not to overwhelm the delicate tuna. Great tuna salad can never, *never*, be bound with that hideous "lite," low-calorie mayonnaise. I use only Hellmann's—about one heaping tablespoon per six-ounce can of tuna—and I may or may not add a crisp leaf of iceberg lettuce.

Oh, yes, the bread. I pile my tuna on soft, plain white—high enough so that the salad can ooze out the sides of the sandwich onto the plate and be eaten with the fingers. And I dare anybody to tell me that's not wonderful eating.

The White Album

by Alan Brown
from *Gourmet*

White bread and mayonnaise may have become synonymous with middle-American blandness, but novelist/playwright Alan Brown refuses to buy that cliche as he sings the praises of Hellman's in a jar.

Mayonnaise and I go way back. Almost a cultural chronicle of the past half century, our deliciously sordid affair began in the Eisenhower era, in the small Pennsylvania town where I was born. Mine was an ordinary, precholesterol family: We drank so much chocolate milk that in our house the unadulterated version was referred to (without irony) as "white milk." And my older sister's favorite dinner was a bowl of elbow macaroni with an entire stick of salted butter melted on top.

I was an innocent in a Zorro mask and a Howdy Doody hat, a finicky eater whose favorite lunch was a tuna salad sandwich on Jewish rye, hold the lettuce and tomato. And only my mother's version would do: snowball-size scoops of mayonnaise mashed into a bowl with the canned tuna—no relish, no spices—until the mixture became a luxurious paste. Heaven.

Food, I quickly surmised, was invented solely as a vehicle for mayonnaise. A gourmand friend taught me to smother cheeseburgers with it. A Dutch exchange student showed me, with missionary zeal, how to dip French fries in it. At lunch, I began to alternate tuna with egg salad. At summer barbecues, I gorged on potato salad. And when, in my high school years, my mother introduced green salads to our dinner table, she coaxed me into eating my plate of iceberg lettuce by dousing it with an exotic ketchup and mayonnaise concoction called "Russian dressing." Licking the dressing bowl, and loving it, felt daringly unpatriotic. Could the Soviet Union really be so bad? I wondered.

I went to college. And when fate brought me an Orthodox Jewish roommate who managed to keep kosher by limiting his diet to canned tuna and mayonnaise, I knew I was lost. After graduating, I headed west to San Francisco, where I moved into a dysfunctional commune (was there any other kind?). I'd never seen an avocado until one was served to me on seven-grain bread with Monterey Jack cheese, alfalfa sprouts—and mayo. In California, I was shocked to discover, mayonnaise was cool with the counterculture. *Mao* and *mayo* were only a letter apart. Joan Baez and Alan Watts surely must have been eating it. From the look of him, Jerry Garcia indulged daily.

Then, without warning, the cultural climate shifted. Baby boomers discovered exercise, and California cuisine reared its ascetic head. In the cultural wars, mayonnaise was suddenly the culinary equivalent of Ronald Reagan and Wonder Bread. A zealous zeitgeist follower, I signed up for yoga classes, bought a juicer and a rice cooker. *Miso* replaced mayo in my fridge. I stopped eating tuna sandwiches. In fact, I stopped eating sandwiches, period, because, well, what was the point? Nothing tasted good on bread anymore.

Mayonnaise-free decades passed. I was clean, and I never looked back. Then, last winter, I was given a month's residency to work on a new stage play at the Virginia Center for the Creative Arts, an artists' retreat in sight of the Blue Ridge Mountains.

At VCCA, lunch is delivered each day to the artists' studios, so that creative work can continue uninterrupted. When my lunch pail arrived on my first day there, I carried it to my desk, turned off my computer, and put on my Discman headphones. I opened the pail and looked inside: A sandwich wrapped in wax paper; a bag of carrot sticks; a cookie; an apple.

I still remember what I was listening to when I unwrapped the wax paper and took my first bite of that sandwich down there in the snowy Virginia hills. Ella Fitzgerald singing "These Foolish Things" from her *Ella in Rome: The Birthday Concert* recording (her best, I think). The sandwich was a BLT on supermarket wheat bread: a generous helping of greasy bacon; crisp iceberg lettuce; a slice of tomato; and a sensuous blanket of mayonnaise. Mayonnaise, I quickly learned, is one of the basic food groups in Virginia; it's on every menu, at every meal. It was a harsh winter; the snow fell and a chill wind howled. Inside my warm studio, though, I listened, transported, to Ella, Stan Getz, Art Pepper, and Anita O'Day, wiping mayonnaise off my chin and typing fingers.

I will refrain here from a Nabokovian rhapsody on the very sound of the word, the slippery slope of those syllables. But, I confess, mayonnaise did become the culinary Lolita of this now-middle-aged man. It became my laudanum, my opium. I begged the kitchen staff for extra sandwiches. And—surprise!—the words flew across my computer screen. My muse had not just paid me a visit, she'd moved right in, seduced by ambrosia-in-a-Hellmann's jar. I wrote my new play with a speed and lucidity I'd never known before.

It is summer now, and I am revising a new novel, a daunting

undertaking. Yet I am oddly confident and serene. Friends attribute it to my yoga classes and lap swimming. But those who spot me late at night slinking down New York's steamy streets and into the corner grocery store—those with a similar, telltale sheen to their skin—know the shameful truth. Virginia Mayo, I am your slave.

Home
Cooking

Secrets of Saffron

by Pat Willard
from *Secrets of Saffron*

In her elegant culinary history of a most precious spice, Pat Willard (author of *Pie Every Day*) offers poetic tribute to how a single special ingredient can influence civilization—or, as in this excerpt, illuminate a life.

E very child has a master teacher beyond her parents, and Mrs. Coogan was mine. The Coogans lived at the top of our street in Philadelphia in a row house just like ours. But they were different from everyone else in our working-class neighborhood because the parents had not only gone to college but they were both writers of some note. When they moved into the neighborhood, they had two children—a boy, Kevin, and a girl, Nell, who became my best friend. Forty years after they met, my mom would still tell with astonishment the story of Mrs. Coogan's audacious first visit to our house. One afternoon, the

doorbell rang, and my mom opened the front door to find standing on our stoop a tall, large-boned, handsome woman with the
brightest shade of fuchsia lipstick freshly painted on her generous mouth.

"My name is Jean Maria," Mrs. Coogan announced in her
breathlessly girlish voice. "I just moved in up the street and I've
heard your husband is a college graduate and that you're a great
reader. Well, we are too, and I'd like us to be friends because I
really don't understand how I'm going to live here if I don't find
someone to talk to."

It was clear to my mom that the woman was upset and in need
of help, so even though she was still trying to sort out what Mrs.
Coogan had said, she invited her inside, and within an hour,
over coffee and one of my mom's pies, the women became fast
friends.

According to my mom, Mrs. Coogan's main misfortune in life
was in having had an overly protective and doting mother, who
instead of teaching her to cook and keep house had sent her off
to a fancy convent school and university. The women in the
neighborhood simply could not figure out what Mrs. Coogan did
all day while her tables gathered dust and her children were selling potato chip sandwiches to the rest of the kids on the block.
Surely this was a woman (and therefore a family) headed for
trouble, and many took the precaution of steering clear of the
entire clan.

But my mom understood Mrs. Coogan, for although my mom
was a remarkable cook and a meticulous cleaner, she was also a
great reader who was thrilled to find someone she could talk to,
especially in those afternoon hours of a young housewife's day
when there was nothing more to clean, the children were down
for naps, and dinner and her husband's return from the world
were still hours away. The two women fell into the habit of
spending this time together, each in her way helping the other
to navigate through the tangled straits of ordinary life.

In particular, Mrs. Coogan relied on my mom to show her how

to cook. She seemed not to have any natural talents in this regard and was, in fact, capable of being completely flummoxed by the intricacies of even the simplest recipes. The neighborhood grew accustomed to seeing her fly down the hill from her house into ours with a cookbook flapping in her hands, all in a state, needing my mom to translate some elementary cooking instruction. She did this most often when she was about to give a party, because she always wanted something gala and extravagant for her guests, and in the days before she could afford a caterer that meant she had to make it herself, usually with my mom's timely intervention.

The Coogans gave a lot of parties. It doesn't seem to me now that Mr. Coogan was a very social man, because he was always in his study writing, but they had a wide circle of friends, and Mrs. Coogan liked the excitement a party brought to the house. She often heightened the excitement by taking to her bed in the days or hours before the party, resisting the cleaning and shopping a party requires. At the very last possible moment, when everyone else had given up hope, Mrs. Coogan would burst from her room and, in a whirl of activity, somehow got done what needed to be done. What she did love was the party itself—the hosting and the greeting, talking and laughing with her guests, drinking and eating and talking some more until well into the night. Their house appeared always to be in a state of animation, with a party being planned or just hours away. The only time all seemed quiet was in the suspended hush of the "day after," when our parents remained in bed and Nell and I would make a game of finding all the small silver bowls of nuts and mints and half-empty glasses hidden about the messy rooms.

"Patty, sweet puss, do you think you can help me with this?" she asked one day when my mom wasn't around. Mrs. Coogan had called me in from the yard where I had been playing with Nell. She helped me up on a stool beside the counter to show me a magazine spread of something I had never seen before—a bowl of golden rice.

"We need to make enough for twenty and the recipe is only for six. So I guess four times everything?"

That sounded good to me, and when she put four green peppers down in front of me and asked me to cut them up, I thought that was pretty good, too. I was not allowed to touch knives at home, but her faith in me was complete, and I boldly took the small paring knife from her hand and began to cut the strips of pepper as carefully as I could. Mrs. Coogan kicked off her shoes and disappeared into the living room; when she came back, she was carrying a martini glass and rowdy music suddenly exploded around us. I cut the peppers. She chopped onions. Nell came in from the yard, asked if she could cut something too but quickly grew bored with all the peppers. Her eyes watered from the onions, and she soon wandered off. Mrs. Coogan took a sip from her glass and began to sway her hips to the music as she sautéed the vegetables together in an enormous black skillet. She didn't seem to mind, or even see, the bits and pieces of onions and peppers that splattered to the floor, for she kept up a lively patter between us and continued to stir the vegetables in the pan. I can't imagine what it was we talked about, but it was thrilling to feel all her interest zeroed in on me, on whatever it was I was telling her. Best of all, after I opened some cans of tomatoes for her, she whisked me down from the stool and, to a particularly raucous tune, swung me across the floor in a lively, all-the-way-down-to-the-ground-and up-again manic version of a twisting jitterbug.

When we had finished dancing, I climbed back on the stool and she dug around in the cupboard until she found a glass tube full of red threads. She pulled the cork from it and put it under my nose.

"Smell," she commanded. I took a big whiff and reeled my head away from the cold acerbic scent that curled from the vial.

"Now look at this." Mrs. Coogan shook the tangled ball of threads out into her palm, dropped a few in a coffee cup, added a little hot water, then stirred the mixture with her finger. The threads seem to swell and burst open, bleeding yellow across the water like the sun setting behind a still lake. The scent rose lightly off the water, almost sweet but as citric as a lemon. Before she poured the threads into the rice, she told me to dip a fingertip into the water and place a drop of the liquid on my tongue.

"Isn't that something?" She laughed at the frown I made as the taste melted like warm metal across my mouth. As she stirred the water into the rice, the white kernels began to turn yellow—first a pale creamy shade and then a darker, almost orange hue.

When I got home later and excitedly told my mom about what Mrs. Coogan and I had cooked, my mom appeared horrified. I thought it was about the knife or the funny stuff Mrs. Coogan let me taste. But a few minutes later when my dad arrived home from work, I heard her talking about the single bowl of rice that would feed the party that night. My dad opened a bottle of beer and said something about making a snack. My mom shrugged her shoulders and, casting a suspicious eye toward me, hoped out loud that the party wouldn't be spoiled.

I lay in bed that night with my sister curled asleep against my back and listened to the music from the Coogans' house flutter down the hill. I wondered whether Nell had been allowed to stay up, as she sometimes was. Maybe she had put on a party dress and was twisting with her mom in the living room. I thought about slipping past the babysitter downstairs and skipping up the hill, through the back door, filling my belly with perfumed rice, and dancing, dancing. When I awoke again, it was pitch dark and the music had stopped. I heard my parents on the stairs, their voices slippery, excited, and I knew the party had been a success. I was sure the rice Mrs. Coogan and I had made had contributed at least a little to the merriment. As the door closed softly behind my parents, as the night once more quieted, I lay awake hankering to cook up a party again and tickled by the strange taste still lightly simmering on my tongue.

The Kitchen That Could

by Bryan Miller
from *Food & Wine*

Turning out a great meal is not necessarily a matter of having a fabulously appointed professional-grade kitchen—quite the opposite, in fact, discovered former *New York Times* restaurant critic Bryan Miller.

I t's been said that all you really need in order to cook are heat, a good knife and a couple of sturdy pots and pans. I agree in principle, although it might be tricky whipping up a lemon meringue pie. Still, I always feel envious when I see photo spreads of spectacular home kitchens with massive stoves, turbo-charged convection ovens, runway-size counters and more storage than the Yankees' locker room.

But impressive as these setups are, for most home cooks they are culinary overkill—like gunning a dragster to the corner deli. Does it really take a great kitchen to make great food, or can you do equally well in humble spaces? I have had the opportunity to investigate this question rigorously: Since retiring six years ago as restaurant critic for *The New York Times*—after a decade-long stretch during which I never ate a home-cooked meal—I have made up for lost time by staging many elaborate dinner parties at my 100-year-old farmhouse. It has a kitchen that some of my more diplomatic guests have described as "different" or "rustic," the way you might compliment the mother of a homely infant by observing that the child seems "bright." The space is large, about 12 feet by 20, and it has a lovely view of the fields and woods out back. It also has a five-foot-long counter with a Formica surface in a faded dalmatian pattern. But as best I can tell, it was last renovated the year Truman rabbit-punched Dewey.

If I had to single out the kitchen's biggest challenge, it would be the stove, which I bought 11 years ago for $75 at a front-lawn tag sale. (I haggled down the price from $80.) Manufactured by a company aptly named Caloric, it is a petulant creature that requires endless negotiation and cajoling before it goes to work. The exterior is a mottled brown, sort of like a baseball infield after it's been watered. Two of the four gas burners have been on strike for years, making cooking for a crowd a slow process. On the back panel is a clock frozen at 7:02. (I often wonder what was cooking, so many years ago, at the moment time stopped.) To the right of the clock is a fogged-over oven timer that also expired long ago, likely resulting in more than one desiccated roast; eerily, though, it continues to buzz every three or four days, precisely at noon. Then there is the third dial, which simply says STOP. Stop what?

I know how to improvise a meal without a timer, but the lack of overhead light presented a problem. My remedy was to clip onto the stove's back panel a big aluminum spotlight, the kind mechanics use to view the underbelly of automobiles. One could perform surgery on my range now.

The gas oven puffs on when (and only when) you place a match to one of the two functioning stovetop burners. Even then you have to wait about three minutes and then slam the oven door two or three times (I am not making this up), before it starts. The thermostat is 30 degrees off, on the hot side. And the woefully underpowered exhaust fan, which could barely ventilate an ashtray, emits a high-pitched screech that frightens the neighborhood dogs. Whenever I sauté or grill, the house fills up with so much smoke that disoriented guests have to clasp one another's hands, like schoolchildren, to find their way out.

After World War II, the General Electric Corporation developed a clunky if crudely effective prototype dishwasher, a miraculous invention that transformed American housekeeping the way the cotton gin had ameliorated plantation work. My dishwasher, in the opinion of the repairman, must have been one of the first off the line. For a time in the late '40s it may have sudsed up some plastic dinner plates and barbecue spatulas, but, like the *Mercury* space rocket, it quickly became obsolete. The marvel of this machine is that you can fill it with dishes, turn it on and hear all kinds of spraying and sloshing, but when you open the door the dishes are untouched. Actually, they are worse off: The circulating air ossifies the food stuck to the plates. The machine makes a good dish rack, though.

And yet, for all of its shortcomings, my little kitchen has nourished more spectacular and raucous parties than many of the showiest kitchens in Manhattan. I'm not saying that everything goes seamlessly—fish have disintegrated, soufflés have imploded and one evening lamb shanks came out of the oven so black and granitic (a visiting chef trusted the timer) that they could have been used as billy clubs. All in all, though, a little improvisation has almost always pulled us through.

Only once has my eccentric kitchen led to major embarrassment, and even then it wasn't really the kitchen's fault. Two years ago, I invited a couple of Manhattan chefs—Cesare Casella, a Tuscan who owns the restaurant Beppe, and Bill Yosses, now pastry chef at the new Citarella restaurant—to prepare a dinner. The guests were a discriminating group: Tim and Nina Zagat, of the Zagat guides; Myles and Lillian Cahn, the owners of Coach Farm goat cheeses; and my parents, who had been frequent dining companions when I was reviewing restaurants for the *Times*.

Fifteen minutes before everyone arrived, we were running way behind. The stove was huffing like an out-of-shape jogger on a final hill. In the midst of the confusion, Cesare realized he was missing a critical ingredient: "Basil!" he cried. I took off like a Roman messenger, roaring into town, grabbing the basil and screeching home again. I dived out of the car and, instead of going in the front door as I usually do, charged around the side of the house to the kitchen. But like a train speeding helplessly toward a broken rail, I couldn't slow my momentum, and I slammed right into the sliding glass door. At once everything seemed to move in slow motion. The door floated toward the floor, crashing in a shower of glittering glass. The chefs froze in mid-chop; the stove hissed mockingly. In that brief moment of suspended silence, I heard a car pulling into the driveway. "Keep cooking!" I shouted, leaping around the floor as I brushed up hundreds of glass nuggets.

The Zagats walked in and took in the scene with horror. "Wouldn't you like a glass of Sancerre?" I asked, feigning nonchalance. Soon we noticed that a frosty November was blowing into the house, a situation I remedied with duct tape, plywood and plastic trash bags. (They are still there.) The cooking recommenced.

All things considered, the dinner was a rousing success. We had a fantastic Tuscan bread salad (with plenty of basil), bruschetta with zucchini and Romano cheese, a peppery mussel-and-clam casserole, braised loin of pork stuffed with fresh herbs, and roasted baby potatoes with rosemary. For dessert there was chocolate mousse with vanilla génoise, farmer's cheese strudel stuffed with glazed apricots, and English trifle with cinnamon plums and blueberries.

Was the meal as enjoyable as any of the ones I had sampled from million-dollar kitchens? Damn right it was—and a lot more memorable, too.

Who's In Chris Walken's Kitchen?

by Andrew Goldman

from *The New York Observer*

From Manhattan's often-snarky weekly newspaper comes this deadpan celebrity profile, wherein Andrew Goldman shows how an actor who rarely eats his own cooking can perform superbly in the kitchen.

At 1:50 p.m. on September 7, screen and stage actor Christopher Walken sat in the driver's seat of his black Cadillac Seville sedan, in a parking space on the street in front of his second residence, a ground-floor apartment on West 80th Street. He was wearing a black T-shirt and faded black cotton pants with an elastic waistband. A pair of tortoise-shell reading glasses hung from his shirt.

He entered his apartment, a duplex that is mostly utilized by his wife of over 30 years, Georgianne, who works in Manhattan as a casting agent. To the right, in the spacious living room, were two enormous canvases painted by his good friend, Julian Schnabel. To the left, with a breakfast nook looking out onto West 80th Street, was the kitchen. Pottery bowls with chopped vegetables—zucchini, summer squash, and onion—sat on the counter, above which, on a shelf, was an old cigar box painted with the word "Smile" next to a photograph of a cute cat, who, he explained, crestfallen, succumbed to "that feline leukemia." In the corner, near a telephone was a black-and-white print of Jerry Lewis, doing his signature drinking-glass-in-the-mouth bit, taken at the Tony Awards.

Christopher Walken crushed a whole bulb of garlic with alarming force on the countertop, as though he were performing CPR, and began chopping the garlic with a menacing-looking butcher knife. He pulled out a Lincoln Wear Ever fry pan outfitted with a blue plastic Cool Handle II, put it down on the white Whirlpool electric stove, and began rummaging through the drawers for a spatula, which he seemed unable to find.

"It's a long time since I was cooking here," said Christopher Walken. "My wife uses this place. She buys this stuff. I have gas in Connecticut, which is much nicer. This is hard. An electric oven isn't bad, but a gas top is much better. In Connecticut I have an electric oven with a gas top. This is hard. I don't know what's going to happen. You don't look very comfortable. Why don't you sit down? Oh, great, I forgot to turn the burner on.

"Cooking is like the family business. My father was a baker all his life. He comes from a big family in Germany. His father was a baker. His brothers are bakers. He came to America and opened a bakery in Queens and had it for 60 years. That's where I came from this morning. My mother broke her hip. It's a drag, because they live in a house and suddenly they can't go up and down stairs."

Christopher Walken began his first dish, Zucchini Linguine, by heating olive oil in the skillet.

"I'm putting some garlic in. New York is great for produce. Those Korean markets always have very fresh stuff.

"My brothers and I were in show business when we were kids, but we also worked in the bakery. I used to deliver cakes in a station wagon and work in the back. I was the guy that put the jelly in the doughnuts. In those days, you'd have a huge can with a plunger on it. It had these two really big needles sticking out each side. You'd take two doughnuts—they'd already be cooked—stick them on those needle things. Then you push the plunger down, and you feel them fill up. There'd usually be a little dribble of jelly on the end. Actually, it was rather sensual."

To the sizzling pan, Christopher Walken added onion first, then red pepper, then the zucchini and summer squash.

"My mother wasn't much of a cook. I mean she was *okay*. She used to overcook everything. She came over from Scotland and used to make interesting things, things that I never see anymore, like oxtails—you know, real...I guess the word is 'peasant' food. Things like the linings of things.

"My father likes that German food. He used to drink sauerkraut juice. He's 97 years old and he eats this incredibly high-cholesterol stuff. All those big sausages. He eats knockwurst and washes it down with beer. And he eats head cheese, which is basically these big chunks of fat in gelatin and made into a loaf. It's like eating solid fat. And he's a skinny guy. My cholesterol is good. Every time I go to the doctor, he swoons in ecstasy over my blood pressure. I've got some incredible blood pressure. When I was a kid, I'd pass out sometimes, because I'd get real slow. The blood, you know. But when you get older, that's good."

Christopher Walken tossed vegetables, added dill and juiced a lemon into the pan, picking out the seeds afterward. He immersed dry pasta in boiling water.

"This is good pasta, De Cecco," he said. "At one point I had a pasta machine. I tried that. They make it look easy. But it's not. Making your own pasta is not easy.

"Now I could put some olives here. You like olives? I put some lemon juice in there, too.

"When I was a kid, every day in the house there was cake,

cookies, chocolate cream pies. Every week, the cleaning lady would take home a huge bag of stuff. You'd think it'd be great. In the bakery, I used to make these big vats of melted chocolate. The smell of sugar in that quantity is overwhelming. It's almost too much.

"Now, I never eat dessert. I eat sweets very rarely. I don't eat sugar. In the morning, when I have coffee, I put molasses in it. It's very good. When I go to a restaurant, people always have dessert, and I always skip it. I might have some cheese or something like that."

Christopher Walken poured the sautéed vegetables into a bowl and put them aside, then tasted the pasta, which was not yet done. He reached into the refrigerator and emerged with a white-paper-wrapped package, which he began to unwrap.

"On pasta, they say 12 minutes," he said, "but I always try to keep an eye on it. This is salmon from Citarella. There's one right down the street. I was just working in Nova Scotia and Halifax. You get the most incredible fish there. Mussels that don't really taste like mussels you ever had before. The salmon, it's unbelievable. Chilean sea bass, you know you don't get it a lot here, but when I go to California, they have it a lot. It's such a gorgeous thing. You get a great big chunk of it and you bake it. It's just fabulous. In California they have all these great things like abalone. It's fabulous. But it's very expensive.

"For me, cooking is something that I do when I'm studying scripts. I put the script on the counter and I cook and study my lines at the same time. It's the power of distraction, I find. I've read that a lot of people do one thing while there's something that they're doing at the same time. Some people play cards or garden. I cook. My wife doesn't cook. That's actually common. I think more men cook than women cook."

Christopher Walken laid the salmon on the counter and began cutting into it.

"I don't cut through the skin," he said. "I just score it in portion sizes and leave the skin hanging off.

"You need to watch your weight in the movie business. It's just a practical thing. Actors are always on some sort of diet. There's a lot of sitting around on movie sets and actors are always sitting on their chairs and talking about food. It may be because they're on a diet and thinking about it a lot. It's true that the camera is very cruel. It makes you look heavier than you are. And movie food is generally very good, because they have to make sure the technicians are happy. They like a nice big lunch with dessert. It's tempting. You've got to watch yourself.

"Buffets are very dangerous. A lot of actors I know gain 15 pounds when they make a movie. I was in a movie once—I don't want to say which—that took eight months to make. Movies are not shot in sequence, so you could watch it and see the people in the movie getting bigger and smaller. Sometimes I go to these movie events, and there'll be a buffet with very good food. You'll see all these important, wealthy people standing on line getting huge plates of it. They don't need it. But psychologically, I guess it's some primitive thing. Somebody's got to eat it.

"I try to keep the icebox fairly empty, and just buy things as I want them. I only eat once a day. Usually about 7 o'clock. If I have things to do, eating slows me down. I feel like I'm under water."

Christopher Walken left the fish for a moment, and ripped open a paper-wrapped jar, the dark, gelatinous contents of which he spooned into a mixing bowl.

"That's chutney," he said, "and I'm going to put a big thing of it in there. And I have some garlic that's already chopped. And sea salt. I'm going to put a little lemon in there and mix it up. I have some cilantro here. People don't use cilantro much, but it's really good.

"I eat slowly. It takes me a long time. I usually watch TV, just flip around and find these great movies that I didn't even know existed. That's the best thing about that cable. I just saw an incredible musical with a lot of black performers called *Stormy Weather*. The last 20 minutes of that are as good as any musical I ever saw. Then I fall right asleep.

"I don't go out to eat much. Occasionally I go to these very fancy restaurants on an anniversary or a birthday or something. I don't want to name any names, but I haven't really been knocked out in the last few years. In the old days—this is 20 years ago—I used to take my wife to Lutèce on her anniversary or birthday. That used to be wonderful. It probably still is. But I went to one of the big ones recently. The check was unbelievable. For three people it was like 300 bucks apiece. I had duck or something like that. Anyway, it was good. But I make a tremendous duck. You have to steam a duck first. I don't think many people do that. This amazing amount of fat comes off. Then you put it on a rack. You stuff it with garlic and oranges, you know, salt, pepper, some herb, whatever that might be. And you put it on the rack and roast it, and it comes out really crispy. I got that from the Julia Child cookbook. Her cookbooks are wonderful, Julia Child."

After tossing the linguini into a collander, Christopher Walken brought the chutney sauce over to the salmon fillet and began massaging the sauce into the fish.

"Oh, incidentally," he said, "my hands may look dirty, but that's paint on them. I was painting. I'm going to take this sauce and put this on the top. You scored it, so it kind of gets down into the holes.

"I love Mexican cooking. It's so much more than people know. Here it's, you know, guacamole and enchiladas. I like eating spaghetti. I could eat it every day and I have to watch that. I like French food but sometimes it's very rich. I was in Japan once, and I said to the people I was with, you know, 'I love Japanese food, so I would like to have some real authentic Japanese food.' And they took me to this restaurant and gave me a bowl of what looked like some pasta. I looked at it. There were all these little eyes, and the whole thing was moving. I think they were little white eels. I did have some of it to be polite. That was tough. I had to take it down with some beer."

Christopher Walken carried the fish over to where a baking

tray is arrayed with a bed of onions, and slapped the fish, sauce-side down, onto the onions.

"All right now," he said. "I have this pan with all these onions I did. I sautéed them a little bit.

"During movies, I bring my own food. I have various Tupper-ware containers. And every time I go away for any extended time, I'll stay in an apartment or a hotel that has a kitchen. When I was a kid, I was in musicals, and there'd be the dancers, you know, these crazy Gypsies. They'd show up in the little hotel with a suitcase, open it up, and it had every kind of cooking utensil. They would cook these incredible dinners from nothing. Thanksgiving would come and they'd cook this huge turkey in the room. I don't know how they did it."

Christopher Walken popped the salmon into the oven.

"It's on broil," he said. "I don't time it. You can sort of tell by touching it.

"I've had to stay in places where there only was a microwave. It's not recommended, but you can actually cook certain fish in a microwave. Salmon you can cook practically anywhere. And if you're living like a hobo in a hotel room, you can make amazing things in crock pots. You can stick a chicken in there with some vegetables. Turn it on real low and just leave it there all day. And when you come back it's fabulous."

Christopher Walken pulled out a package of jumbo shrimp from the refrigerator and, grasping them in his hands, cut through them with the butcher knife, then ran them under water.

"This is a little dangerous," he said. "You know you're never supposed to cut like this. You can cut your hand off. You see, you butterfly it. And then there's this vein in there. You want to get rid of that. It's guts, I guess. You want to get those nice and clean.

"I almost did a cooking show. I went to Bravo and MTV and the Comedy Channel. I had meetings with these people and I was going to do this show. It was either 10 or 12 segments. I can't remember. I was going to have some sort of kitchen set-up. I wanted it to be a little like *Pee-Wee's Playhouse*. I love that show.

And I'd have maybe a showgirl, you know, with a little thing on, chopping my vegetables. Maybe some musicians. And an audience. Some people to talk to."

Christopher Walken laid the shrimp into a sizzling frying pan, in which he had sautéed some chopped garlic in olive oil. He squeezed an orange into a coffee mug that read "Notre Dame High School, 25th Class Reunion, Class of 1967."

"I'm going to throw a little more garlic in there," he said. "You want a little more cilantro in the shrimps. You put them in shell down in the hot oil—but the next part is a little tricky, some say dangerous. What I got here is some rum, and I'm squeezing a little bit of orange juice in the rum. You got to wait until these shrimps get a little white. These are big, so they're taking a while.

"I remember Dean Martin's old shows, when he had the Gold Diggers. It was a fabulous show. They say they had the whole thing set up and he'd get in his car and drive from his house, park the car, walk into the studio and do it completely off the cuff. You watch it and you could tell that he didn't really know what was going on. And every time things got a little rough, these showgirls called the Gold Diggers—these gorgeous girls—would come on and do this dance number. That's sort of what I had in mind."

Satisfied the shrimp were sufficiently opaque, Christopher Walken grabbed the rum, turned the burner up and tossed the rum into the pan, then quickly covered it with a lid. It sizzled loudly.

"This top isn't quite tight enough, but it works," he said. "It's like a big sudden steam bath.

"With the cable, the thing was, when it got down to it, every one of them wanted something much more precise. They wanted it to be much more planned. Much more of a pragmatic, fabricated thing that could be repeated. They wanted to have a comic actor with me. They wanted to have a script. Jokes. I like jokes. But I wouldn't want to have to say the jokes, you know. Because certain times things are funny anyway. I mean, funny people are funny. And I said to them I wouldn't be able to do that. I wanted it to be like the Dean Martin show."

The meal was done. Christopher Walken tossed the vegetables and pasta together, pulled out some small wine glasses, a couple of plates and a half bottle of 1998 Corvo, a white Italian table wine. He carried a canister of sour cream over to the table for the pasta.

"I usually put some sour cream on that," he said. "It's up to you. I'll tell you a really simple thing if you're going to have people over. It's expensive, but you get a thing of caviar—but you can use the red caviar. But one of the best things in the world is linguine, a big thing of sour cream in the middle and a big scoop of caviar. With some pepper. It's like the best. Anybody can make it. Piece of bread? It's nice bread. Just a little corner? I'll get you a napkin. I'm gonna give you food. I'm not going to eat today. I'll eat later."

Christopher Walken washed the dishes. He cleaned the sink with a sponge. He put the leftovers in Tupperware. Then he tossed a few paper towels on the ground and wiped the floor by skating around on top of the towel with a stockinged foot.

"Cilantro is very hard to clean," he said. "All these little green things.

"If I wasn't so lazy, I'll tell you what I would do. I saw this thing on television. This whole thing with people putting cameras in their house, for the Net. I understand that people outfit their houses with these things, and some guy's girlfriend finds out that she's been naked all over the Internet. You hear about that. If everybody can do it, it can't be that hard. You just need to figure out where to tune in, right? I would need some help with this. I don't quite understand how the Internet works. I don't have a computer. You know, 12-year-old kids know all about that.

"I thought I'd get a couple of those cameras and put them in my kitchen in Connecticut and just, you know, turn it on whenever I felt like it. Maybe I would have a particular time of day I would do it, or something like that. You could charge people to take hits, or something like that. And it would just be me cooking. And I thought to make it amusing, I thought I would have a hotline—you know, a red telephone. And they could call and I could give them advice about their love life. I mean silly stuff, personal questions, about them, you know, 'What should I do?' In the old days, there used to be these things—I can't remember what they're called, but it's a Spanish word. Like a bodega, but something else. They'd be on the corners. You could buy a love potion. You could buy, you know, something, if you were mad at somebody, you could buy a hex. They even had aerosol, I remember—you could spray somebody to get them to fall in love with you or something. I could provide services like that. Or just talk while I'm cooking."

Christopher Walken sat down at the kitchen table.

"And you remember a program called *This Is Your Life*? I thought I'd have a curtain over to one side and once in a while I'd have a mystery guest. You know, actors are always coming over to my house. Maybe Joe Pesci comes over and makes his tomato sauce. Everybody makes something, you know what I mean. Don't you think that might be amusing?

"Or I could do restaurant reviews. Like Ruth Reichl, I could walk in with a big disguise. Like a great big wig. Like everybody would know, they'd be like, 'Oh, here comes Chris with a big wig. Who's he kidding with those big dark glasses?' Or I could dress up like a woman. Get dressed up with a big fur coat, and I could pretend it's not me."

Christopher Walken said he would eat later.

Perfect Rice

by John Thorne with Matt Lewis Thorne

from *Pot on the Fire*

In several books, articles, and his *Simple Cooking* newsletter, John Thorne is a source any serious home cook can trust—like a lively, curious, and utterly unpretentious friend cooking alongside you.

For most of my cooking life, I paid hardly any attention at all to ordinary rice, except that I thought I did a good job of making it. Early on, I used converted rice, not because I liked it especially but because it kept in all those "essential" vitamins—Wonder Rice—and because I had somehow imbibed the idea that rice, real rice, was difficult to make. Then, during a stretch when I was pinching every dime, I switched over to plain, supermarket-label long-grain rice. This rice was not only much cheaper, it also tasted better. Like frozen vegetables, converted rice has a vague "cooked" taste; all its flavor edges have been rubbed away in some distant processing plant. By comparison, even bargain-basement ordinary rice had a noticeably sweeter, brighter taste.

Consequently, when money started coming in again, I switched, not back to Uncle Ben's but to various premium brands of standard American long-grain rice—Carolina, River, Alma—and stayed with them. I made this rice by following the instructions on the package, performing the ritual so often that I knew the formula by heart: one cup of rice, two cups of water, a tablespoon of butter, a teaspoonful of salt. And so the years went.

Then, one evening after Matt moved permanently into my life, we had my friend Dave over for supper. I don't remember what we cooked up that night, except that it was served with rice. As I was dishing this out over at the kitchen counter, Dave said to Matt, "You know, all the years I've known him, John's always made perfect rice." I glanced over at Matt, expecting, I guess, to see a faint flush of pride or, at least, an assenting nod. Instead, I was just in time to catch, flitting across her face, a look of sheer incredulity.

I was dumbfounded. I looked down at the fluffy white stuff on the plates in front of me and poked it with the serving spoon. So, what was I doing wrong?

> There are over one hundred varieties of rice grown in Burma. . . . Their price and taste vary. *Nga kywe* is the most expensive and the easiest to digest. It is the favorite for the table of the wealthy. *Nga sein,* which has a harder texture when cooked and is less expensive, is eaten by the farmers. *Londei* is the hardest and cheapest and mainly used in feeding the inmates of prisons and livestock. Many of the other varieties, such as the sweet, pink, and black rices, are used in making snacks and confections.
> —Aung Aung Taik, *Under the Golden Pagoda*

Matt and I were then in the process of integrating our rather different cooking styles. Consequently, when we had dishes like rice and peas or tripe gumbo or dirty rice, I made the rice; when we had other dishes, like a vegetable curry or a kedgeree, Matt made it. Or rather, she made basmati rice, which she much preferred to American long-grain rice—certainly, at least, to my version of it.

Early in her wonderful book on the rice culture of the Carolinas, *The Carolina Rice Kitchen,* Karen Hess explains what she intends by the phrase "rice kitchen." It is meant to capture less a body of particular dishes than the almost spiritual presence that a much loved and entirely depended-on ingredient can have for a cook, serving as the basic ground in which all the other cooking in the kitchen has its roots and in relation to which it finds its meaning.

Ours is not and never can become such a kitchen, even if we wanted this. But when I read that phrase the image immediately came to me of Matt preparing rice. I saw her bent over the spread-out kernels and carefully sorting through them, grain by grain, picking out the tiny pebbles, the strange-looking seeds, the discolored and broken grains, and the dead (and sometimes not-so-dead) insects. Following this came the washing and soaking rituals, which sluiced away every trace of the stale bran dust and excess milky-white rice starch. Finally, she carefully calibrated the amount of water to add to the cooking pot. When the rice was done the pot was completely dry, the rice itself light, delicate, and fluffy, a collation of distinct and tender grains as different as day is from night to the dense, gummy stuff I made.

Talking to her about it I discovered that her devotion to all this sprang from something more than her natural fastidiousness. She found it calming, even pleasurable, this sorting. Picking through the rice meant not only removing the detritus but establishing an anticipatory connection with the rest. Raw rice has a lovely translucency and rolls under the fingers with the soothing smoothness of abacus beads. To try to put this experience into words is to exaggerate it, she said; it's something that, doing it, you just feel. Even so, it was clear she felt an affinity to rice that I did not. And her complete absorption while preparing it made me, for the first time, begin paying attention myself.

What there was to pay attention to, however, wasn't at first exactly clear. I was already curious about "gourmet" rices like Italian arborio and Asian fragrant rices. But rice itself—the plain, unparticularized fluffy white stuff—was always in the background of my imagination the way it was in my meals, like a slice of sandwich loaf in a peanut butter and jelly sandwich.

In a way, that was the price I paid, coming from a culture so absurdly wealthy that it lacks an essential starch to connect all the basic dishes of its cuisine, framing them within its own distinctive taste. For the Chinese—at least those who come from southern China—that grain is so central, so much the meal, and what is served with it merely the enhancements, that, as E.N. Anderson writes in *The Food of China:*

> the phrase *chih fan* (to eat rice) also means simply "to eat," and the word *fan* (cooked rice, cooked grain) also means simply "food." A southerner who has not eaten rice all day will deny having eaten at all, although he or she may have consumed a large quantity of snacks. A meal without rice just isn't a meal...[A meal] is made up of cooked rice and *sung*..., a Cantonese word that may best be translated as "topping for rice" or "dishes to put on the rice." *Sung* includes everything else, all combined into dishes that are, indeed, put on the rice (and in a poor-to-ordinary home are little more than flavorings for it).

If I got hungry an hour after eating in a Chinese restaurant, it was because, ordering some fan with my sung, I had got the thing the wrong way around. That tiny bowl of rice that came with the roast duck and chicken with cashews and vegetable moo shi was ordered out of politeness, a bit of "When in Rome . . ." I hadn't come there to eat rice; I didn't even particularly want it. Consequently, reading that the average Chinese still nourished by the traditional cuisine eats eight cups of cooked white rice a day, I unreflectively imagined the stuff as a kind of undifferentiated starchy filler crammed down out of sheer, driving hunger.

This, of course, reveals a naive (but still embarrassing) cultural prejudice. It never occurred to me that such a Chinese eater might actually look to the texture, flavor, and aroma of rice for the same aesthetic nourishment that I had come to search for in a piece of bread, and, furthermore, might find it there. Having fought my way to that relationship with my daily bread, you would think that by extension this connection would be obvious. But no, if life teaches us anything, it is that such provincialisms must be uprooted one by stubborn one.

Indeed, as I was about to discover, a forest of cultural confusion stood between me and that simple bowl of perfect boiled rice. Matt, reading Julie Sahni, had spent months mastering the art of preparing basmati rice, a naturally perfumed (the word in Hindi literally means "queen of fragrance") long-grain rice with a distinctive "tender spongy" (Julie Sahni's phrase) texture. Although I didn't confess this to her for some time, I was finding it very hard to accept basmati rice as rice. For me, it was always "*basmati* rice." When this finally spilled out, I had to admit further—still more cultural chauvinism— that its sandalwood-tinged aroma and ephemeral texture vaguely irritated me. Basmati seemed to me the rice of a thin people; all fragrance and ephemerality. I wanted our house rice— our rice—to have *body* to it, the familiar, firm resiliency of American long-grain rice.

So, after bringing into the open this secret ambivalence that existed between us—my uncomfortableness with her rice and hers with mine—we were faced with either pursuing a two-rice cuisine or finding a rice and a way of cooking it that brought to table the qualities that both of us wanted from that grain. So, together, we plunged into several months of experiment, trials… and errors.

The English, or rather the Anglo-Indian, method of boiling rice is more laborious but less likely to yield a glutinous mess. Set on your stove three large vessels of water. When all are boiling cast the rice into the first. Ten minutes later drain the partially cooked grains in a colander. Wash them with the boiling contents of the second pot and then put them into the third to complete their cooking.

—Peter Gray, *The Mistress Cook*

Plain boiled long-grain rice*: how can something be easy to do if almost every cook insists on a different—sometimes *entirely* different—way of preparing it? Pick up a handful of cookbooks and you experience a riot of conflicting instructions. I don't think there's a single step in making rice where you will not find one instruction countermanded by its opposite, argued with equal authority. Wash/don't wash; wash before cooking/wash after cooking; cook in lots of water/cook in just enough water; cook for a long time/cook for a short time...and on and on.

Compare rice with pasta, a basic starch that comes with its cooking method already built in. You don't need a cookbook to teach you how to prepare spaghetti. It cooks up fast, it cooks up easy, and it cooks up right. That is why there's no such thing as Minute Pasta or Success Pasta. And it is also why no one tells you what a snap it is to cook. You already know.

Cooking also follows the laws of evolution: successful methods crowd out all others. If there's no simple method for cooking rice, it isn't because the right genius hasn't yet come along to set us straight (there are already too many vying for *that* role), but because rice cooking is attempting the unnatural. It means to force those grains of rice to do something they don't particularly want to do.

*Long-grain rice is "plain" rice to most non-Asian Americans; short-grain rice requires a very different kind of cooking and so is outside the reach of this discussion.

If you come from a non-rice-cooking culture and trust your instinct to cook rice right, your instinct will let you down. Toss a handful of those tiny, pearlescent grains into a pot of boiling water and let them do their thing, and the grains become not soft but soggy. Pressed gently with a finger, they collapse to mush. Measure the water so that the grains absorb it all while cooking, and you get that familiar dense, gummy, sticky mass.

What, though, is wrong with that? Abstractly—nothing. The French, for instance, cultural chauvinists from birth, seem quite happy with it: their description of perfectly cooked rice is *crevé*, or (to translate roughly) "burst." Taste rice prepared by someone who knows what they're doing, however, and your ignorance will lose its bliss. Well-made rice is something else again.

Still, it isn't all that easy to say what, exactly, that "something else" is. The best way to approach it, I think, is to answer an implicit question that has been hovering over this text from the start: why *white* rice at all? I know that readers convinced of the superiority of the unpolished grain have already started muttering, "Brown rice is natural, it is more nutritious, it is obviously less tampered with, and it has more flavor than polished rice."

All these things are true. The problem is that brown rice is also not really rice. Plain boiled rice has become, like bread, an artifact of culture, as much idea as thing. Brown rice, on the other hand, is just another edible seed—one among many equivalent grains that fill the bins of the natural foods shop: barley, millet, rye, and wheat berries, not to mention such exotics as spelt, quinoa, kamut, and hato mugi. Those who find our civilization too much for them turn to such foods as a portal to an unsullied, primal world. But the Thai or Gambian or Chinese peasant who becomes prosperous enough to set aside the coarse, rough stuff for the refined does so to acquire identity with their culture: white rice wraps the family meal with connection to the common way. For them, white rice is a doorway *in*.

This connection is at the heart of what rice is all about. And for the participating cooks of a rice culture, shared agreement on what rice should be lifts its preparation out of the realm of merely boiling and propels it into the platonic. To cook rice correctly requires not only patience and skill but an abstract conception of an idealized form. In perfectly cooked rice, to let one expert speak for all, "each grain is separate and dry, yet tender, not gummy or sticky."

Taken literally, these familiar adjectives most *exactly* describe Quaker puffed rice, or, for that matter, Rice Krispies. In rice cooking, these terms serve to create a tension between what the rice wants to do and what the cook persuades it to do. It is the vegetable equivalent of dingo becoming dog. (This, by the way, is why the dullness of instant rice extends beyond its taste; it is all obedience, its rice spirit broken instead of tamed.)

Every rice culture has its own definition of perfect rice. For the South Carolina cook, the cooked grains literally pour out of the pan like popcorn. For the Chinese cook, they are similarly individually distinct, whole, and dry, but they also hold together, so that the fingers, or chopsticks, can pluck them up in a bite-sized clump. For the Thai or Indian cook, the ideal rice is transcendentally light and soft—and the talented rice cook can take the longest, most fragile grains and cook them until exquisitely moist and tender, but still unbroken and unburst. All these are results that truly deserve that ultimate accolade.

We Americans have no such cultural consensus, which is why our notion of perfect rice is so murky and undefined—and the directions in our cookbooks so contrary. After all, much of the ritual surrounding rice is only superficially about its making. There is a short Japanese nursery rhyme about rice:

> *Hajimé choro choro* First it bubbles
> *Naka pa ppa* Then it hisses
> *Akago naité moé* Even if baby is crying
> *Futa tore na.* Don't remove the lid.*

On the surface, this is a neat little onomatopoetic lesson in rice cooking (listen carefully and never peek under the lid, even if baby is wailing for its breakfast), but the Japanese housewife who, plugging in the electric rice cooker, chants it to her daughter is really instructing that little girl (and reminding herself) *how nice it is to be Japanese*—and, consequently, how comforting it is, doing this most Japanese of tasks.

We have no such little songs. No part of our American identity is bound to rice. Trying to prepare it, we have no established standards to absorb, no accepted method with which to test our mettle against our neighbor's, no firmly fixed feelings about texture and taste that we want our own rice pot to produce. We don't even, most of us, *have* a rice pot. In other words, we share no oneness through our rice. And so we don't—excepting a few Southerners, many of them black—understand the first thing about cooking it.

> Unlike spaghetti and potatoes, which have their devoted fanciers in lands to which neither is indigenous, rice must be lived with to be loved—and well cooked. In non-rice-producing regions the grain is a poor thing poorly dealt with, and the passion for it which unites all people to whom it has been the cornerstone of family life is never quite understood or even believed by outsiders.
> —Sheila Hibben, *A Kitchen Manual*

Well, what is one to do? I knew for sure that I didn't want to build my rice cooking either on an arbitrary recipe or on a romanticized identification with some arbitrarily chosen rice culture/kitchen. So what I turned to for help was the basic artisanal sense of *task*. Make it simple by making it particular: what can I do with *this* rice, *this* rice pot, *this* need, *this* temperament? In other words, to learn to make some facsimile of perfect rice, I had to learn to anchor it to my life.

*Quoted, with slight adaptation, from Elizabeth Andoh's *At Home with Japanese Cooking*

My starting point was Alma, our choice of the supermarket brands of long-grain rice. It had the texture I wanted but not the aroma or taste. We set out to discover which American rice—if any—might possess all three. Soon, the UPS truck began rolling up the driveway with sacks of rice from Arkansas, Texas, and Louisiana, some sent directly from rice mills, others from the actual growers.

Simultaneously, we worked on method. We ransacked the literature and tried out the most appealing-sounding of the techniques, including Elizabeth David's method of boiling the rice and then putting it, casseroled and buttered, to dry out in the oven. They all worked well enough, but none of them produced rice equal to Matt's basmati. The problem, I gradually realized, was that I wanted to simply follow a set of instructions, whereas what was required of me was to establish a close working relationship with a particular cooking vessel—my personal rice pot.

Although it would, in fact, become a pot almost solely devoted to rice-making, that designation as "rice pot" came from the fact that I chose it because its shape and weight somehow spoke directly to the point. I walked up and down the aisle of the kitchen-equipment store, hefting one pot after another, until a one-and-a-half-quart Calphalon saucepan made of heavy anodized aluminum, with a tight-fitting glass lid, spoke out to me, simply and directly: "I can make your rice." I believed it, bought it, and brought it home.

The fact that it *is* a very good pot made my work all the easier—an authentic workhorse, its solidity gave me confidence and its stolidity posed no problems of intervening temperament. Having it as my constant, I learned to be increasingly stingy with the water and more aggressive in the cooking than I had before found nerve to be. Because American cooking shares no common rice pot, rice-cooking directions always counsel moderation—but in this instance, moderation leads to mush.

When I began my exploration of rice, I happened to be baking all the bread we ate. This task required continual consideration, which, in turn, meant a slow accretion of observed detail. Part of the pleasure of eating your own bread lies in contemplating the result of today's efforts, in comparing the crust, texture, and taste of this loaf with the one made yesterday or the day before, which, in turn, brings to mind other flours, other approaches, other loaves.

The same is true with rice. In ways that matter as much as they are hard to quantify, it has gained increasing substance, presence, weight. For an inattentive eater sitting down to dinner at our table, the difference most likely would elicit no more than an appreciative grunt. However, for us, now, the shared discussion of choice of rice and the gradual articulation of a method have lent a quiet but deeply pleasing richness to the meal.

Perhaps our favorite rice right now is the long-grain Della-type grown in Cajun country and called popcorn rice after its familiar aroma (the two share a highly aromatic chemical compound). To our surprise, we found that distinctions could be made between batches of the rice grown in neighboring parishes; they were all delicious, but in subtly contrasting ways. Now when the rice is done, I bring Matt a forkful from the pot, and we taste it together consideringly, the way the mouth works a first sip of wine.

When the rice is good, this tasting is an act of unmitigated pleasure. Part of it, of course, is just whetted anticipation of the meal, but there's something else there, too...only more difficult to explain. Dingo into dog—that connection wasn't gratuitous. A dog acquires dogness learning to sit, shake hands, roll over, and other, similar dumb pet tricks. When I got my dog Mick to sit and shake hands (rolling over was beneath his dignity), I felt silly with pleasure—exactly how I felt when I first lifted the lid of that Calphalon pot and saw that the rice had *risen up* of its own accord into a white and fluffy mound.

With Mick, as with rice, I wasn't showing my talents as a trainer (negligible) or his at accepting discipline (laughable)—or even the bond between us (he would do the same for anyone who offered him a biscuit). No, I was simply delighting in what I can only call his "dogness"—in which at that moment I was somehow allowed to participate. That is what the phrase "my dog" is really all about. In the same way, when I bring Matt a forkful of rice at the end of cooking, what we both delight in is neither my rice-cooking talents nor the savor of the thing but— what else can I call it?—its *riceness*. Our rice—we, together, have somehow managed once again to pull off the trick. And now, at least as far as Matt is concerned, I know how to make a pot of perfect rice.

According to Karen Hess, the first rule of good rice cooking is not overcooking. Perfectly cooked long-grain rice is tender but resilient, faintly sticky but not gluey or mushy. She also insists that the rice must be left unmolested during its recovery time. This is similar to letting a roast "sit" after it's been brought out of the oven, so that the juices can redistribute themselves throughout the meat. In the rice pot, this resting time allows the moisture to penetrate to the center of each kernel and the excess to evaporate, producing firm-textured, separate grains.

Whether Karen Hess would approve of our method or its results is something we'll discover only should we ever have her over for supper. For us, though, it does the trick. Even so, I want to stress again that every instruction that follows was built on our growing familiarity with our own rice pot. So far as your own "perfect" rice is concerned, surely the right approach is to get a basic grasp of the issues involved and to work them out after your own fashion and to your own satisfaction, and at your own pace.

All the rices that are most commonly eaten around the world come from the Asian variety Oryza sativa. This rice is usually divided into two major groups: indica rices, such as basmati and jasmine, which are more fragile-grained and often fragrant; and japonica rices, which have sturdier, plumper grains and are more tolerant of cold weather and so can be grown in more temperate climates. (A third group, javanica, consists of tropical rices, mostly grown in Indonesia.) Whether a rice is short-, medium-, or long-grain is dependent less on type than on the length of the growing season. Similarly, "sticky," or glutinous, rice may be long-grain or short-grain, indica or japonica.

Basmati rice, grown in the foothills of the Himalayas in northern India and Pakistan, is the perfumy, fragile, long-grain indica rice most associated with Indian cooking. Dehra Dun is considered the choicest; patna is the more abundant and less expensive, although connoisseurs consider it to be not quite as good. American-grown basmati rice (such as Calmati) is acceptable but does not completely capture native basmati's unique aroma or texture.

Brand names to the contrary, there hasn't been a commercial rice crop grown in South Carolina since 1927. With it went the distinctive Carolina Gold, which had made the word *Carolina* a synonym for quality rice. Said to have originated in Madagascar, it is a fragile long-grain variety described as possessing a distinct if delicate flavor, firm texture, and astonishing whiteness. Recently, Richard and Patricia Schulze persuaded the United States Department of Agriculture, after a hiatus of more than sixty years, to propagate authentic Carolina Gold from the grains stored in its seed bank in order to bring it back into cultivation on their plantation on the Savannah River. The Schulzes grow the rice as an avocation and donate their tiny crop to charity.

Della is an American cross between basmati and standard long-grain American rice. When cooked properly, it produces a fluffy-textured rice with dry and separate grains. Della is often sold as Louisiana "pecan" or Louisiana "popcorn" rice, because its distinctive aroma (but not its taste) is uncannily reminiscent of those two foods.

Japanese rice is of the japonica type, medium-grain and slightly translucent. When cooked, the grains are distinct and firm but slightly sticky. (This rice absorbs much less water than other kinds, which can be confusing to those accustomed to preparing indica-type rices.) Japan does not export its rice; the Japanese-style rice available in America is grown in California. Preferred brands include Kokuho Rose, CalRose, Nishiki, and

Matsu. Sushi rice is cooked Japanese rice delicately seasoned with rice vinegar and sugar.

Jasmine is an aromatic, long-grain indica rice native to Cambodia, Vietnam, and Thailand, which export large quantities to this country. Introduced to American rice farmers in 1989, it is now grown in Texas and California. When properly prepared, it possesses a spongier, slightly stickier texture than Della or basmati, but its cooked grains are still firm and easy to separate.

Sticky rice has a predominance of amylopectin, a rice starch that becomes gummy when cooked, causing the grains to adhere. Sticky rice is easy to eat with the fingers because it can be gathered in clumps; the same quality—along with its sweeter taste—makes it perfect for a wide variety of Asian rice pastries. The sticky rice grown in warmer areas, like Thailand, is long-grain; that grown in more temperate areas, like Japan, is short-grain.

Plain Boiled Rice
Serves 2 to 4
    1 cup (6 ounces) long-grain white rice
    1½ cups minus 2 tablespoons (11 fluid ounces) water
    ¾ teaspoon salt
Choosing the Rice. Although Indians believe that aged rice increases in flavor (and, consequently, let some develop for as long as ten years), in our experience—with rice as with flour—the fresher it comes from the mill, the brighter the flavor notes. Age also affects the amount of water needed to cook it.

Choosing the Rice Pot. Here is Diana Kennedy on this subject, as set out in The Art of Mexican Cooking:

Choose a heavy pot for cooking the rice; it will be less likely to scorch on the bottom. The shape of the pot is also important; if it is too wide, the water will cook off too quickly and the rice will not be as tender; if it is too deep, it is liable to be mushy at the bottom. As noted, we use a Calphalon one-and-a-half-quart saucepan with a tight-fitting lid.

Sorting the Rice. Matt finds all sorts of detritus (seeds, pebbles, chaff, insects, and, mostly, damaged and discolored grains) in the rice we use, especially when it is processed in small, old-fashioned mills. Spread the rice out on a paper towel and look for yourself.

Rinsing the Rice. Washing rice rinses away polish dust, bran particles, starch, and sprayed-on vitamin powder, so that the grain's own subtle favors can come through. Barbara Tropp argues—and our experience confirms—that mere swishing under running water accomplishes nothing; you have to give it a good *wash*. Pour the rice into a small sieve and insert this into a bowl. Fill the bowl with cold water and stir the rice with your fingers until the water is milky. Lift up the sieve, pour off this liquid, refill the bowl with fresh cold water, and repeat several times, until the water stays clear and the rice grains are translucent.

Cooking the Rice. Again, the secret to perfect rice cooking is to cook the rice aggressively and quickly, so that the grains are given just enough time to swell and soften but not to begin breaking up. Different writers have different strong feelings about when that moment is; I have taken my time from H. Pearl Adam. I add the salt and washed rice to the water, bring everything to a brisk boil, cover the pot, and lower the flame to the point where the tiniest amount of additional heat would cause the pot to bubble over (to make sure this is so, I follow the hint supplied by our electric-rice-cooker experiments and *let* it boil over—just a bit). The rice is allowed to cook in this manner for exactly *12 ½ minutes.*

Resting the Rice. At this point I remove the pot from the heat, turn the flame down as low as possible, set a flame tamer over the burner, and put the pot back on this. Then, quickly, I remove the cover of the pot, wrap it in a dish towel, and press it back firmly onto the pot, folding the ends of the towel so they sit on top of the pot, out of the way of the burner flame. The rice is allowed to rest for *17 ½ minutes,* making an even half hour of cooking time. The rice will be dry all through—there should be no wet patch on the bottom of the pot, and hardly any rice stuck to it, either. The rice in the lower part of the pot will be compressed, but not soggy or damp. It will easily fluff up when turned out of the pot into a serving bowl. The result is about 3 cups of cooked rice.

Adventures with An Electric Rice Cooker

We came across so many recommendations urging us to purchase this device during our rice research that we were finally persuaded to order a Chinese model from a mail-order discount firm that specializes in selling off the buying mistakes of other companies at prices too good to refuse. Our unit arrived with a host of accoutrements, including a videotape, which we could not bear to watch, and a set of instructions, written in barely comprehensible *Chinglais*.

Even so, we soon got the hang of its operation. One was to add strictly determined proportions of (carefully washed) rice, water, and salt, plug the thing in (there was no on/off switch), and then stand back while its contents began to boil furiously. Soon the lid was jiggling ominously, the signal, we soon learned, that a steady flow of rice scum would soon be oozing down the side of the machine and creeping across the counter. When, at last, the indicator light changed from "cooking" to "warming" and we removed the cooking insert, we found a thick crust of rice firmly burned onto its bottom and lower sides.

The rest of the rice, however, was the closest we had ever come to preparing genuine Chinese—or, at least, Chinese restaurant—rice. Perhaps our cooker was defective? After a few more experimental runs, each of which resulted in the same behavior, we returned it for another, which behaved in exactly the same way. Our tentative conclusion—as we sheepishly returned this second unit—was that these machines were designed by people who couldn't imagine anyone preparing so *small* an amount of rice as amply feeds us two.

The Zuppa Club

by Molly O'Neill

from *The New York Times Magazine*

Long-time dean of the Sunday *New York Times Magazine*'s regular food column, Molly O'Neill writes thoughtful, meticulous pieces along with recipes well worth clipping.

There should be soup all the time, but especially in the winter. Like the steam that fogs windows as a caldron simmers, soup gives the body a sense of safety and satisfaction.

And though it's pretty easy to make, soup can also be as risky as a road trip in a blizzard. Concocted in a blast of excitement, soup can be great or blah or revolting. It's always a mystery.

"What do you think it will taste like?" writes the American poet Charles Simic in "Soup."

And then he imagines: *"Like barbed wire, like burglar's*

tools/Like a word you'd rather forget/The way the book tastes to the
goat/Who is chewing and spitting its pages/Also like the ear of a
girl you are about to undress/Also like the rim of a smile."

I am not sure whether it is my love of soup or my unflagging belief in happy endings that makes me a soup maniac. Call it soup, zuppa, broth, consommé, bisque, chowder, porridge or potage, but make it a meal; that was the original intent. The European notion of soup as a first course came later and, to my mind, underestimates the power of the dish.

Soup has taught me to be as content with the process of simmering and seasoning as I am with eating the stuff. Early on, my habit of hurrying left me with assorted disasters: big bland pots that had been boiled rather that simmered, scorched soups, over-salted soups, misbegotten soups. Delving into the mystery of soup forced me to slow down. Building a soup is like building a home. The foundation—the fundamental aromatics and broth—needs to be firm. The structure, which in soup is a skeleton of ingredients carefully built from the foundation, needs to be joined as strongly as a wood-framed house. Everything else is decorative.

Begin by imagining the flavors you want, by projecting how ingredients need to be cooked—sweetened in oil to mellow or simmered in broth—to bring out their best qualities, as well as to temper their flavor to meld with other flavors.

Garlic or onions, for instance, need to be sautéed very slowly in fat to become pliable enough to play well with other ingredients. If using the subtle sweet-and-salty blend of carrots, celery and onions to give background flavor, the same slow cooking in fat provides more depth. Sweet peppers acquire a toasty sweet flavor if slowly sweated in oil or butter. Added later in the cooking, they give a blast of sun.

A good, sturdy broth requires a strong body. Chicken, beef, veal, mushroom or seafood broths can be made in huge quantity, defatted and frozen in quart containers as future elixirs.

Season lightly at every stage. Adjust the final seasoning

toward the end of cooking. Salt, in particular, gets strong in the evaporation involved in simmering a soup. Spices like curry and saffron and dried herbs like basil and oregano tend to become bitter; add them just five minutes before serving.

Use sulfureous vegetables as you might a hand grenade. They need to be sweated to lose their bossy attitude.

Within these basic parameters, face your overstuffed refrigerator and summon the soup state of mind. In the end, the two most important things are patience and palate. The dance of soup goes like this: add, simmer and taste. Add, simmer and taste. And its mystery lies in the relationship between heat, time and ingredients. As Simic writes: *"We'll dive into the soup/With a grain of salt between our teeth/And won't come up/Until we learn its song."*

The Crock-pot That Saved Dinner Time

by Janet E. Keeler

from *The St. Petersburg Times*

When we overlook what everyday cooks are up against, it's good to have someone like *St. Petersburg Times* food editor Janet E. Keeler to bring us back to earth.

It is noon on Wednesday and I have a secret.

To the casual observer, everything appears as usual. I peck away on my computer keyboard, interrupted occasionally by the jangle of the phone or the enticing conversation coming from the pod to my right. They laugh, but I am the clever one.

It is noon on Wednesday and I am making dinner.

While the world wobbles, a 3-pound London broil cooks slow and low in my new Crock-Pot. I feel a little bit superior, a little more together knowing that a hearty dinner awaits my family. I will no longer be one of the thousands of Americans who at 5 p.m. still don't know what's for dinner.

I so want my Rival Smart-Pot Programmable Crock-Pot to change my life. I don't want to fret postwork about making dinner or, worse yet, feel guilty because I planned nothing. The science lab corners of the fridge are no place to find nourishment. I envision thoughtful conversations around the table, facilitated by stress-free cooking, to be the coda for our busy day.

I have been watching too much TV.

As 2000 yawned into 2001, we ate Crock-Pot fare four nights out of seven. No one really complained, despite raised eyebrows all around the table on Day 2. The chicken and cabbage didn't turn out as planned, colorwise or tastewise. I pressed on. After all, Santa had left the six-quart gleaming behemoth under the tree, and it was going to turn our lives around. (For the record, I'm the only Keeler who thinks our lives are going the wrong way.)

It wasn't long ago that the avocado green Crock-Pot was lumped with the lava lamp and peace sign as relics from groovier days. Now, like almost everything '70s, the Crock-Pot is cool again. Rival, the originator of the species, celebrates its 30th anniversary this year and touts the Crock-Pot's more seductive name: slow cooker. Who wouldn't want to eat something savory that has been simmering in an earthenware pot all day? Apparently lots of us do. Rival sells about 7-million Crock-Pots a year and is just one of several makers including Hamilton Beach.

Day 1 of our dinnertime makeover began with Navajo Beef and Chile Stew from "Healthy Crockery Cooker" by Mable Hoffman (HPBooks, 1998), also a Christmas present. I unnecessarily doubled the recipe because my Crock-Pot is nearly twice as big as the 3 1/2-quart appliance specified. The spicy stew was welcome on a chilly night, our bellies warmed by its heat. I don't remember particularly rousing or deep dinner conversation, but it was the first day, after all. I was less rushed when I got home from work, and that was part of my mission. Leftovers went into the freezer for another meal, another time.

(A confession: the 5-year-old thought the stew smelled terrific but refused to eat anything from "Mommy's new machine." On his perpetual menu are beans and franks, applesauce and broccoli with ranch dressing.)

Not all is wonderful in Crock-Pot world, though. It's easy to muck up a recipe by cooking the ingredients too long until it's a thick, stewy brown. Not everything should be cooked for 8 to 10 hours, the time most people are at work.

Chicken especially should be cooked for the time noted in the recipe. I gave Chicken with Cabbage and Apples a few extra hours for good measure. Bad idea. The chicken fell from the bones, and I had to fish them out of the soupy mess along with the skin, which looked like jellyfish. It was greasy, too. Skinning the thighs and cutting off any other fat would have helped. In addition, I should have followed the directions and cooked it for 6 hours, rather than 8 with an additional hour on warm.

(The programmable Crock-Pot has this cool feature by which the appliance automatically clicks to warm after the programmed cooking time. The directions suggest not warming food for more than four hours or the taste will be affected.)

Besides the unappetizing grease and bones issues, the dish was bland. For 3 1/2 pounds of chicken pieces, the recipe calls for only 2 tablespoons of soy sauce and 2 teaspoons of grated fresh ginger. Next time I would double that, if there is a next time.

My Day 2 failure overshadowed my Day 1 success until Day 3, when I was redeemed by Roasted Red Pepper and Eggplant Soup, a spicy, meaty melange of veggies.

Thank goodness the peppers came from a jar so I was saved the time of roasting them. The red pepper along with diced eggplant, chopped onions, garlic, white wine, canned chicken broth, fresh bread cubes and spices simmered all day, and the adults lapped it up in the evening. (See note above for the 5-year-old's dinner.) A last-minute addition of minced parsley and medallions of goat cheese added freshness and flavor. A salad and crusty bread rounded out the meal.

Life was good. Dinner was lovely and tasty and we were sharing the news of our day, right on schedule. Perhaps I should do a testimonial for Rival about the Crock-Pot that Brought My Family to the Table.

On Day 4, I shrugged off the cookbook. With cocky abandon, I mixed a can of chopped tomatoes with a couple of teaspoons of minced roasted garlic from a jar, salt and pepper in the Crock-Pot and placed a 3-pound London broil on top. (In hindsight, I should have browned the beef first to make it more appealing and to seal in juices.) It cooked for 8 hours on low and 2 hours on warm waiting for my dear to come home from work.

He was late, the beans and franks routine long over, and I was steamed. My plan was thrown off, and my Crock-Pot offered no company. The waiting time did allow me to bake an acorn squash, delicious with salt, pepper and butter.

Dinner was even good an hour later when the straggler made it home. The London broil was wonderfully tender, falling apart in strings made tangy by the chunky tomato broth. The warm meal was quite a change from the usual self-serve available at that hour.

Things will never be the same at our house. At least that's the plan.

Do-It-Yourself Ducasse

by Peter Kaminsky

from *Food & Wine*

For all the hoopla that has surrounded Alain Ducasse this past year, perhaps the piece that most illuminates this multi-Michelin-starred chef is this feature by Peter Kaminsky (author with Gray Kunz of *The Elements of Taste*), which casts Ducasse in a wholly different— and very likeable—light.

L ast summer, the world's reigning French chef, Alain Ducasse—he of the multiple Michelin stars and the cele- brated restaurants in Paris, Monte Carlo, London and Tokyo—opened his first Manhattan restaurant, Alain Ducasse at the Essex House. The buzz was all about how high the prices were (a $160 prix fixe) and how hard it was to get a reservation (the restaurant has a single seating each night for 65 people). It looked like the only way I would ever taste Ducasse's food was if I made it myself. All right, then. I came up with a plan: I would try to buy the same ingredients Ducasse uses, dig up his brand of pots and pans, knives and plates, pick some recipes from his books and get my wife and daughters to join me in preparing a do-it-yourself Ducasse dinner. And for the pièce de résistance— or perhaps the coup de grâce—we'd invite Ducasse over for the meal. He'd have no trouble getting a reservation *chez nous.*

I wasn't afraid of cooking for a culinary demigod. I've found over the years that chefs are pretty easy to please when they're off duty; after all, the reason they're in the business they're in is that they like food. The tough part, I thought, would be the same thing I find problematic with a lot of great chefs' cookbooks. The recipes are easy—but only if you have a platoon of culinary-school graduates chopping hard-to-get and harder-to-afford ingredients into atoms. Would my wife and daughters be a suitable substitute?

I sat for a few days in our little cabin up in the Adirondacks, thumbing through Ducasse's books, and after much page turning and mental tasting, I began to feel a menu coming together. First, a steak: The recipe I chose, from the 1998 *Ducasse Flavors of France,* called for a sauce made with a reduction of sour cherries and cherry vinegar combined with an equally reduced red-wine-and-beef stock.

"Aha," I can hear you say. "Cherry vinegar? Where do you get that?"

A peek at the back of the book revealed substitutions for unusual ingredients, and an early-morning visit to the supermarket yielded everything else the recipes called for. I returned to the cabin, unpacked and began to reduce stockpots of ingredients to little saucepans' worth of sauces for a practice run. Working alongside me, my 15-year-old daughter, Lucy, made Ducasse's jasmine crème brûlée and learned that the delicious custard would require second-by-second monitoring when she put a blowtorch to the top. (On the first try, she charred it.) Her 10-year-old sister, Lily, helped me strain the sauces and plate the pan-seared shell steak.

Once we were back home in Brooklyn, it was decided that my

wife, Melinda, would do the starter, Ducasse's tomato confit tart with young lettuces. I would concentrate on the steak with sour-cherry sauce and a daunting-sounding but relatively uncompli-cated dish of sole in fig leaves with vanilla bean, Sumatra pepper and a confit of fig and lemon. The fig leaves threw me for a sec-ond, but I live in an Italian neighborhood, and Carmine, my greengrocer, reminded me about Tony Didio's tree on Second Place. Tony got up on a stepladder to snip off the broadest leaves.

Our preparations occupied most of the weekend; there was always something bubbling on top of the stove or roasting inside it. I made the sauces, Lily made a trial pear bread, Melinda roasted tomatoes and assembled a practice tart. Monday morn-ing we packed up our goods and headed to a Manhattan loft about midway between Ducasse's restaurant and our house and began the countdown. Lily mixed up her batter and folded in her honeyed pears. Lucy's ramekins went into the oven, followed by Melinda's crusts. Meanwhile, I put all the ingredients for the fish and meat courses onto little plates, which I covered with plastic wrap. (I've learned, from watching chefs, the tremen-dous virtue of getting ready in advance: *mise en place,* as the French say.)

We began work about 9:30, and for the next several hours we barely looked up. By 2:00, when Dana Cowin of F&W arrived, everything was ready enough that we could chat semirelaxedly. We hardly noticed when, a few minutes later, Ducasse eased into the kitchen, accompanied by his companion, Gwénaëlle Guéguen, a glamorous Bretonne who made me think of a French Lauren Hutton. Her fashionable Courregès outfit and his suit, tie and crisp white shirt struck a more serious note than my polo shirt and Mickey Mouse apron.

I wondered if I was in for a going-over from a no-nonsense big-shot chef; I was relieved when Ducasse removed his suit jacket and glided around the kitchen muttering what I took to be grunts of approval. As we began to chat, he insisted that we speak French, a language I feel rather than really know. But I was game, and Ducasse quickly dropped the persona of serious chef. He was enthusiastic and, best of all, he was hungry.

Melinda cut her tomato tart, wincing at the sounds of the crust cracking where it wanted to rather than along the neat lines her blade was suggesting. Hey, no problem—we heaped the mesclun and tomato confit on top, and nobody knew the difference. It tasted great and Ducasse chowed down. Whew!

I was up next. When I removed my sole-and-fig-leaf bundles from the oven, I decided to leave the fish sitting on the leaves because they looked so nice and rustic; I plopped a roasted fig on one side of each and a roasted lemon slice on the other. This is a very Ducassian dish. Rather than layering taste upon taste, the approach is minimal—not sushi-minimal, but not complicated. If you added anything else, the light sweetness of the fig and the roundness of the vanilla would be overwhelmed. Here, they are left alone to work their shy sorcery on the light and delicate white-fleshed fish.

"Fig leaves!" Ducasse was surprised. "Where did you find those?"

"You can get anything in Brooklyn," I answered.

So far the chef had neither tsk-tsked nor given that Gallic heaven-help-us raising of the eyebrows that signifies chefly displeasure. His basic criticism was "More salt, more pepper," but most chefs will say that about anything they taste.

The next course was the steak. I was curious as to whether, away from his kitchen, Ducasse would first spoon the sauce onto the plate, the way fancy restaurants do, or slice the steak and spoon the sauce over it, the way normal people do. So I told him I'd like to know how he would serve it. That was all he needed to hear—give a chef an opening and the next thing you know he'll have an apron on and a spoon in his hand. True to form, Ducasse shook and stirred my sauce, tasted, added salt, tasted, added pepper, tasted, added salt again. Meanwhile, I seared the steak in the pan and sliced it. Ducasse plated it and then spooned the sauce over the meat, just like a short-order chef putting pan gravy on his meat loaf down at the diner.

At last dinner was ready. We sat. We ate. We finished everything.

"Lucy, your crème brûlée," I barked in chef-like fashion.

Lucy ignited her little blowtorch and crisped the tops perfectly. She placed the finished desserts on a larger dish, leaving room for Lily's pear bread. Emboldened by Ducasse's seasoning foray into my steak sauce, I poured off some of the honey, butter, and juice Lily had cooked her pears in before she folded them into the dough. I dumped the liquid into a saucepan, threw in some salt (eliciting a "Good idea!" from Ducasse) and added some lemon juice. With Lily's collaboration, I spooned the lemon sauce over the pear bread, and the kids served up the desserts. We all fairly licked our dishes clean. If I counted right, Gwénaëlle, who had forgone her meat, polished off three of the creamy desserts.

"Very good," Ducasse declared as he put on his jacket. "It's the ingredients," I answered. That's what chefs say in an interview when nothing else comes to mind. But I knew the recipes had something to do with it too.

An Insincere Cassoulet

by Michael Lewis

from *Gourmet*

Author of best-sellers *Liar's Poker*, and *Next*, and *The New New Thing*, Michael Lewis here turns his hand to food writing. What emerges is a searing exposé—of the male ego unloosed in the kitchen.

A few months ago my parents came to visit us in Paris, to see their new granddaughter and to see how we were getting on. They hoped to be shown around the city, of course, but they didn't need us to help them find the Louvre. They already knew how to be tourists in Paris; what they wanted to know was what it was like simply to live in Paris. This raised a question: Around which quotidian Parisian experience might I structure a week with my parents? I was able to think of only one: a cassoulet. A cassoulet is less a French dish than an athletic event capable of eating up large chunks of time. It requires at least a day and a half of scavenger-hunt-style shopping; two more days of cooking; and then another two days of digestion. To do it well, you must travel from one end of Paris to the other.

When informed that the centerpiece of their week in Paris would be the creation and consumption of a single meal, my parents had radically different responses. In 40 years of marriage my father has been cooked approximately 14,600 dinners by my mother. He couldn't find his own kitchen with a map, and he tends to assume that I'd do well to follow closely in his footsteps. When he heard about the cassoulet, his face instantly became a mask of ironic detachment that as much as shouted, "What? *You* are going to cook? So how am I going to eat?"

Just as instantly my mother assumed the expression of maternal concern that typically precedes her intention to meddle.

Both reactions I fully understood. My personal culinary history has never been anything to write home about. Around ten years ago, for the first time in my life, I was seized by the desire to learn how to cook. I got over it soon enough, but before I did, I pretty well determined that I had no talent for it, for the same reasons I'm slow to learn new board games and to assemble Christmas gifts that arrive in boxes filled with parts. I take instruction poorly, especially when the instructions are written, and I have yet to encounter an oral recipe. So, you might well ask, "Why on earth did you think you should learn how to cook?" I admit, it's a good question. The answer is that I was a single heterosexual American male looking for a quick and easy way to fool single heterosexual American females into believing that I held enlightened, up-to-the-minute attitudes about gender roles—which, at the time, seemed more important than it in fact turned out to be. Also, I liked to eat.

But that's the catch. To become a cook, you not only need to be able to read instructions, you must want to cook when you don't feel like eating. It only ever occurred to me to cook when I was hungry, and by then, of course, it was already too late. Chinese takeout beckoned; Domino's whispered its deadly pickup line into my ear: *"Why bother?"* Realizing that I lacked the self-discipline to cook for myself, I took to forcing myself into must-cook situations. I invited friends to dinner and practiced on them. But my dinner parties tended to be long on the party and short on the dinner. I don't think the guests actually suffered any real harm, but I don't think they ever felt fed. Occasionally, I found them rummaging through the back of my refrigerator on their way out the door. Years later, a friend who came early and often confessed that before he came to my place for dinner he routinely stopped at McDonald's.

In any case, six months or so into the cooking life, I abandoned it.

Then, last year, we moved to Paris. We arrived in the dead of winter with 15 suitcases and a trunk full of assumptions. One of the assumptions was that we would learn how to cook French food. Of course, if you are the sort of person who believes that it is pointless to cook when Domino's is just around the corner, you are likely to find it even more pointless to cook when there are several dozen monomaniacal French chefs around the corner whose sense of self-worth depends entirely on the expression that crosses your face as you masticate. But it's more complicated than that. There may be no point in knowing how to cook when you live in Paris, but there is every point in knowing how to cook when you *have lived* in Paris.

Permit me to explain. As anyone who is honest about it will tell you, Paris is a city of vulgarians that has somehow cowed the world into believing it is the global capital of worldliness, a living and breathing arbiter of good taste. The Parisians treat each other and everyone else with a crudeness and contempt that would make a New Yorker blush. Yet for reasons as deep as they are mysterious, they retain the unique ability to convey an air of sophistication to anyone unlucky enough to experience prolonged contact with them. You don't live in Paris for the fun of it; you live in Paris to acquire, or seem to acquire, a bit of the Parisian ability to impress others with your worldliness.

Put another way, the whole point of living in Paris for a year is to let others know that you are *the kind of person who might well have lived in Paris.*

Put yet another way: Though I have arrived at the point where I can't wait to leave Paris, I don't exactly want to leave Paris behind.

To that end, ten months ago, for the second time in my life, I set out to conquer our new French kitchen. Knowing how to prepare elaborate French meals, I figured, might well inspire future dinner guests in the United States to inquire, "However did you learn how to cook this terribly classy French meal?" Whereupon I might reply, "Oh, it's just a little something I picked up while living in Paris." And my American dinner guests would just stare, slack jawed, in awe.

Sincerity of purpose is in many respects an overrated attribute, but it is extremely useful when setting out to learn to do something new. In the ten months or so since I set out to learn how to cook French food, I have learned how to cook exactly one French dish—my cassoulet. The good news about my cassoulet is that it tastes great. The bad news is that it will do nothing to enhance your reputation as a French sophisticate. Cassoulet isn't what most people imagine when they think "fine dining" or "classy food." It's what they imagine when they hear the phrase "peasant slop." But that, in a way, is also a virtue. Perhaps because it has its origins in the peasant culture of southern France, the typical cassoulet recipe is sufficiently fault-tolerant to be passed along orally, with happy consequences. The recipe that I settled on for my parents' visit, for instance, is not so much a recipe but a few simple rules of thumb.

Rule #1: Nothing should be permitted to distract from the importance of the beans. You will spend a lot more money, and a lot more time, on the other ingredients, but you must always remember to treat the beans as the stars of your show. This isn't as easy as it sounds. The cassoulet cook is subjected to endless entreaties from his fancier ingredients; he is a bit like the director of one of those independent films in which the leading actor is a humble unknown and the walk-on parts are played by glamorous celebrities. The cook who lacks the discipline and resolve to keep these prima donnas in their assigned places will find his entire production undermined. When he shops for ingredients, when he fiddles with his recipe, when he makes those slight adjustments to taste that allow him to feel less a dutiful craftsman than an improvisational artist, he must keep in his mind's eye the simple white bean.

Rule #2: Do not attempt to flatter the beans falsely by juxtaposing them with inedible pseudo-foods. The French tend to ignore this rule. They include in their finished cassoulet many disgusting shards of animal fat and rind. The cassoulets you find in Parisian restaurants, in particular, are minefields of animal parts. This does not flatter the beans; it insults them. It suggests that they cannot hold their own in polite company. They can.

Rule #3: Avoid reminding your guests that they are eating meat. In my view, the well-cooked cassoulet should be able to fool a vegetarian for a bite or two. This is a radical departure from the French view of the matter, which assumes that cassoulet should be presented as a hearty meat dish. But, like many Anglo-Saxons, I am a hypocritical carnivore. I realize that there are people in this world, many of them French, who when they drive past a field of sheep, crave lamb. I am not among them. I enjoy a piece of meat from time to time, but not if I'm reminded where it came from. Of course, the English language encourages this hypocrisy—we don't eat "cow," we eat "beef." People don't say "Pass the deer" because it conjures up a mental picture that

ruins everybody's dinner. But I take the hypocrisy one step further—I like meat less the more it resembles its former owner. Fat
and gristle and large chunks of dripping flesh put me off, and so
I keep all of them out of the pot. All meat is sliced and diced to
be as un-meatlike as possible.

Rule #4: Take off your watch. The pleasure of making cassoulet is precisely that it is an unsophisticated dish, created by
unsophisticated people whose lives were so different from our
own that we can barely imagine them. The cooking of their dish
hauls you away from modernity and its time-is-money sensibility and throws you back into 18th-century French peasant life.
There is no such thing as instant cassoulet; when you set out to
make this dish, you have to acknowledge right up front that it
will require the better part of three days. The mere thought that
you will be spending that much time on a single meal is annoy-
ing at first (at least it is to me). But I find that once I've settled
into the cassoulet's deliberate rhythms, I lose all sense of time.
For this reason and others—the main one being that I can't cook
anything else—I have found that cassoulet is well suited to those
special occasions when you have cut a deal with your mental
diary to abandon your ordinary rushed habits.

Rule #5: If you want to preserve your authority in the
kitchen, keep your mother out of it.

At some point between the vegetable stands and the butcher
shops, my father simply vanished. I'm still not sure where he
went, but he was gone for most of the week. The moment he did
this, my mother took charge of my cassoulet. In apparent harmony, we passed from the glorious indoor market at Le Bon
Marché—Paris's devastating answer to Dean & DeLuca—to the
glorious outdoor market on the Rue Mouffetard, but just below
the surface there simmered a power struggle that will be familiar to any man who has ever tried to cook for his mother.

In addition, my mother is one of those people who does things
her way or not at all. She's the only person I've ever met who

becomes irritated when someone else tries to help her wash the dishes. As a result, she can't really understand what others mean when they ask her to lend a hand. She assumes they mean that they want her to do whatever needs doing for them. Often they do—nearly always I do—but whether they do or they don't, she winds up doing all the work.

As we ducked beneath the animal carcasses into the French butcher shops, I could feel my authority shrink. It began with seemingly harmless suggestions ("Shouldn't we really have some bacon?"; "Are you sure that's the *best* duck?"). By the time we arrived back in the kitchen with the sacks of ingredients, I realized that I was already the victim of a coup d'état. I had intended to serve the cassoulet straight, with maybe a little side salad. Somehow, my mother got her mind set on an elaborate concoction of green beans and carrots that I won't bother to describe because I can't. Once the cooking began, I became a puppet dictator in my own kitchen. In a blur of activity, the new regime rejiggered the cooking order, reduced the cooking time for the beans by 15 minutes, and restored the bacon to the pot—all of which, I admit, were improvements on my design.

Her insistence on bacon was a good example of her kitchen politics. I initially opposed the bacon. As I say, the biggest mistake that the French make in their cassoulets is their lack of discrimination about the meat. One solid chomp on a piece of loose goose rind can ruin your week. And what the French call bacon is not the light and crispy breakfast food so relished by red-blooded Americans. It's a thick, ugly wedge of ham with a repellent brownish rind and thick streaks of glutinous white fat; there's no disguising where it comes from. You could cook a piece of it for a week without rendering it any more appealing unless, of course, you're a meat fanatic.

Ignoring all these obvious objections, my mother diced the bacon and eliminated every trace of brown or white. It took an hour or so, which to my mind was a huge waste of time for a few scraps of bacon. But each time I complained she'd say things like "I'll just put in a little bit" and "I'll chop it up so you won't even notice" and "It really won't change your recipe at all." As it is impossible to cook a cassoulet and, at the same time, monitor another human being intent on taking control, the little pile of meat was ready to drop into the pot before I knew what had happened. It was all done with such subtlety that I nearly forgot it wasn't my idea.

On day four, the guests we had invited arrived, and my father finally emerged from whatever hole he had disappeared down. The cassoulet came out of the oven at just the right moment—which is the moment everyone is ready to eat. My daughter, Quinn, took the first bite—then another. Soon, everyone was tucking into seconds and proclaiming the dish a smash hit, which they always do. "This is *really* good," said my father, with something like shock. "You did a wonderful job," said my mother. I didn't, of course, but what does that matter? The cassoulet was nothing to me, the applause everything.

Michael Lewis's Cassoulet de Canard
Serves 10
Active time: 2 hr
Start to finish: 2 days
My recipe was adapted from Julia Child's Mastering the Art of French Cooking. *I've changed the meats (a lot) and the seasonings (a bit). I've also tinkered with cooking times and sequence.*

  2 ½ lb dried white beans such as Great Northern
  ½ lb fresh pork rind
  2 ½ lb confit duck legs
  6 fresh parsley stems (without leaves)
  4 fresh thyme sprigs
  5 whole cloves
  12 garlic cloves

1 (1-lb) piece smoked salted slab bacon, halved crosswise

3 cups chopped onion (1 lb)

1 teaspoon salt

1 lb meaty mutton or lamb bones, cracked by butcher

1 cup rendered goose fat

6 large tomatoes (3 lb)

5 bay leaves (not California)

1 qt beef stock (not canned broth)

1 (750-ml) bottle dry white wine

2 teaspoons black pepper

2 ½ lb fresh garlic-pork sausage (not sweet or very spicy) such as *saucisson à l'ail au vin rouge, saucisse de canard à l'armagnac,* or a mixture of the two

1 ½ cups plain dry bread crumbs

1 cup chopped fresh flat-leaf parsley

Special equipment: a small square of cheesecloth and a wide 10-quart enameled cast-iron pot

Day 1
Act 1: Nasty Work
   1 hr

Bring 5 quarts water to a boil in an 8-quart heavy pot. Boil beans, uncovered, 1 ½ minutes, then turn off heat and let them soak 50 minutes.

While beans soak, do all the really disgusting work with the meat. Put pork rind in a 3-quart saucepan three-fourths full of cold water and bring to a boil. Boil pork rind 1 minute. Drain and rinse under cold running water, then do it again. (Sometimes you know it's ready because it grows nipples.) After draining, cut the truly repulsive boiled pork rind into pieces that are big enough to identify (about 2 inches), so you can fish them out before serving.

Scrape off and discard fat from confit duck legs and shred meat (the more it shreds the better). [Editors' note: Those who have no problem with identifiable meat in their food might want to keep the shredding to a minimum.]

Act 2: Slightly Less Nasty Work
   1 hr and 20 min
Put parsley stems, thyme, whole cloves, and 8 garlic cloves in cheesecloth and tie into a bundle to make a *bouquet garni.*

First seasoning of beans: Add rind pieces, bacon halves, 1 cup onion, *bouquet garni,* and salt to beans. Simmer, covered, 1 ¼ hours, skimming regularly. Cool, uncovered.

While beans simmer, brown mutton bones. Do this by heating goose fat in enameled cast-iron pot over moderate heat until it smokes, then cook mutton bones, stirring occasionally, until browned, about 5 minutes. Set them aside on a plate. Drop remaining 2 cups onion into pot and brown that, too. This can take as long as 15 minutes. Stir regularly.

Peel..., seed, and chop tomatoes.

Act 3: Nasty Gets Nice
   1 ¾ hr
Flavoring the meat: Add browned bones and shredded duck to onion. Add bay leaves, beef stock, tomatoes, remaining 4 garlic cloves, white wine, and pepper. Simmer, covered, 1 ½ hours. Cool to room temperature, uncovered.

Put pot with meat and pot with beans in refrigerator, covered, overnight.

Day 2
Act 1: Crescendo
   1 hr
Poke holes in sausage with a fork and grill it slowly in a well-seasoned ridged grill pan over moderately low heat 20 minutes

(to get the fat out). (Sausage should still be slightly undercooked on the inside when you're done.) Transfer to a cutting board and cool slightly. Slice into thin (¼-inch) rounds.

Remove and discard bones and bay leaves from meat pot. Remove duck with a slotted spoon and put on a plate. Reserve cooking liquid remaining in pot.

Remove bacon from beans and cut into tiny, fat-free pieces. Put pieces on a plate and discard remaining bacon fat. Discard pork rind and *bouquet garni* from beans.

Julia Child says: "Now is the time to drain the beans and dump them into the ample, leftover meat cooking juices." In my experience, there is nothing left to drain. What you are looking at, when you stare into the bean pot, is a fairly solid wall of beans, with some gluey goop in between. So, pour reserved meat cooking juices into bean pot. Bring to a simmer over moderately high heat, stirring occasionally, and simmer 5 minutes, skimming any scum. Then turn off heat and let sit another 5 minutes.

Act 2: Final Assembly
  1 ½ hr
  Preheat oven to 375°F.

Spread a layer of beans on bottom of enameled cast-iron pot. Layer half of sausage and bacon on top, then another layer of beans, then half of duck (and any mutton), then another layer of beans, et cetera, ending with a layer of beans. Then add enough remaining liquid from bean pot until beans are submerged. Sprinkle with bread crumbs and parsley.

Bring the whole thing to a simmer, uncovered, over moderately low heat. Then stick it in oven 20 minutes. Break through bread crumbs in several places with a spoon, allowing the liquid to mess up the look of the thing. Then reduce heat to 350°F and leave it in another 40 minutes. Serve very hot.

Fred and Ginger, Lamb and Cabernet

by Dorothy J. Gaiter
and John Brecher

from *The Wall Street Journal*

In their wonderful weekly wine column, the husband-and-wife team of Gaiter and Brecher dispenses level-headed advice to help *Wall Street Journal* readers navigate the transition from boardroom to wine cellar.

S ince Spring is a traditional time for lamb and many people prepare it for their Easter dinner, we thought it would be a good idea to write about the perfect wine to have with such a special meal. But let's talk first about *From Russia With Love.*

Our favorite scene in that old James Bond movie takes place aboard a train. Sean Connery is having dinner with Robert Shaw, who is pretending to be a fellow agent, and they both order grilled sole. Bond tells the waiter: I'll have a bottle of the Blanc de Blancs." The bad guy says: "Make mine Chianti—the red kind."

Minutes later, Robert Shaw knocks Bond unconscious. When 007 wakes up, with a gun in his face, the first thing he says is: "Red wine with fish. Well, that should have told me something."

The message is clear: Drink the wrong wine with dinner and you might as well be a paid assassin. But what is the "right" wine?

We're asked about wine-and-food matches all the time. This is fun for us because we enjoy helping people create special matches, and, frankly, as serious eaters ourselves, we love hearing about the remarkable meals that people cook. Who wouldn't enjoy the question from Rick and Lola Henderson of Las Vegas, who asked what would go with "oyster stew made with fresh oysters, celery, onions, cayenne and black pepper and whole milk?" (We suggested a sparkling wine.)

Let's start with common sense. There's no one-size-fits-all match between any wine and food. So much depends on what you like. A classic match with roast chicken, for instance, is red Burgundy, but if you don't like red Burgundy, clearly that won't work for you.

The match also depends on how the dish is prepared. Late last year, Dr. M. Dean Jacoby of Dallas wrote to suggest that we try a smoked turkey from a company called Greenberg with a Riesling, which sounded like a fabulous combination to us. We tried that, along with other wines Dr. Jacoby recommended as good combinations. To our surprise, we preferred a creamy Pinot Noir to the Riesling. That discovery, in turn, brought a note from Gil Smith of Helotes, Texas, who wrote that he smokes turkeys himself and "we always go for the Riesling, usually a Spatlese.

"So why the different results?" he continued. "I checked the Web for information on the source of your turkey, the Greenberg company in Tyler, Texas, and found, in a *Texas Monthly* article from 1997, that they use a hickory fire for smoking their birds. Hickory produces a very distinctive flavor in any meat that is smoked over it, and needs a fairly robust wine to stand up to it. On the other hand, I use nothing but South Texas live oak in the smoking process, and the result is a smoked meat with a more neutral flavor. That allows a gentle white wine like the German Riesling (especially a Mosel) to blend wonderfully with the bird."

Even experts rarely agree on the "perfect" match. We looked at some good Internet sites for advice on matching wine with roast leg of lamb. They suggested Merlot, Chianti, red Burgundy, Pinot Noir, Syrah, Dolcetto, Beaujolais, Cotes-du-Rhone, Bordeaux, Barolo, Barbaresco, Shiraz, Petite Sirah and Zinfandel. Wow. What's a cook to do? We decided to conduct our own test. As it happened, we were on our way to Atlanta for a family reunion, where Dottie's mother always prepares her famous roast leg of lamb.

This is the lamb she cooked for our after-wedding dinner in 1979 and always prepares when we visit her. Like many of the world's best cooks, only she knows how she actually makes this dish, how much of this and that she uses. But for the record, this is what she's willing to share. She marinates the lamb for a day or two in onion, garlic, salt and pepper, ground ginger, oregano, curry powder and either sugar or vinegar. Then she roasts it for an hour at "400 something," then she turns it down lower "for a while" until it's ready.

We dropped in on two wine stores to find enough different wines for a wide array of possible combinations. They were the first two stores we saw, so our experience in buying the wine would be very much like yours. If we were at home, we'd almost surely open a fine old Bordeaux—not just because we think the elegant but supple red would be an excellent match for the lamb, but because a visit from Dottie's mom is special, and the wine should match the occasion. We didn't have that luxury, though.

In the stores, we focused on wines under $20, and looked for wineries that are widely distributed. When we got back to Dottie's sister Juarlyn's house—sister Karen, her husband David and their kids had come up from Tallahassee—we opened them all up and conducted a pre-dinner tasting (we didn't conduct this blind since we were tasting different kinds of wine). Then, during dinner, we tasted them again.

When we look for a good food-wine pairing, we try to walk a line. We don't want the wine and food to be too similar or too different. If they're too similar—rich lobster with a big, luscious Chardonnay, for instance—they just duplicate each other. If they're too different—pot roast with a floral, acidic Riesling—they don't complement each other. What we look for is a combination in which the food will make the wine taste better, and vice versa, a classic case of the sum being greater than the parts. Think Tracy and Hepburn, Astaire and Rogers, Ashford and Simpson, Brecher and Gaiter.

We all agreed that the Chianti was wrong—far too fruity for the elegant, earthy tastes of the meat. We felt the same way about the Pinot Noir. The Pinot was fruity and creamy, with nice perfume and even some lilacs. But the tastes of the lamb made the Pinot seem almost sweet. They clashed.

On and on we went. One Merlot was too grapey and simple, adding nothing to the complexity and different textures of the lamb. We had great hopes for one of the Zinfandels. It was a Rodney Strong "Old Vines" Zinfandel from 1997, and we were all impressed with it during our pre-dinner tasting. It was massive, rich and classy, with nice pepper and tastes of the earth. All in all, it seemed like it would be a perfect pairing. But it wasn't. The big wine overwhelmed the tastes of the lamb.

A couple of tasters, including Dottie, believed a Merlot from Bogle (1999 "Old Vine Cuvée") was the winner. Before dinner, it was simply soft and pleasant, a nice "glass of Merlot" at a smoky bar. With the lamb, Dottie felt that the creaminess, softness and simple smoothness of the wine created something special—not just a good taste pairing, but a "warming effect" that made the whole meal seem more homey and delicious. She also felt a little acid kick at the end of the wine—generally wines with good acids go better with food—was a nice finish with a bite of lamb.

We had a very interesting experience with a Ravenswood Zinfandel (1998 Vintners Blend). Ravenswood is a great name in Zinfandel, but before dinner, this one, though pleasant, seemed diluted and simple. With the lamb, though, it was a different wine. Tastes that we'd barely registered before—cream, pepper and a slight bitterness—seemed more obvious. At the same time, the lamb, with its subtle herbs, became more vibrant when paired with the wine.

We ultimately decided that our favorite wine with the lamb was a Cabernet Sauvignon—in this case, a Hess Select 1998. The wine was classy, with nice structure and some hints of herbs and spices. Its combination of good fruit, structure and earthiness paired beautifully with the juicy, melt-in-your-mouth tastes of the lamb. They seemed to bring out the best in each other.

So next time we have Grandma Dot's lamb, if we don't have access to an older Bordeaux, we'll likely have a Cabernet Sauvignon or a somewhat soft young Bordeaux, like a Margaux. But that's just us. Make your own decisions based on what you like. After all, in that whole list of the experts' recommendations, there's not a single white wine. And while roast lamb seems like a red-wine dish, there are many people who don't like red wine. Does that mean they should give up lamb altogether, or have no wine with lamb? Of course not. They should just think about a "bigger" white wine—a Viognier, for instance.

Even assassins know that "perfect" wine-food combinations aren't everything in life. As Robert Shaw responds to James Bond when 007 wakes up on the floor: "You may know the right wines, but you're the one on your knees."

My Best Friend's Wedding Cake

by Melanie Thernstrom

from *Food & Wine*

For every cook who ever set out with grand ideas for a high-profile culinary project, here's writer Melanie Thernstrom's tongue-in-cheek account of her rash offer to bake her friends a wedding cake.

Cynthia, my best friend, was not touched or overjoyed or even grateful when I told her I wanted to make her wedding cake. Her e-mail did not mince words:

Ahem. Have you ever made a cake for 120 to 150? I don't mean to sound like I lack faith, but this is what I fear: The caterer's assistants will have to be working around you as you ice the cake, the kitchen will be in an uproar, icing everywhere, the layers of the cake

> not adhering, and the assistants will have to pitch in
> to help. Besides, I really love our caterer, Gracie . . .

Some people might have found this reply discouraging, but it only piqued my resolve. Was I going to allow her to place more faith in the hired help than in me? A privilege of best friendship is to never take no for an answer, in the certainty that the person will thank you later. I was determined: I would make a cake she would forever thank me for.

Although my baking history is checkered, each cake's problems were unique, and, as I reminded Cynthia, only the initial experience was a half disaster. A decade ago, my first college friends, Annie and Mark, decided to become prematurely grown-up and got engaged. They had no money, and when the caterers informed them the cake would cost $500 (the standard fee), they were shocked. I told them I could make them a free cake in a jiffy.

Modern friendship sometimes strikes me as a sadly attenuated affair, more talk than action. I like a friendship with a lot of tangibles—and what is more tangible than a five-layer English fruitcake blanketed in marzipan? I was in graduate school then, with work to avoid, which I did for many a week by drying and candying cherries and apricots and pineapples, piping marzipan roses and converting the British recipe's measurements from pounds to cups. I was a tad anxious as I increased the baking powder tenfold. What if it rose a hundredfold? Would it explode? I felt as though I was making a bomb.

The layers did emerge from the oven as round as bombs, so they didn't balance on top of one another. (I didn't then know the trick of lopping off the curved tops with a dental-floss guillotine.) Far from stabilizing the layers, the glossy icing that went over the marzipan was slippery. On the day of the wedding, although I got the cake assembled on a table in the reception tent, it soon began to resemble the Matterhorn, the top layers sloping precariously to one side. When we got back from the church, it looked like an earthquake had struck: a deep fissure had formed, revealing the dark fruit-and-nut innards of a slab that appeared to be minutes away from toppling to the floor.

Panic. I downed a tall glass of Champagne, and the giddiness of catastrophe began to set in. The great thing about a baking disaster, I realized, is that it is, after all, merely a dessert; just because the cake is unsound doesn't mean the marriage will be. I repeated this to myself as I jury-rigged the cake with barbecue skewers and frosted over them; they held the layers together long enough for the pictures—but the ceremonial first cut couldn't be too deep.

My mistake turned out to be simple. A cake of substantial height and weight needs a supporting beam. I hadn't known that caterers use a special system of cardboard disks supported by dowels inside the cake to hold up the layers.

I didn't do any event baking for a long stretch after that. But when, five years later, an old boyfriend decided to get married, I saw an opportunity to redeem my previous maladroitness by making the groom's cake—a Southern tradition of having a second smaller cake of a different variety. I settled on a Lady Baltimore, an almond-flavored cake iced with a nerve-racking frosting. (Why had I volunteered, I wondered as I struggled with the frosting. To demonstrate I *was* happy about his wedding? I was happy, but not while making the frosting.)

A candy thermometer is a portent of trouble: A recipe that requires it is always a pain. My frosting required caramelizing sugar and then pouring it slowly into stiffly beaten egg whites in such a way that the boiling liquid doesn't cook the eggs and turn what is supposed to be a stiff frosting into a warm, soupy mess. Even if you manage all that, cleaning rock hard, caramelized sugar out of the pan afterwards will do you in.

I managed it all, however, and the cake was flawless. I was the only one who thought so, though, because the hotel staff forgot to serve it! Two hundred and fifty dessert plates went out to the guests with the hotel's Sanka-colored slice while my beautiful creation, dressed in white roses and ribbons, sat forsaken on a banquet table. I like to think the kitchen staff tasted it before they discarded it.

That might have been my finale if the experience hadn't been so maddeningly purposeless. But then, five years after that, my dear friend Elizabeth got engaged. Nuptial symbolism was anathema to her and her intended—they could barely bring themselves to call their small ceremony a "wedding." (The invitation was to help celebrate—in this order—their friends, their family, their new house and, finally, their marriage!) Elizabeth's only requirement for the cake was that it not look like a wedding cake. I decided to make a family favorite, a bourbon-pecan cake—or rather, three of them, each birthday-size.

Shortly before the wedding, I came down with pneumonia. So I ordered emergency cakes from my parents' local bakery. But when my father and I went to pick them up, they were so disappointing, with that awful faux look—why do bakery cakes look fake? they aren't—that my father offered to take the afternoon off and help me bake. I sat at the kitchen table drinking tea and coughing instructions as he chopped and stirred.

My father doesn't bake, he grills. But the bourbon-pecan cake—which he had eaten countless times, because I started making it when I was 10—is fool- and father-proof. It has three main ingredients: pecans (or walnuts), raisins (or prunes or dried cherries) and decent bourbon (Southern Comfort won't work). It's easy to make in any multiple without fear of a baking-powder incident, because it barely rises—and therefore can't fall. It's hearty: It can sit around for weeks, and it freezes more or less indefinitely. (Our record-holder kept for three years and still tasted merry.) Blessedly, powdered sugar suffices for frosting. The cake bears the same relationship to fruitcake that mock turtle soup does to real turtle soup: People prefer it.

The cakes were still warm when I arrived at the ceremony, trying not to cough on them. Everyone treated me like a hero. And although I forwarded the thank-you note to my father, I was not displeased to get all the credit.

But I had a last chance to make a perfect wedding cake. Cynthia apprehensively agreed. She and her fiancé, Jim, had turned away from their Christian upbringing but felt the formerly religious person's need for a ritual, so they'd decided to have a Wiccan ceremony—one modeled on the nature-based pre-Christian faith—in their 1740 farmhouse. The bourbon-pecan cake seemed right because just as red, the color of her dress, had been a common wedding-gown color in eighteenth century England, fruitcakes had been traditional for weddings before the advent of refrigeration. After the celebration, the cake was soaked in liquor, wrapped in cloth and eaten a year later, when it would still be good.

I had had the revelation before Elizabeth's wedding that what makes a wedding cake riskier than others is not that it has to feed so many but that it's one cake. If a single cake is supposed to represent the unity of the couple, I decided, a multiplicity of cakes could represent richness, heterogeneity or even a subversion of the genre. (Cynthia and I met in graduate school.)

Knowing that Cynthia liked vintage things, I spent a long evening on eBay searching for "vintage wedding" items and discovered scores of antique "toppers," the miniature bride-and-groom figurines that used to routinely adorn wedding cakes. I agonized between a pale porcelain childlike couple stamped "Made in Occupied Japan" and a hale 1954 California bisque couple, and finally—eBay mindset—went for both. Then I decided to purchase four more, so that each of the six cakes could have its own topper.

Surrounded by garlands from Cynthia's garden, the figurines looked great on the cakes. Gracie, the caterer, made caramel and fudge sauces to drizzle over the slices, which she served with cut-up strawberries, mangoes and kiwis. People asked to take pieces home.

A few days after the wedding, I received an e-mail with the heading "Apologia":

> I apologize from the bottom of my heart for all my fears. Your flock of cakes was gorgeous beyond belief—like a Mardi Gras parade on the table. To have friend-made cakes gave the wedding a sweet, old-fashioned touch, as if we lived in the same small village instead of different cities. The cake toppers, a century's worth of happy couples, are now awaiting their next duties—as attendants at your wedding? I wonder who will make those cakes (she says, glancing around nervously). I know you said it was easy, but—really—how easy?

"Easy as duck soup! Quick as hasty pudding!" I wrote back. Two supposedly easy projects that I've yet to attempt.

Someone's in the Kitchen

Comfort Me with Apples

by Ruth Reichl

from *Comfort Me with Apples*

In this second volume of her memoirs, *Gourmet* editor-in-chief Ruth Reichl shows how a chef from a Berkeley commune became one of the country's most respected restaurant critics. Here she learns by watching a truly great cook in action.

'd recognized the voice at once: masculine, slightly high, with the polish of the theater and just a whiff of New York. It was straight out of my childhood. The very sound of it had made me laugh.

"Danny Kaye phoned you?" said my mother during her daily call. "Why?"

"He's very interested in food," I replied. "He said he liked my writing, and he invited me to his house for dinner next Monday night."

"Danny Kaye invited you to his *house* for dinner?" she repeated, actually sounding impressed. "He's supposed to be a wonderful cook!"

"He certainly seems to think he is," I replied. "He told me that Paul Bocuse and Roger Verger say that the best restaurant in California is Danny Kaye's house."

"He must have been joking," she said.

"No, Mom, he wasn't."

"Too bad Daddy's not alive. Danny Kaye was his favorite actor. He'd be so pleased."

I thought of my father, singing "Hans Christian Andersen" to me as I fell asleep. I saw him laughing at *Me and the Colonel*. "Do you think he might finally approve of the work I'm doing?" I asked, hating the needy tone of my voice.

My mother ignored it. "He just loved Danny Kaye," she replied, making no concessions.

At first the thought of going to Danny Kaye's house was thrilling. But at the last minute Michael couldn't come; three gunmen had held up a bank in Santa Monica, and he was needed at the station. As I drove through Beverly Hills, alone, looking for San Ysidro Drive, I began to have doubts. What on earth were we going to talk about? By the time I found the house and walked up the path I was so nervous that I panicked as I was about to ring the bell. I stood there for a second, then ran back to the car.

"You're late," Danny said when I'd finally composed myself enough for a second attempt. He glanced at his watch. "Six minutes late. You could have ruined dinner."

"It's nice to meet you too," I heard myself say. He let out a short bark of laughter, shook my hand, and led me into the house.

He looked just as he had in all the movies of my childhood. He was not so much older as more wrinkled, like laundry that had not been ironed. His blondish hair was a little too long and fluffed around his face, and his lean body no longer moved with the boneless grace of an acrobat, but otherwise he seemed unchanged.

The best restaurant in California was huge—and echoing. We seemed to be alone as we walked through one silent decorator-designed room after another, and I began to hate those gunmen who had sent Michael back to work. It was a relief when we reached a cheerful sitting room and found it filled with other guests.

"Don't get comfortable," said Danny as he introduced me to his friends, "because I want to show you my kitchen." He rushed through the introductions as if they were an irritating chore and led me out the door. I felt like a very special guest of honor. For the first time since I had been in Los Angeles I was glad I had taken the job.

"Wow." I actually said it, then put my hand to my mouth and blushed. The kitchen was a theater, and the round table in the middle was set so that the people seated there would be facing the stove. The cook would be the star of this show, and as Danny strolled possessively around the stage, showing off exotic pots and expensive gadgets, I saw that the entire room had been built with this in mind. It was a one-man kitchen, designed exactly for his body: Each counter was precisely calibrated to his height, so that he could stand at the stove and reach anything he might need.

Danny picked up a cleaver lying on the butcher block and held it out. "Try it," he urged. "I have them hand-made just for me."

I took the cleaver, feeling the comforting heft of the thing. Danny handed me a carrot. "Cut it," he said, and I understood that he was conferring a rare privilege. "I don't normally like people to touch my tools, but I want you to." The cleaver felt good in my hand. I swung and felt it bite cleanly through the carrot.

"Great cleaver," I said, handing it back.

"Knives are very important," he noted, solemnly caressing the edge.

He went to the big refrigerator and took out something wrapped in white paper. "I hope you eat liver," he said, opening the paper and holding up a thick maroon slab.

"Of course I eat it," I replied. "I'm a restaurant critic. I eat everything."

"You have not eaten liver like my liver," he said confidently.

"Just wait. There's only one butcher in the entire city worth buying it from. And then you have to slice the meat just so, on the diagonal." He demonstrated.

He showed me the vegetables, the fruits, the cheese, reciting the pedigree of each. As he offered to introduce me to his purveyors I realized that my opinion really mattered to him. I hoped, with all my heart, that he cooked as well as he believed he did; I did not think I would be able to lie to him.

Danny led me back to the sitting room, and then he disappeared for a while. The rest of us chatted, distant and polite, but the room seemed empty without him. Suddenly he was back, standing in the doorway imperiously calling, "Dinner, now!" Everyone in the room jumped up, scattering crumbs and spilling drinks, scrambled into the hall, and made a mad dash for the kitchen.

I stood in the doorway, staring at the scene. The table had been set with bowls of clear, golden broth that sat steaming at each place. The fragrance drifted intoxicatingly through the room. "Lemongrass!" I said.

"Sit down!" Danny shouted irritably from his post at the stove. We stopped milling and each of us rushed for the nearest seat, as if this were a game of musical chairs. We threw ourselves down as he commanded, "Eat!" We obediently picked up our spoons.

With the first bite I knew that no lies would be necessary. Danny's soup was extraordinary, with that resonance that goes on and on, like a bell still humming, long after the last note has been struck.

Danny did not sit down. As we ate he stood at the stove like a mad scientist, enveloped in the steam that billowed about him from a huge cauldron. I heard the sizzle of butter hitting a hot surface and sensed the high, clean note of lemon juice being added to the pan. Now there was a richer scent—cream, I guessed—and then the aromas began to mingle, so that lemon and cream and butter were dancing through the air.

Water drained; wet pasta hit a skillet with a hiss, and a cover went crashing down. Then Danny was rushing to the table with a plate in his hand and setting it in front of me. "Eat it now," he insisted, "don't wait for the others. This is a dish that can only be served to people eating in the kitchen. In a few minutes it won't be any good. I made the noodles myself."

I twirled the pasta around my fork and took a bite. And then, in spite of myself, I gasped. The pasta was so thin that it seemed to have vanished, leaving only a memory behind. What was left was simply the subtlety of the sauce, pure and light, as if the liquid had somehow taken solid form. It wasn't food; it was magic on a plate, and for a moment I disappeared into the flavor. When I returned Danny was standing over me, watching me so intently and with such pleasure that I knew I didn't have to say a single word.

I didn't listen to the conversation after that, or think about much of anything at all. I just ate, conscious of my luck at being there, trusting that each dish would be extraordinary. The liver was like little pillows of velvet between satin slivers of onion, and so sweet it was as if it had been dusted with sugar. "It's the onions," he said, answering my unspoken question. "They're grown in special soil. And, of course, the way they're cut."

The conversation flowed around us, background music, but I didn't try to join it. I understood that in his kitchen Danny was desperate for an audience; cooking for people who didn't pay attention ruined it for him. He was a creator, not a consumer, and the only thing he required was appreciation.

And so I said nothing as he snatched the lemon souffle from the oven and rushed it to the table. High, light, rich, and eggy, it fell, slightly, as it was cut, collapsing onto itself with a fragrant sigh. I ate it slowly, savoring the way it disappeared in my mouth, and drank the espresso he served me at the end without sugar, liking the bitterness against the sweetness of the soufflé.

"I think it's the best meal I've ever eaten," I said as I left. Danny nodded. "You have to come back," he said. I understood that this had been a test, and I had passed.

Lobsters at Five Paces, Knives and Egos Bared

by Rick Marin
from *The New York Times*

In this, the age of the celebrity superchef, could there be any weirder expression of the zeitgeist than the Food Network's Iron Chef competition? Reporter Rick Marin's feature story covers the cook-off with all the drollery it deserves.

They called it "The Tango in Tokyo."

On Sunday night, the Food Network ran its "Iron Chef" rematch between Bobby Flay and Masaharu Morimoto, after Mr. Flay's humiliating home-kitchen defeat a year ago in New York. This time, victory belonged to Mr. Flay. But some viewers of this strange, dubbed Japanese import—a bake-off with the trappings of professional wrestling—must have come away wondering if Mr. Morimoto was robbed.

The five judges sampled five dishes by the challenger, the chef and owner of Mesa Grill and Bolo (and a resident Food Network star) and were . . . pleasantly surprised. "Quite good," a matronly

Japanese food critic said of Mr. Flay's blue-corn deep-fry, though a Japanese actor on the panel found his tamale "a bit too floury and—how do you say?—not as good as the previous dish."

The tasting tribunal, which also included a retired sumo wrestler and an officer of the American Embassy, then moved on to Mr. Morimoto, the former chef at Nobu in Manhattan. Eyes popped and rolled. Fingers were licked. Bouillabaisse shabu-shabu was slurped to the last drop. "So good!" "Such luxurious flavor." "Some kind of magic."

The score: 89 for Mr. Flay, 83 for Mr. Morimoto. But even without tasting the food, that result was a little hard to swallow.

This was a "grudge match," heavily hyped by the Food Network. No expense was spared. A truck advertising the event patrolled Times Square pelting bystanders with refrigerator magnets saying, "Hail to the Iron Chef!" while megaphones blared, "Let's get ready to rumble."

Last time around, Mr. Morimoto beat Mr. Flay at Webster Hall in the Food Network's highest-rated program ever (960,000 viewers). It got ugly.

"He's not a chef," Mr. Morimoto said after Mr. Flay jumped up on his cutting board to raise his arms in premature victory. "Cutting boards and knives are sacred to us." Mr. Flay, for his part, complained about the fairness of the fight. "I cut myself," he said. "I was getting electrocuted every three minutes." (Water had leaked onto the floor under his cooking station.)

But revenge is a dish best served with your own line of Southwestern-theme spices. So Mr. Flay flew 8,000 miles to Kitchen Stadium, the Tokyo television studio where the Iron Chefs traditionally square off. He was back for blood, this time hopefully not from his finger.

To kick off the rematch, Takeshi Kaga, the "Iron Chef" impresario and the chairman of the so-called Gourmet Academy, entered on a white horse. He was costumed in his usual 18th-century nobleman's get-up. One look at this guy's white feather boa and black O.J. gloves and you know there's no way this isn't a totally legitimate operation.

"Settle your unsettled duel!" the chairman commanded Mr. Morimoto and Mr. Flay, who was called the "No. 1 chef in New York." (Daniel and Jean-Georges: phone your publicists.) Let the trash talk begin!

"As long as the fight is fair, we will win," Mr. Flay said.

"Don't complain about the battle," Mr. Morimoto said, through an interpreter.

The "secret ingredient" was unveiled. Sixty Japanese lobsters, valued by the chairman at $10,000. Despite the secrecy of the ingredient, the Iron Chefs always seem to have conveniently prepared everything they need to build four or five elaborate dishes around it. Mr. Morimoto happened to have a bucket of sake, into which he dropped some squirming lobsters. Mr. Flay had bottled carrot juice and canned mango at the ready.

"The way he sliced the corn off the cob is so bold!" a Japanese actress-judge said, after Mr. Flay stood a cob on its end and sliced the kernels off with a knife. It was not particularly bold, though not bothering to use fresh carrot or mango was.

It was quite a coincidence that the actress kept describing Mr. Flay's every culinary move as "bold," considering that the word is trumpeted in the titles of all his cookbooks. Perhaps the actress had read them.

When he slathered brown powder from a Bobby Flay-brand spice jar onto a giant slab of kobe beef (the most expensive substance on earth) and threw it in a frying pan, the actress seemed stunned and also a little worried.

"Oh!" she said.

Mr. Morimoto was more concerned about Mr. Flay's bold American treatment of the secret ingredient.

"With all those spices, he's killing the subtle flavor of the Japanese lobster," he said.

As Mr. Flay concocted his surf 'n' turf, Mr. Morimoto performed unheard-of feats of Japanese cuisine. Drunken lobsters. No soy, but a sauce of Gorgonzola and fresh cream for his deep-fried sushi rolls. White truffles and caviar.

As the Japanese studio audience did the wave, the excitement drove the Japanese color commentators to new heights of jocularity.

"I didn't have anything to drink last night, but I feel like I have a hangover," one said.

Mr. Morimoto had assistants but seemed bent on doing everything himself. Mr. Flay had airlifted a small army of sous-chefs. One wore a stars-and-stripes bandanna around his shaved head and always looked hard at work, while Mr. Flay opened jars, dribbled honey into his horseradish and mugged.

He also solidified his reputation as the John McEnroe of the competitive food circuit.

"You're doing it to me again!" he cried, when one of his burners went out.

"Lighten up, Bobby!" the commentator shot back, pointing out that it was the same equipment the chef in the undercard had used to win. "He seems to be getting more and more irritable as time goes by."

Mr. Morimoto, meanwhile, had bigger shellfish to fry. Those drunken lobsters may have been over the legal limit, but they were clearly not yet dead.

The bold American finished his dishes first and, once again, made a victory leap up onto the countertop. As a nod to Mr. Morimoto, he took the hygienic precaution of tossing the cutting board onto the floor. (Note to self: avoid chopped foods at Mesa Grill and Bolo.)

The chairman announced the new champ.

"Bobbyyyy Flayyyy!"

The agony of defeat was probably less painful for Mr. Morimoto, soon to open his own restaurant in Philadelphia, than for his No. 1 fan.

Little Tommy Mothershead had flown all the way from America to watch his hero defend the title. Cute little guy, with an uncanny resemblance to the 70's child actor Mason Reese. Could it be?

Nah. Not even the chairman would stoop to that.

To Live and Dine in N.Y.

by Frank DiGiacomo
from *The New York Observer*

Navigating the high-end New York culinary world in the wake of the celebrated chef Jean-Louis Palladin, reporter Frank DiGiacomo gives us a glimpse of a rarified world, populated by a very exclusive fraternity.

Midway through our meal at the restaurant Daniel—after the caviar and tiny rosettes of salmon tartar, after the rolled fillets of Portuguese sardines filled with sweet peppers, and after a few glasses of white and red Châteauneuf du Pape—I asked Jean-Louis Palladin what goes through his mind when he is in the kitchen.

Mr. Palladin—the 54-year-old French chef formerly of the restaurants Palladin in New York, Jean-Louis at the Watergate Hotel in Washington, D.C., and now Napa in Las Vegas—bolted upright in his chair, as if someone had dropped a tray of dishes behind him. Bushy-haired with big chopper teeth, he was wearing dark slacks, a cream-colored wool turtleneck and a black Catalina jacket. He looked at Tanya Bogdanovic, his Greek-Yugoslavian girlfriend, a flirtatious woman with dark eyes and a boyish haircut.

"It's like making love to a lady like that," he said as his hand reached out and grazed Ms. Bogdanovic's slender arm. "I believe there is a very fine line between making love to a woman and doing food. It is all, uh, sensual."

Delivered in his French baritone, the word "sensual" became onomatopoeic.

"When I cook for myself," Mr. Palladin said, "I believe I make love with the food."

As I watched him sitting in Daniel that evening, lost in the simple, visceral pleasure of eating good food well prepared, a dark cloud of a thought formed in my brain: How can a man wrestling with death be so alive? If you were to see Mr. Palladin on the street, you would not think, *There goes a sick man*. His hair is thick, his stride is strong, the woman on his arm is compelling. But in December he was diagnosed with lung cancer, and by the time you read this story, he will be waiting to learn if his second round of chemotherapy shrank his tumor sufficiently to allow his surgeons at Memorial Sloan-Kettering Cancer Center to remove it. Waiting almost as anxiously is the population of chefs of New York, many of whom Mr. Palladin brought to the city.

And yet, for all his shortness of breath and for all the bags of heinous chemotherapy circulating in his bloodstream, I can assure you that Mr. Palladin is a man more alive than either you or me.

Across the table from him at Daniel sat Rod Mitchell, a husky fish purveyor from Maine and a good friend. "He has the passion for ingredients," Mr. Mitchell said. "I believe it is exactly like when you touch a lady. You feel that—"

"That stimulation," Ms. Bogdanovic filled in.

"When I go to the market and touch a leek," said Mr. Palladin, "*oh-hh-h*." He hunched his shoulders as if shuddering with delight. "Somebody work a lot to provide that leek." He pointed to Mr. Mitchell. "Just to go to fish and to feel the fish [fighting]!"

Mr. Palladin let out a little sound of exclamation.

"It's like coming," he said quietly.

If you spend any time in a first-class restaurant kitchen during the lunch or dinner rush, you will immediately understand that in the ballet of pots, knives, and fire there is no time for intro-spection—only instinct. New York rewards those who can per-form in such a theater. But until I ate dinner with Jean-Louis Palladin, I hadn't realized how clueless I was about the begin-ning of that equation.

Mr. Palladin made me understand that a leek or a salmon, plucked from the earth or the sea, was not an inert object. That inside every good thing we eat is an after-life force, if you will, which the great chefs take joy in releasing—an act of resurrec-tion performed daily. Animal and vegetable are brought into the kitchen freshly extinguished, and by the time they are delivered to the dining room they are alive again, in new flavors and tex-tures. Clearly, the man revels in this power. But like the hunter who worships the prey he kills, Mr. Palladin has an almost sacred respect for the meshing of life, death, and food.

"He has an instinct when he cooks," said Lespinasse executive chef Christian Delouvrier, who has known Mr. Palladin since their culinary-school days in France. "He comes to the moment, and he knows exactly what to do at that moment. He is right there." Even the ingredients that Mr. Palladin favors speak to the essence of life. Long before organ meats were in vogue, the chef was working with calf hearts and brains, pig bladders and the blood of lamprey—ingredients that even today give us pause—and working his transformational magic on them. The chef Eric Ripert, a man who filled the shoes of Le Bernardin's legendary co-founder Gilbert Le Coze, said that in his life, he has had three mentors. "Joël Robuchon taught me technique and discipline. Gilbert showed me how to run a kitchen and restaurant. But Jean-Louis," Mr. Ripert said, "opened my mind."

In 1979, Mr. Palladin arrived in America, settling in the nation's capital with his then wife, Régine Palladin, a culinary figure in her own right who owns the Washington restaurant Pesce. At the end of that year he had opened Jean-Louis at the Watergate, and by 1985 he and Régine had two children. But Mr. Palladin, part missionary, part voluptuary, was determined to teach the country that French cuisine was much sexier and more challenging than Dover Sole, no matter how much we resisted.

He began to tour the states, cooking charity meals and exploring the farmlands and the backwater towns for purveyors who could provide him with the oddities and the quality his cooking demanded.

"While all these French chefs were busy bullshitting about how their butter was better, he was here sourcing American products," said Drew Nieporent, co-owner of Nobu and Tribeca Grill. Mr. Palladin, he said, was "unquestionably the most influential food person in my life" and "the greatest chef in America," adding: "There's an intricacy about his food, but there's also a simplicity of presentation. He has a knowledge of food and a love for it that surpasses someone who's book-read on the subject." Mr. Palladin facilitated a virtual French invasion of chefs to America, helping Daniel Boulud and Eric Ripert land their first jobs in New York. "He's shaped the culinary map," said Michael Ginor, the owner of Hudson Valley Foie Gras.

Mr. Palladin's stories are those of a man who believes in protagonists and antagonists. For example, Mr. Palladin said that when he was nearly 16, his formal training ended when he was kicked out of culinary school for punching a teacher. "I was not a very good student . . . . I was the No. 1 joker at school. And this [teacher], he was punishing me." Mr. Palladin pronounced it "poo-nish-ing."

"Every Sunday, he was punishing me. Until the day I went with three guys, and boom, boom, boom, we left him in his office flat on his desk. We close the door, pull out the key. By the time they find the guy—" Mr. Palladin finished the sentence with his husky chuckle.

When they can get away from their kitchens, Mr. Ripert and renowned French chefs Alain Ducasse and Paul Bocuse have accompanied Mr. Palladin on his obsessive explorations of the city's markets and restaurants. In one recent week, he took colleagues to an Italian restaurant called Peasant on Elizabeth Street and a Basque restaurant called Marichu on East 46th Street, near the United Nations.

Mr. Ripert, Mr. Boulud, Jean-Georges Vongerichten and others are bolstering Mr. Palladin's spirit by giving him open reservations at their restaurants, knocking themselves out to please and surprise him. The chefs of New York are also helping with Mr. Palladin's extensive medical bills. The sad irony is that the mentor never attained the financial success of his protégés. Mr. Palladin's ascent came before chefs regularly parlayed their fame into books, TV projects, and product-licensing deals. When he did earn well, he lived well.

So in late February at New York's annual Restaurant and Food-service Show, Mr. Ripert auctioned off a week of training in Le Bernardin's kitchen and seats to a series of dinners at Le Bernardin, Jean-Georges and other local restaurants, and raised more than $20,000. Two lots of knives autographed by Mr. Palladin, Mr. Boulud, Chicago chef Charlie Trotter and others sold at La Paulée, a wine event in San Francisco, for a combined $40,000. The money is going into the Jean-Louis Palladin Medical Fund, which the chef's friends—Mr. Ripert, Mr. Boulud, Mr. Nieporent and Mr. Ginor, among others—have started for him. In June, Mr. Boulud will host a $500-a-plate dinner in the private banquet room of his restaurant featuring 11 French and American chefs preparing dinner. Mr. Ginor has started Mr. Palladin writing a new cookbook on the *cuisine bourgeoise* of his native country. He is also organizing a late-summer all-star chefs' dinner to be hosted by Mr. Ducasse at The Essex House.

As for Mr. Palladin, "he's amazingly strong," said Mr. Ripert. "He still eat like a pig, fuck like a rabbit, drink like a fish."

This became apparent upon my arrival at Daniel, where Mr. Palladin sat waiting for me with Ms. Bogdanovic and Mr. Mitchell. The moment I sat down, Mr. Palladin said, "You need to eat." There was a three-tiered silver tray of hors d'oeuvres.

"Here you have salmon," he said, pointing to little tarts piled with slivers of salmon tartare. "Here you have truffle." He motioned to a puff pastry filled with a sharp earthy mix of Parmesan and truffle cream and topped with black shavings.

He has always been a wiry, fit guy (in 1999 he posed naked, save for a strategically placed Vita-Mix blender, in an ad for the appliance, telling *The New York Times,* "You are a chef, you are a sex symbol . . . ") and he did not look like he had lost much weight during his ordeal. Somehow, he had managed to keep his hair. All in all, he looked damn good for a man who said he'd undergone eight hours of chemotherapy the day before.

"I don't think I'm sick. I don't think I'm sick," he said. "But I know I'm sick. My breaths. It's tough, but that's the only moment I see I'm sick."

Mr. Palladin made a fist with his left hand and placed it over his heart and left lung. "It's right here," he said. "Right here, on the top of the lung." The tumor, he explained, is also perilously close to his aorta. "You can play tennis with it," he said matter-of-factly. "Incredible. He is in the body for six years. He never move. For six years. And six months ago, boom." Mr. Palladin opened his fist like a blooming flower.

"You knew about the tumor six years ago?" I said.

He explained that after a long period of excessive fatigue, "I told my doctor, 'That's enough.' I said, 'Put me on the scanner'—his term for the X-ray machine—'because I cannot continue like that.' "

On Dec. 12, Mr. Palladin said, the diagnosis came.

"I said, 'Another shit in my body.' " Mr. Palladin laughed. He then added resolutely: "I need to fight it. It doesn't matter what. I'm a survivor."

Mr. Palladin has given up a two-pack-a-day cigarette habit, but regarding his other vices, he has a different understanding from that of his doctors. "Today is a little special, not to drink too much," the chef said, reaching for his glass of white wine. "But last night, I drink like a—"

He laughed.

"You know, last night it was Valentine's Day," he said. He and Ms. Bogdanovic were at Jean-Georges and "open and open and open," he said, meaning the wine. "The nurse tell me, 'For today, because you have everything in the blood right now, today you need to be very careful, you need to drink a lot.' I said, 'What—wine?' " Mr. Palladin shook his head and smiled. "Lucky I didn't say what I drink last night. Oh boy, she will kill me."

Then he admitted, "Tonight, I'm a little low."

Later in the day he and Ms. Bogdanovic were flying to Las Vegas to check up on Napa. And then, Ms. Bogdanovic said, there was a meeting with potential investors for a new restaurant in San Francisco. After all that, Mr. Palladin said, pointing at Mr. Mitchell, "I'm going to Maine, and this guy is going to produce all the fish."

Mr. Mitchell, a marine biologist by training, was running a small wine and gourmet food concern in Camden, Me., when one day Mr. Palladin walked in, observed how Camden was like Bordeaux on the coast and "made my business." Mr. Mitchell was game to get Mr. Palladin whatever he wanted, no matter how hard it was to catch or digest. No dish better illustrates both than Mr. Palladin's signature *Lamproie à la Bordelaise*.

Lamproie is French for lamprey, eel-like creatures that attach themselves parasitically to other fish. The lamprey is a hideous, wrinkled black creature with a serrated hole for a mouth and impenetrable, milky-gray eyes. Lamprey, Mr. Mitchell said, "is the only organism that can take fish blood and synthesize it into protein directly." His Browne Trading Company nets the eels and keeps them writhing until just before they're served.

"They need to be as close to alive as possible," Mr. Mitchell explained, "because you need to take the blood before it curdles."

Mr. Palladin himself dispatches the lamprey. He drains their blood, then skins them and cuts them crosswise into two-inch sections and marinates the pieces overnight in Bordeaux wine, a mixture of chopped leeks, onions, unpeeled carrots, celery, turnips and shallots, and crushed garlic, thyme sprigs and bay leaves. Mr. Palladin lightly sautés the lamprey sections in extra-virgin olive oil and seasons them with salt and pepper. To this, he adds some of the marinade, more Bordeaux and lean, finely chopped prosciutto. He brings this concoction to a boil, then reduces the heat and lets it simmer for a half hour.

Next, Mr. Palladin puts the lamprey cuts in a covered bowl. He adds *Fond de Veau,* a thick, rich sauce that is made from calves' feet, veal bones and V-8 juice. The resulting mixture is reduced again and then strained through chinois cloth. To this, the lamprey blood is added.

Braised leeks complete the plate. There is something about the paleness of the leeks contrasting with the blackness of the blood and wine sauce that makes it seem as if the struggle between light and dark, that which thrives in the sun and that which lurks in the depths, has been captured on a plate.

"This is a national dish of the Basque area," Mr. Palladin said. He grew up nearby in a town called Condom. "Very easy to remember," he added.

Daniel Boulud recalled that when he was in his 30's, he cele-brated a birthday at Jean-Louis in Washington. Mr. Palladin went all out for the occasion. "Almost everything he cooked for me that night was live before he cooked it," Mr. Boulud said.

"And Jean-Louis liked the theatrical side of the restaurant. So, of course, he had live crabs, and before he served them he brought them out and let them run around the table. And, at the third course, he came out into the dining room with a towel wrapped up around the lamprey which was jiggling all over the place. It was about three feet long. Very scary," he said, sounding as if he still hadn't quite gotten over the experience. "He gave me a blast. When he starts to cook, he is just out of control."

A man of Mr. Palladin's culinary convictions is destined for moments of genius and failure. Mr. Nieporent described an important culinary showcase in Carmel, Calif., in the late 80's. Mr. Palladin had planned to cook his own twist on an ambitious dish, *Poularde de Bresse en Vessie,* in which a chicken is cooked inside a pig's bladder, which resembles a veiny, translucent, flesh-colored balloon. Mr. Palladin's rendition involved using squab.

There was the small problem that pigs' bladders aren't legal for culinary use in this country. This, Mr. Palladin said, required him to retrieve the 150 bladders—more than enough for 140 or so diners—under cover of night and spend a day personally cleaning them by hand. He borrowed an air compressor from a local Carmel garage to inflate the bladders.

As Mr. Nieporent explained, the bladder is used merely to keep the bird moist and is discarded before the pigeon is served. But Mr. Palladin wanted his audience of food V.I.P.'s to understand what was involved. "He's done all of this work, and I remember he said to me, 'Drew, how do they know? How do they see it?' "

So Mr. Nieporent suggested floating a couple of the bladders on a pool of hot water that had been placed in a chafing dish. Mr. Palladin liked the idea, and they marched it past the dinner guests. "For me, that was an absolute coronation," Mr. Nieporent said. "He had let me collaborate with him." But when the dish was served, "he had undercooked the pigeons," Mr. Nieporent said, adding that the critics reamed him. "But that's the point of Palladin. He's never afraid to take a risk."

The photos for Mr. Palladin's new cookbook make this abundantly clear. In one, you see the top half of a baby pig, head and all, stuffed with black truffles and sweetbreads. It looks like a Damien Hirst exhibit. There is also an entire stuffed veal heart.

"They're very carnal," Michael Ginor said. "Very vivid and in-your-face." In many cases, these are specialties that Mr. Palladin has been cooking since his Condom days; still, he is pushing the envelope. In the past, Mr. Ginor said, the chef would have applied a little bit of *nouvelle cuisine* sleight of hand to appeal to his less adventurous clientele. "When I'm doing a brain pancake or tempura Rocky Mountain oysters . . . people love it and they don't know what it is, and at the end I tell them what they ate," said Mr. Palladin. "And they say, 'Whew!—but it was so good.'"

The waiters at Daniel delivered plates of glistening Portuguese sardines that had been fashioned into thick rings and stuffed with a subtle mixture of tomatoes, olives, sweet peppers and basil and bathed in a fragrant lemon vinaigrette.

"So what happened with Palladin?" I asked the chef.

"It didn't fly" is all that he would initially say about his ill-fated New York restaurant.

Palladin was positioned as a bistro, which some critics found odd, given Mr. Palladin's ability to produce much more challenging food. "No Reason for Palladin to Get on High Horse—Yet" read the *New York Post*'s May 5, 1999, review, which took issue largely with the service ("Starbucks-trained") and the decor ("factory-outlet [Adam] Tihany.")

"You cannot hide the truth," Mr. Palladin said as he wrestled with one of his sardines. "I believe I was not in the right spot. No big name is going to do something in Times Square. It was a challenge. I lost the challenge."

Certainly New Yorkers pride themselves as being on the cutting edge of the culinary world, and I asked Mr. Palladin if, in his experience, that was true. "No," he replied. "They are very conservative. Very, very conservative. Incredible. Even in Las

Vegas, they are more creative than here." A little smile appeared on his face. "Coco Pazzo gonna do well," he said.

The problem, he said, is that "you need a lot of money to open in New York City, and you need to have a lot of investors. Or you need to go downtown and try to find a shack," like 71 Clinton Fresh Food.

An artistic success but not a financial one, Jean-Louis in Washington in the 80's defined Mr. Palladin as a chef who made memorable food but not profits. Mr. Boulud, who was in Washington around the same time, said of the Watergate restaurant: "Nobody would have been able to make that restaurant work except Jean-Louis. I mean, it was in a basement next to a parking lot. It was a 40-seat restaurant, where unless there was a genius there, no one was going to come."

"The restaurant was not there to make a profit," Mr. Palladin said. "It was there to put the hotel on the map." He did, taking D.C. chefs on picnics and game hunts, and then he had a run-in with a food critic in the dining room of the restaurant.

The writer, Robert Shoffner, had killed Jean-Louis in two reviews. And, Mr. Palladin recalled, "I say, 'One day or another, this one upstairs is going to send him to me.' And five years later, the *maître d'* come and say to me, 'Shoffner is in the dining room with a lady.' Holy moly!"

Mr. Palladin's voice had descended to a growl. "I start to be white like my jacket. I go to the dining room. Packed! I say, 'Good evening, Madame; good evening, Monsieur. I need to talk to you. I'm sorry, man, you gave me enough shit like that. Now if, in five minutes from now, you are not out of the dining room, I kick you out."

Mr. Shoffner didn't tell it quite this way. He recalled that though Mr. Palladin refused to serve him, he never threatened to kick him out of the restaurant. But both agree that Mr. Shoffner called the cops on Mr. Palladin.

"I'm all shaky," Mr. Palladin said, remembering how he felt at the time.

Mr. Palladin's restaurant lasted 17 years. But it was the very act of coming to the U.S. from France—where, at age 28, he had been the youngest chef to earn two Michelin stars—that made him "a global figure," as Mr. Boulud put it. Venturing to Jean-Louis, Mr. Nieporent remembered, was becoming "a kind of pilgrimage" for the country's culinary elite.

One of those pilgrimages was made by a group of surgeons. About seven years ago, Mr. Palladin received a call from a chef friend, Robert Del Grande of Cafe Annie in Houston. Mr. Del Grande said that some physicians from The Johns Hopkins Hospital wanted to eat dinner at Mr. Palladin's restaurant.

"I said, 'O.K., come, guys.' Eight or nine people. I take care of the menu. I take care of the wine."

After the meal, he met the doctors—"nice guys," he said—and during their conversation he was asked what his life's dream was. "To be a surgeon," Mr. Palladin said. "But my parents, they didn't have any money. That mean, I'm a surgeon for dead animal, you know."

Six months after that dinner, Mr. Palladin received a phone call in which a trade was proposed. The Johns Hopkins doctors were having a party at the home of the chief of pediatric surgery, Paul Colombani. Mr. Palladin went to Baltimore and let the surgeons help him prepare a multi-course feast. And early the next morning, the chef accompanied Dr. Colombani to the operating room and looked over his shoulder as he performed four procedures. "Ten hours. I was blown out. I was like a kid with John F. Kennedy," he said, his eyes wide.

Mr. Palladin was in Vegas when he got the news about his cancer, and Ms. Bogdanovic called Dr. Colombani late that night in Baltimore to tell him. Dr. Colombani said they were not to worry and to call back at 7 a.m. Eastern time.

"The next morning," Mr. Palladin said, "he's got the doctor at Sloan-Kettering for me. He's got me an appointment there. Boom. Boom. Boom."

• • •

Mr. Palladin was finishing his dish of scallops, made with a meaty, gelatinous stew of calves' feet, tomatoes and olives, when Mr. Boulud emerged from the kitchen. "How was your fish?" he asked, his kind eyes peering shyly at the table.

"So good," Mr. Palladin said.

"I'll bring you a good wine when I come back," Mr. Boulud said, and then he returned to his kitchen.

"Merci, Daniel," Mr. Palladin called after him.

When Le Cirque's Sirio Maccioni told Mr. Palladin that he was looking for a new chef at his restaurant and was considering Mr. Boulud and others, including Christian Delouvrier, Mr. Palladin's boyhood friend from culinary school in Toulouse, Mr. Palladin recommended Mr. Boulud. "I told Sirio, 'I bet you Daniel can get you four stars in six months after he start.' That why he went with Daniel. I tell Sirio, '[Christian] is going to be ready, but he's not ready yet.' " Mr. Boulud and Le Cirque got their four stars in six months. "He fly and he fly well," Mr. Palladin said. And Mr. Delouvrier got his four stars at Lespinasse in 1998.

Similarly, Mr. Palladin influenced Eric Ripert's career. Mr. Ripert came to the restaurant Jean-Louis from Paris, but the two did not immediately hit it off. About two months into Mr. Ripert's employment there, the two men got into it in the middle of service. Mr. Ripert handed Mr. Palladin his apron and told him he was quitting. Mr. Palladin followed Mr. Ripert to the employees' locker room. "You need to prove to me that you can be the best chef in the world, but right now you are nothing," he said. For good measure, Mr. Palladin said he told Mr. Ripert that if he left, he was never to mention Mr. Palladin's name again, and that, by the way, "you have nothing between your legs."

Mr. Ripert put on his apron.

He worked for Mr. Palladin for three years, eventually graduating to the position of sous-chef. He said Mr. Palladin was instrumental in getting him the Le Bernardin job—the restaurant's co-owner, the late Mr. Le Coze, was another Palladin friend. "I didn't want to come to Le Bernardin. I never showed up at the appointment," Mr. Ripert remembered. "And Jean-Louis said, 'Are you fucking crazy?' "

"You're like the Godfather," I said to Mr. Palladin.

"Yeah," he said, sipping his glass of red Châteauneuf du Pape. "But the nice one."

The next course showed up. A slender woman at an adjacent table peeked over enviously at what was being unveiled.

"Madame," a waitress said to Ms. Bogdanovic, "you have the ravioli with nine herbs, black trumpet and Yellowfoot chanterelles and a black truffle cream." Then she turned to Mr. Palladin. "Monsieur, you have the sautéed frog legs with tomato compote, asparagus, black truffle and almond milk emulsion."

The black truffles sat on top of the frog legs like a rain cloud. And when you put your fork into the dish, the fungi crumbled and mixed with the almond milk and the tomato to form a black sauce that coated the tender frog legs. Eventually, the black stuff blanketed everything. If you gave yourself over to it, the taste was like a symphony of light. The rarefied, slightly briny taste of the frog legs somehow both absorbed and reflected the earthy musk of the truffles.

Little grunts of approval could be heard around the table.

"Daniel took the truffles out of his office, I can see," Mr. Mitchell said almost reverently.

"Perfect," declared Mr. Palladin.

Then, for a while, all that could be heard was the life-affirming clink of silverware against china.

"Oh my God," Mr. Mitchell said. "We're in heaven again, Jean-Louis."

In the 10 p.m. glow of Daniel's lounge, Jean-Louis Palladin bowed his head almost as in prayer, focused on the frog legs and ate.

A Chef's Eye View of Dining Out

by Bill St. John

from *The Denver Post*

Like most local restaurant critics, Bill St. John spends an inordinate proportion of his life in restaurants. Here, he gives Denver chefs a chance, for once, to let us see the business the way *they* see it.

Laws and sausages, it's said, should not be witnessed being made.

But even so, we know the benefit of keeping watch on lawyers, lobbyists and legislators. And, sometimes, finding out how our food is prepared—what work's really like behind the kitchen door—can be a revelation.

We typically see only one portion of a restaurant, what's called "the front of the house," essentially everything but the kitchen. The dining room and bar, the restrooms, all the tables and booths—even the valet and service staff—make up "the front of the house."

"The back of the house" is made up of the kitchen, the pantry, the dishwashing area and any other rooms not commonly used by the public, say, a locker room or an office [although an office can be considered, paradoxically, part of "the front of the house"]. In most restaurants, a strict division of labor separates the front from the back of the house, although if the chef is owner, he or she will oversee both.

The front of the house is run by a general manager who hires and fire servers, pays for linens, liquor and licenses and generally manages the business side of the restaurant. The general manager is often the first person you encounter when entering the restaurant, for she is the likely maitre d' [a term cycling out of use] or "host" or "greeter."

But dinner doesn't happen in the front of the house.

I spent four days bagging snapshots of two chefs—Steve Smith of Dixons in LoDo and Dan Landes of WaterCourse Foods—while in the thick of their workdays. Here's what it's like for two toques to sling sausage [or, in Landes' case, tofu] during their busiest times.

"I get in around 8 a.m.," says Smith, "and out around 9 [p.m.], 4 [p.m.] if I'm lucky. If the Avs [Colorado Avalanche] are in town I stay later—or if there's a wine tasting or any kind of party." Smith spends those 13-hour days, in large part, on his feet, which explains two things: why so many chefs wear Birkenstocks and why so many smoke. A cigarette break is like manna from on high.

One typical Thursday, Smith makes a "start list" of things he must prepare that very morning before the Dixons lunch crunch happens at noon. Imagine doing all this in three or four hours: "Prep [trim] 12 salmon; make 20 ahi [tuna] skewers; cut up 1 tray of roasted vegetables; make 1 gallon beef sauce; make 2 gallons beef stock; trim 2 sirloins into 20–24 9-ounce steaks; roast 6 chickens; prep [cook] 2 gallons black beans; make 2 gallons poultry stock; mash potatoes; make soup."

By himself.

"It's just pretty chaotic around here," says Landes about the Capitol Hill health-oriented eatery he owns with his wife, Michelle. "You have to combine some amazing elements: food made with precision standards and also dealing with a pretty transient staff, a lot of 18-year-old kids who are not committed.

"The other day, after I had just given him a raise, the dishwasher totally bailed on me, right in the middle of the busiest morning of the weekend."

"On the other hand," he says, "one Saturday at 9 o'clock, the water main broke in the basement and the prep cook [the cook who prepares foods to be cooked later, such as cut-up vegetables] must've carried out 50 to 60 gallons of water, by herself, all the time she was prepping and we were cooking and feeding."

"But that's nothing. We blow the electric transformers down the block all the time," says Landes. "So, we just go with gas and candles."

Dixons' kitchen is like many in a large restaurant, divided into stations, each with its own cook [or, in some cases, one of Smith's "sous" or "under" chefs].

"I have two [sous-chefs]," says Smith, "13 cooks and five dishwashers. That's for the whole day. Two of them speak no English at all, but we can usually get by, although I wish I spoke more Spanish."

The kitchen is in four parts: the pantry, where salads, desserts, sandwiches and any cold foods are made; the broiler, for things such as burgers, steaks and fajitas; the "flat top," where salmon and chicken filets are grilled; and the sauté area, where anything cooked in a skillet is prepared [sautéed onions or peppers, some sauces made to order].

Irma DeLeon is Smith's pantry cook. She sets up her station so that she knows where—and how far away from her hands—her many minions are: slices of avocado, tomato wedges, crumbled blue cheese, pickle spears—dozens of things. She assembles them into salads and cold plates, in a flurry of movement between noon and 1:30 p.m., with an economy of movement and grace that simply makes her dance.

And then there are the characters.

"Our dishwasher, Eeyorr Theobald Eecitro—that's his name—is someone you cannot forget," says Landes. "Every word out of his mouth is like the King's English, perfectly phrased.

"One morning, he called in late: 'It seems that I have slept in. I shall be there in 10 minutes.' "

In person, Eecitro is unprepossessing, his face trimmed in black-rimmed eyeglasses and a fop of sand-colored hair. Then he opens his mouth. Like the time he cut his finger on a broken mug.

"All of a sudden he yells [an expletive]. Just way out loud," says Landes. "But immediately, he pipes down and gets back into character. 'Oh, excuse me,' he said, 'When you have lacerated your finger, the words of Beauregard are not the first to come to mind.' "

"The most favorite part of my job," says Smith, "is the cooking. But because there's so much more management, I don't get to do that much cooking anymore.

"Running a restaurant's come down to personalities," he says. "It's 'The day cooks did this,' 'The night cooks did that.' Ugh.

"Or a waiter comes up to me and asks 'Are we still out of hot chocolate?' Well, I didn't know that we were out of it in the first place!" he says. "Out of the 10 or 12 things that we need to do each day, about four or five never get written down. I find out about those, you know, later."

Smith gets out to cook once a month or so, with his friends

Jennifer Jasinski, executive chef at Panzano restaurant at the Hotel Monaco, and Daniel Fennessey, executive chef at Wolfgang Puck Cafe in Denver Pavilions.

"They're my friends and we team up and do a menu with a theme at one of our restaurants," Smith says. "It's great relief."

"A restaurant is like a ship leaving the harbor," says Landes. "No matter what happens—a no-show dishwasher, a flood, a run on food—you cannot turn the ship back around. You've just got to feed the people who show up that day.

"The philosophy of [our] restaurant is the name, Watercourse," he says. "Water follows the path of least resistance. When an obstacle comes upon me, I just have to move around it.

"I am the captain of the ship and I love it," he says. "I accept the obstacles and I surrender to the cause of feeding these people and working with these others the way that I do. I accept the chaos.

"A cook is the only profession, so far as I can see," says Landes, "who truly deals with the five base elements: metal, earth, fire, water and air. I love it, I truly love it."

SLINGING SLANG FILLS SHORT ORDERS
One aspect of the restaurant business that the common diner rarely comes across is the special language chefs and servers use to communicate.

Restaurant workers have evolved a hip, verbal shorthand to communicate among each other. Many phrases—for example, "wreck a pair" for "scramble two eggs"—have gone the way of waitresses named Dot or Madge. But some language is here to stay.

Perhaps the most common term is "86," to mean that the kitchen is out of something, as in "Eighty-six today's special." It's also a verb, meaning discard ["Eighty-six that spoiled cheese"] or, even more potently, "eject a customer" ["Eighty-six the bum"].

The strangest thing is that no one knows for sure the origin of the term.

In the kitchen, hot foods, trays and pots are of the most concern. Someone will yell "Coming down, hot!" when wanting to pass through a group. Chefs routinely tell each other where they are in the kitchen by shouting "Behind you."

When a customer wants something immediately, he wants it "on the fly" [or "on the rail"]. When servers or cooks are as busy as they can get, they're "in the weeds."

"Covers" means both customers and table settings, as in "They're two covers." A "two-top" is a table for two [also called "a deuce"]. Likewise, "four-top," "six-top" and the like.

Customers who tip below 15 percent may get a "squeak, squeak" from their server in the direction of the other servers. A "PIB" is a "pain in the butt."

And if a customer gives a server an extra-difficult time, she might make an "L" shape of her thumb and index finger and point the customer out to the other servers. She's saying that this guy is a "loser."

Food for the Crew

by Greg Atkinson
from *The Seattle Times*

As head chef at Seattle's esteemed Canlis restaurant, Greg Atkinson is privy to all the rituals that form a kitchen's distinctive character. Here's a look at a side of restaurant life that we mere diners never see.

Behind the scenes at every great restaurant, cooks make certain meals that customers never see. These are staff meals, family meals, or as we like to say in my kitchen "crew chow." By any name, these are the meals that keep the restaurant going. Every restaurant is different and each one has its own policies about feeding the staff, but far and away, at least among the better houses, a family meal at least once a day is the norm. Where I work, there is a staff of about 60 people, and every day at 5 o'clock we have dinner, and then at 11 or so we have a substantial snack.

This is how its been at most of the places I've worked. In Friday Harbor, when I was chef at a small cafe, the entire crew sat down after service every night with bread and wine, and chicken or fish, and salad, or whatever we needed to use up before the next day's service. There were never more than six or seven of us and the meals were fairly intimate.

Mealtime was an opportunity to meet and go over the fine points of service, and a chance to share news of our lives outside the restaurant. We worked and ate together like one big dysfunctional family. Sometimes one of the employees would bring a boyfriend or girlfriend to the family meal, and it was just like bringing home a date to meet the family, only worse. None of us was shy about asking probing personal questions. Some of us in fact were bold and rude. Still, a good time was generally had by all.

In his runaway best seller, *Kitchen Confidential,* Anthony Bourdain describes the perfunctory family meals that were presented in the various restaurant kitchens where he worked in New York City. Crew chow in Bourdain's book ranged from the ordinary to the hideous. Most common was the ubiquitous chicken leg, noodles, and salad. Worst was the awful thing called a raft, a mish-mash of solids strained out of the stockpot. Most restaurants discard this stuff, but Bourdain insists that at some places, this is all there is for the staff to eat.

When I went to New York a couple of years ago to spend some time as a guest cook in three different four-star restaurants, I saw plenty of that famous trinity of chicken, noodles, and salad. But I also saw roast beef, baked fish, sandwiches, hot dogs, all kinds of ordinary foods that would never have been served in the dining room, and all these foods were consumed with gusto by the hungry cooks and waiters. "We eat really good here," said Daniel Boulud's sous-chef, as we served ourselves chicken legs, noodles, and salad, and I had to agree. But the meals in New York's great French restaurants were not quite as interesting as the staff meals in France.

When I worked for a too-brief time at Moulin de Mougins in Provence, then four-star-rated by Michelin, crew chow gave me an intriguing glimpse into the stratified world of the French. Perhaps it was because my senses were heightened by the excitement of being in a foreign country, or perhaps it was because the food really was extraordinary, but the meals I had there were the most memorable crew meals of my life.

Mealtimes at Moulin de Mougins were segregated into three levels of sophistication. The management ate the finest food, almost as good as the guests, and they drank good wine. The waiters and cooks drank modest wine and ordinary food. The dishwashers ate mysterious things, pots of lentils and polenta with rejected parts of animals butchered for the restaurant, and they drank plain, barely fermented wine from collapsible plastic jugs.

On my first afternoon at the restaurant, I was led into the dining room and seated at a table with a half-dozen well-dressed sophisticates who were introduced to me as the "direction," or management. I smiled weakly. I was uncomfortable with my French and unable to understand much of what was said.

We were presented with tiny plates of smoked salmon and I ate as politely as I could while the "direction" practiced obscure idioms in their brilliant native tongue and asked me very slowly if, since I lived in Washington, did I live with the president. "No, no," one of them answered for me, "He's from the west where they've only just recently chased out the savages." No one spoke a word of English.

I sat quietly and allowed the smoked salmon to be exchanged for a neat packet of veal, tied with strings and stuffed with sausage. My glass was filled with a deep red wine. I struggled with the strings around my veal and glanced nervously at the others who managed to remove their strings with the same fluid ease with which they spoke. My strings wouldn't budge and my tongue would not form a single word in French.

Finally came the cheese course, smooth white Camembert and

bottles of chilled spring water. It was soothing and I felt forti-
fied enough to look the others in the eye, but I was far too hum-
bled to practice anything I had learned from the *Jiffy French
Phrase Book.*

The next day, after shucking two cases of live scallops, I ate
with the cooks. We had lamb's brains in browned butter with
capers. The meat was pale and soft, and not very appetizing, but
the bread and cheese were abundant and so was the wine. Everyone ate quickly so there would be time for cards. The food was
pushed aside and out came the deck. The cooks pounded the
table with their fists as they lost and stood triumphant with
chairs tumbling behind them when they won. I was incapable of
following the games.

On the third day, I was assigned to work in the laboratoire,
a prep kitchen in a separate building behind the main restaurant where all the basic foods were brought in and broken
down before they went into the main kitchen. There, whole
birds were eviscerated and plucked. Rabbits and deer were
butchered. Fresh mushrooms and berries were made into dux-
elles and sorbets.

In charge of the lab was one of the few, honored "Master
Chefs of France." He was in semiretirement and worked at the
restaurant, he said, "just to keep from rotting away." We spent
the morning chopping huge bones on a stump outside the "laboratory," where he would later transform them first into rich
broth and eventually into a rich concentrate known as demi-
glace for use by the other chefs. By lunch time, the stump had
been sprayed down with a garden hose and the bones were
roasting with aromatic vegetables.

We ate at a bare table in an attic room from mismatched
plates. With the tattered sleeves of his monogrammed chef's
jacket pushed unceremoniously up to his elbow, the grandfa-
therly chef served spaghetti with meat and tomato sauce. We
drank country wine from jelly jars and broke bread directly
over the table without bread plates. There was no butter, no

cheese and no pretense. "This, you must understand," he told me instructively in very plain, precise French, "is real food, simple food."

Made with beef from a steer he butchered himself, handmade pork sausage and fresh tomatoes, the sauce was seasoned unpretentiously with dried herbs, fresh ground pepper and a sprinkling of commercial chicken bouillon granules. It was the quintessential spaghetti sauce. A gentle wind came through the open windows from the herb garden outside and, more than at any other time since I had been in France, I felt at home. "This is good," I said. "It reminds me of home."

"Of course it does," the old man said as if he knew me, as if he knew my grandmother's kitchen with its peculiar smells and sounds. "It is real food." Without referring directly to the haute cuisine served in the dining room 50 meters from where we sat, the old master managed to imply that the food served there at hundreds of francs per plate was something less than real. So I came to France to learn the secrets of haute cuisine and learned instead what I had always known, that simple food is the best food.

"This is the way to live, isn't it?" he asked me.

"Yes sir, I think so," I said.

Most of the best family meals at restaurants are like the best family meals at home: simple, familiar foods served without a lot of fuss and fanfare. People in my crew often cook the traditional comfort foods they grew up with, and since they come from Laos, Mexico, Japan, and the Phillipines, crew chow can be pretty interesting. Almost every meal features some kind of spicy condiment. Most often, we have something we call Yoko sauce. It's made with fresh jalapenos, shallots, and soy sauce. Sometimes we have Phouvy sauce made with fresh bird chilies, or crushed red chilies with lime juice and soy sauce.

My favorite staff meal revolves around Jeff Taton's Chicken Adobo, with steamed rice and salad, and a generous splash of Yoko sauce or Phouvy sauce. Even after eating it two or three times a month for the last four years, this dish tastes as good to me as the spaghetti I ate in the south of France.

Jeff Taton's Chicken Adobo
Serves 4

    1 (4-pound) chicken, cut into 12 pieces
    2 cups soy sauce
    2 cups vinegar
    2 cups water
    5 cloves garlic, peeled and crushed
    1 tablespoon cracked black pepper
    2 bay leaves
    steamed white rice

Rinse the chicken and put it in a pot with soy sauce, vinegar, water, garlic, pepper and bay leaves. Bring the mixture to a boil and reduce heat to medium-low. Keep the chicken boiling gently for 45 minutes.

Serve hot with steamed rice.

Dining
Around

Another Roadside Attraction

by Mort Rosenblum

from *A Goose in Toulouse*

Long based in France as editor of the *International Herald Tribune* and an AP correspondent, Mort Rosenblum (who also wrote the award-winning *Olives*) knows French culture as well as he knows French cuisine—and worries over where they're both going.

W hen I mapped out that first trip to Roquefort country, my eye fell on the name Conques-en-Rouergue. Years earlier, my sister Jane had come back stricken with concern after church-hopping in the Aveyron. She had come upon a gem, a hallowed waystation for pilgrims headed toward Santiago de Compostela, and its roof was falling in. Poor Conques, she lamented. Someone has to help save that church.

A fabled tympanum above the great western doors of the abbey church featured 124 polychromatic figures, carved in stone by medieval monks with passion and humor, depicting the Last Judgment. Priceless stained glass colored the light that fell on treasures within.

From its lonely spot in a patch of wooded hills on the small-scale Michelin map, Conques looked as if hardly anyone had been there since Jane's visit. If that precarious Romanesque roof had lasted since the 1200's, chances were it had not yet collapsed in a pile of slate. I'd sound the alarm. This was the stuff of Mother Teresa.

For good measure, I took along Jeannette Hermann, my stalwart companion, who organizes tours to little-known places. Surely, she could help this French backwater find a suitable following.

The first obstacle to our mercy mission, as it happened, was finding somewhere to park. A young woman in a Conques Tourist Board T-shirt and frayed change apron sent me to the annex lot because a great sea of cars, minivans, and tour buses had choked all available spaces at the entrance to town.

Winding around to the back way in, I found an empty spot. A kid hurried up to tell me that since no white lines were painted around the perfectly good space where I had parked, I would have to go another quarter-mile farther. But first I had to fork over the equivalent of four bucks for a parking sticker.

God, I knew, works in mysterious ways. This might be a test, and I was not daunted. In any case, I was in an unflaggable mood. It was time for lunch. No serious crusade in France begins on an empty stomach.

Jeannette and I approached the highly recommended Hotel Sainte Foy, and we located a vacant table on a lovely terrace overlooking the church. It was shaded with wisteria, and planters were ablaze in scarlet geraniums. Succulent aromas wafted from the other tables, which buzzed with happy mealtime chatter.

A waiter approached, pleasant but firm, and informed us that it was seven minutes after two. The kitchen had closed only moments earlier. I explained the parking delay. I pleaded and added the hint of bribery. He consulted the chef. Sorry.

We scurried to the smaller Hostellerie de l'Abbaye across the plaza, much less attractive but with an encouraging clatter of plates echoing from the dining room. I asked the young man at the desk about lunch.

"Are you crazy?" he wanted to know. "It's nearly two-thirty." In fact, it was 2:16.

"Yes, but . . ."

"It's the law in France," the young man said, puffing up as much importance as his scrawny frame allowed. "Restaurants close at two o'clock. Lunch is from twelve to two. Soon it will be less."

"Since when?"

"Since the Socialists," he said, not specifying whether he meant the Socialist president with the conservative prime minister or the subsequent conservative president with the Socialist prime minister. In either case, it was crap.

Jeannette, meanwhile, was desperate for a ladies' room. She asked the bartender, who pointed amiably toward a door across the room. As she headed for it, a stocky woman who looked as if she had just dismounted from a broom ran out and barred her way.

"Where do you believe yourself to be going, madame," she demanded. This was not a question.

"To the bathroom," Jeannette said pleasantly. She has the angelic face of a harmless innocent, which melts most such barriers, and the tidy, bejeweled look of a traveler with real luggage. But she might as well have been Dorothy facing the Wicked Witch of the West.

"The bathrooms are for customers," the woman shrieked. "This is a hotel."

The whole scene was so preposterous—the young prig followed by the old harridan—that Jeannette and I just looked at each other and laughed. We walked out, but I was overcome with curiosity. I went back in and asked the clerk for the name of the proprietor.

"Why?" he demanded.

"Because I'm—"

"Do you have a salesman's license? You have no business asking questions."

When he saw me write the hotel telephone number on a pad, he leaped forward, halfway over the counter, and yelled, "What are you noting down there?"

Just then the old woman approached, shrieking louder still and waving her arms.

"Call the gendarmes," she ordered.

"Exactly," the clerk said. He reached for the telephone and dialed the equivalent of 911.

This was a dilemma. I was dying of curiosity to know what the cops would do, in fact, faced with a foreign perpetrator, who had politely asked for lunch in a restaurant and an accomplice who wanted to use a hotel bathroom. I even had a French press card, which formalized the right to ask questions.

But in a small town in the rural back hills, who knew whose brother-in-law held local authority? And, more important than that, we were hungry. I left, laughing harder, and we found a friendly refuge on a terrace just across the street.

"Ah, yes, them," the waiter said with a little chuckle when I told him what had just happened. Apparently we were not the first to have found an unusual reception. This, in contrast, was a friendly bistro with more relaxed hours. But it was after 2:30, and the kindly waiter, who doubled as assistant cook, said he could only serve us a Roquefort salad.

"Not even an omelet?" I asked.

He shook his head. The stove was just inside the door. Surely, there were eggs in the refrigerator. But I'd had enough fights for the day.

Later, at my request, the owner came over to chat. I complimented him on the sparse, cold salad.

"Paf," he said, making a face. "That's no meal."

It was not actually what we had in mind, either, I told him, but he did not offer to do any better. Instead, we talked about the state of food in France.

"All this fast food, Coca-Cola, it makes me sad as a Frenchman," he said. "It offends my pride. Before, in the cities, everyone left the office at midday and had a proper lunch. And now"—he paused to purse his lips as if to expel the next word quickly and completely—"sandwiches."

The nearby city of Rodez was once thick with fine tables, he said. One could still find a decent meal, but the future trend was unsettling.

"Do you realize there are two McDonald's in Rodez?" he asked, with a snort and a thump on the table. "Two! And that's the only place kids want their parents to go. My own kids! For me, that's a real sign of the times. Two of them. It is *dégueulasse.*"

"Disgusting," I agreed. "Where are they, exactly?"

And there you have it. Nature is not known for its tolerance of vacuums, and the monster international chain learned that lesson early on. For me, it was a simple calculation.

Dinner was impossible until, say, eight p.m. If I worked quickly, I could save the ancient Conques church in an hour or two, and get back on the road toward Draguignan. One choice was to stop at a café for a frozen industrial pizza slice or a baguette, stale by late afternoon, with sliced ham of dubious quality. Another was to shop around for the fixings of something tasty, which could be amusing. But that would take time and might expose me to a lurking big sister of the hotel hag across the street.

Or I could roll up to a McDrive window, say a few words into a speaker, hand over not many francs, and wheel away with an acceptable warm sandwich that, at the worst of it, would probably not give me ptomaine.

It is easy enough to see why an American traveler on budgeted time would want to take every opportunity to find good French food. But the long-termers? M.F.K. Fisher once wrote of being stopped by a young American in Marseille who was in acute culture shock. A luncheon club network had selected him as outstanding student and sent him to France for a grand tour. In city after city, local nobles fed him their specialties. After three weeks, he was ready to kill for a hamburger. Fisher and her daughters sent him after a sort-of hot dog by the Gare Saint-Charles. That was early in the 1960's. Now, he would hardly be beyond sniffing distance of a Big Mac anywhere in greater Marseille.

By the end of 1999, nearly eight hundred McDonald's restaurants were scattered across France, from the Champs Élysées to remote crossroads deep in the countryside. That is not counting the Belgian version, Quick, or all the rest.

McCustomers, in fact, are only marginally American. The French have taken in the place as their own, shortening the name in popular slang to two syllables pronounced "Mahc-Doe." Kids in their late teens love to hang out in the immediate vicinity and do wheelies on their Hondas. A certain sort of young professional stops in for a quick lunch or post-film bite. But just as the Conques restaurateur explained it, the real devotees are very young French people with their parents in tow.

If Americans are used to a certain level of permissiveness, French kids suffer through a restaurant meal. They're supposed to sit in quiet dignity while their elders prattle on about boring stuff. McDonald's, therefore, is kiddie heaven. A *blanquette de veau* might be tasty to a preschooler, but its heavy cream is not a secret sauce you can let drip down your cheeks. *Pommes rissolées* have their place, but as ketchup-bearing missiles to launch against a younger sister, nothing beats *les frites McDo*.

Then there are all those toys, gifts, rides, games, clowns, exotic American names for things. The kid tug factor is massive. And when busy parents calculate the bill and the time spent, compared to real food in a proper place, it is often an easy sell.

Up to now, there has been plenty of resistance among parents. An occasional *attaque de Mac* might be harmless enough, but what about the family table, tradition, a svelte figure, and decent nourishment? The big question, of course, is what next? What happens when all these McDo Generation kids grow up and have their own kids? If the push is equaled by a pull, God help us all.

When the Sea Reaches for the Sky

by Amanda Hesser
from *The New York Times*

Selecting just one piece by Amanda Hesser for this year's collection was no easy task. Her prolific pieces in *The New York Times* are a joy to read, whether your main interest is as a cook or as a gourmand.

Y ou do not forget the first time you have a plateau de fruits de mer.

Shortly after I moved to New York, David, the son of a friend of my family, was assigned to take me downtown and show me a good time. He picked me up in his beat-up convertible, and we sped down the West Side and into SoHo, swinging by Blue Ribbon to put our names on the list.

When we finally got in, I let David do the ordering while I peered around the room jumping with young diners. Champagne arrived, bubbling up in the glass and dancing down my throat. Then a waiter approached our table, walking cautiously under the weight of an imposing tower packed with ice and overflowing with seafood. Heads followed it in a trance, like a tennis ball across a court. He set it down in the center of our table.

I knew what it was—a plateau de fruits de mer—but had never seen one up close. It had eluded me the two years I lived in France. But here it was in all its glory. Towering, resplendent, unrestrained. There were oysters rimmed with their liquor, their shells nestled in the ice. Clams, scallops the size of dice still attached to their ridged shells, crabs poised as if on sand, shrimp with their heads on and a plump lobster, split in half. We were given the tools for our task and three tiny ramekins of sauce.

David had done his job: I was suddenly, utterly infatuated with New York.

What I didn't know at the time—among other things, like where Union Square was and whether Daniel was a restaurant or a hair salon—was that Blue Ribbon's plateau was one of the first to show up in New York. Balthazar followed suit when it opened in 1997. But recently, it seems that restaurants in every corner of the city, from Artisanal and Guastavino's to Next Door Nobu and City Hall, are serving plateaux de fruits de mer.

The stacked platters stand like evergreens among dense forests of diners. Some are lavished with sea urchins and tins of caviar. Others are rimmed with poppy red crayfish. You can indulge in bay scallop-ceviche and carefully pry a whelk from its snail-shaped shell. The one at Next Door Nobu is like a flower arrangement formed from clams, octopus and tuna. City Hall's has a steakhouse air with a big, meaty lobster claw and an abundance of oysters.

There is no precise definition for a plateau de fruit de mer. You won't find it in Larousse Gastronomique or the Oxford Companion to Food. There is no recipe. It is more abstract than that. Think of it as an expression of the sea, a display of the best shellfish and crustaceans a restaurant can find that day, put forth in their purest form. Oysters are simply shucked, sea urchins sliced open, langoustines cooked in salt water. All are arranged on deep aluminum trays that are filled with ice.

A great plateau de fruits de mer gives a sense of excess, with the seafood coming off as if they were jewels nestled in the ice. Like a wedding cake, the bottom layer is largest. It is typically dotted with oysters, clams and scallops, perhaps a few lemon wedges plunged into the ice. This is so the diner can see that they are fresh and plump, and immersed in their liquor. (If they were placed on a higher layer, you would risk spilling the precious liquor as you lifted each shell.)

The second layer, and sometimes the third, each smaller and supported by steel pedestals, are decorated with richer shellfish, like shrimp, mussels and razor clams. Sometimes, periwinkles and seaweed are slipped among them, as if they had washed up on the ice. If there is lobster, it is usually placed on top, crowning the plateau with a flash of red to catch diners' eyes as it passes from raw bar to table.

A plateau de fruits de mer is not so much a dish as an experience. And none is better in New York than that served at Balthazar.

I went with a group of friends recently and ordered the Balthazar, the large, three-tiered, $99 fruits de mer extravaganza. Shortly after the order tumbled from my lips, waiters descended on our table, placing three bowls, one long and slim fork, one small clam fork and a crab cracker before each of us. Minutes later, a phalanx of waiters arrived, one to set down the pedestal, another to place dishes of sauces—cocktail, mignonette and tarragon mayonnaise—in the center and a third to crown the pedestal with the plateaux.

For a minute or two, conversation ceased and a feeding frenzy ensued. "I don't know where to begin," one friend said. "It's too tall for us!" It was true: the top layer was higher than I could reach. The table next to us looked on shamelessly.

As we began plucking away at the oysters and a fresh, peppery scallop ceviche on the bottom, the waiters kept close by like birds on a wire, ready to swoop in—to replace our shell-strewn bowls, rearrange the layers and remove them once they were emptied. As we ate through the whelks, the shrimp and calamari salad in a radicchio cup, and mussels with barnacles still on their shells, the tower lowered until we were faced with the shrimp and lobster, poised regally on the top tier. It was an artful dance between us cracking crab claws, greedily dipping lumps of lobster in the tarragon mayonnaise and sucking the meat from lobster legs, and the waiters pampering us. And when we were finished, our shirts stained with clam juice and hands sticky, they replaced our tablecloths and handed us warm moist towels and a wedge of lemon.

At Next Door Nobu, the plateau is listed on the menu as simply "raw bar," and is best enjoyed by sitting at the sushi bar, where you can watch it be assembled. An opaque green glass bowl is mounded with ice—the canvas stretched on the frame. Shiso leaves are held on the ice with thick red cubes of tuna. Large Hunter Point oysters from Washington State are propped near the edge; Kumomoto oysters are wedged in the sides like outcroppings on a hillside.

Coral-colored top neck clams are laid next to a nest of shredded daikon; giant clams are scored to look like daisies; and slices of octopus are arranged like fans. The sushi chef places a few raspberry-flavored yamamomo berries between the fish and, on top, a glass cradling abalone, sea urchin and caviar. It is like a garden of seafood blooming before your eyes. It arrives with three dipping pools: a Maui onion salsa, a citrusy and spicy ponzu sauce and a tart lemon wasabi sauce. Platters start at $40.

When I returned with a friend to Blue Ribbon, the plateau was as splendid as I had remembered. This time we sat at the bar, and, as at Next Door Nobu, watching it being constructed was as pleasurable as eating it. Perhaps even more so at Blue Ribbon, where the same person has been making them since the restaurant opened nine years ago. You can't miss him: he's the man wearing a headband with "Alonso" printed in big block letters and an "oyster tips" jar loaded with cash nearby.

From the bar, you can watch him pack the trays with ice, swishing his hand through the center, creating a gulley for the lobster to lay in, shucking the oysters and inspecting them critically, swiftly, and in a single motion, prying open littleneck clams and flipping them over so that their fat side buckles above the shell.

There is nothing fancy about the basic plateau at Blue Ribbon, which is $62. There are littleneck clams, Taylor Bay scallops, lobster, shrimp with their heads on, Maryland crab and one variety of oyster, Malpeque, when we were there. The Blue Ribbon Royale, its deluxe version for about $30 more, has a third layer with glasses of Stolichnaya vodka punched into the ice and a tin of American caviar balanced atop a miniature bowl of ice. A few lemon wedges and sprigs of parsley are the only adornment.

But the oysters are clean-tasting and briny, the crab meat is sweet-tasting in the legs and moist and spicy in the body, and the lobster is left with its mustardy roe. "Here are your machines," Alonso says as he hands you your cracker, prong, spoon and tiny fork for digging, cracking and plucking. There is homemade mayonnaise sprinkled with a mixture of cayenne, paprika and dried herbs; cocktail sauce; mignonette; and "Alonso sauce," which is red onion, tomato and celery, chopped into tiny flecks and seasoned with hot sauce, lemon juice and butcher-grind black pepper.

Alonso checks in with you, clearing your empty shells, making sure you taste his sauce. Meanwhile, the plateau's infectiousness takes effect. People filtering in past the bar peer over your shoulder, and the orders roll in, keeping Alonso busy through the night. They sell about a dozen of the Blue Ribbon Royales on a weekend night.

Eric and Bruce Bromberg, the owners of Blue Ribbon, modeled their platters after those they dined on in Paris, at all-night brasseries like Au Pied du Cochon.

"Their doors haven't been closed since Hitler left Paris," Mr. Bromberg said. "Our restaurant doesn't look anything like it, but it embodies the same thing."

When they started serving oysters and shrimp and plateau de fruits de mer, Bruce Bromberg said, "we were told New Yorkers were not going to go for it."

But who would guess that New Yorkers would be buying up $10 bottles of sparkling water with nary a flinch, either?

When brasseries became popular in New York a few years ago, the plateau de fruits de mer was part of the package, as important as hard-boiled eggs on the bar and pastis behind it. The plateau de fruits de mer has long been part of the coastal cuisine of Brittany, served essentially straight off the fishing boats. But the dish really gained popularity as brasseries began opening in Paris at the turn of the 20th century. Brasseries were beer halls, open late into the night, serving simple fare like steak and potatoes. Shucked oysters, crevettes grises and boiled langoustines fit into this idiom.

The idea of presenting seafood so elaborately, though, comes from a much earlier period. Stacking food, wrote Carolin Young, a dining historian, in an e-mail message from Paris, whether it be seafood, fruits or vegetables, began in the 17th century. Then it would have been served at banquets in the homes of aristocrats.

But in a strange way, a plateau de fruit de mer seems better suited to showy New York dining than to France. French restaurateurs are stingy and economical. At a bistro, you will get an excellent piece of duck. Just one piece. Here, the ante is continually raised. Portions abound, and so do extras like caviar and truffles.

At Artisanal, the grand plateau de fruits de mer for $98 is absolutely baroque. There is sea urchin custard, Belon, Cape

Neddick and Island Creek oysters, Australian crawfish called yabbies, ceviche, periwinkles, whelks, shrimp, crab, lobster, and razor clams. It drew wails of shock from my fellow diners.

The plateau seems like something that shows up in a good economy powered with ambitious diners, and disappears in a slump. I hope that's not the case. If things are going to slide, I would like to go down slurping my choice of oysters and clams, squeezing over lemon juice, dipping them in mignonette, sipping on my wine. It's what warmed me to New York, and I'd like to hold on to it.

Gold Plate Special

by Gael Greene
from *New York Magazine*

There was a time last summer when the food world seemed to think of nothing but the opening of Alain Ducasse's new Manhattan restaurant. Gael Greene's article is more than a review; it is a sharply delineated vignette of haute cuisine, circa 2000.

Why is New York so frosty to Alain Ducasse? Can this be the warm and bumptious city that has welcomed millions of immigrants—the hungry, the persecuted, outcasts and dreamers, saints and rapscallions—to our streets paved with gold? We embrace Cuban baseball players and Italian tenors and Indian novelists-on-the-run so warmly yet offer France's emperor of haute cuisine the cold shoulder and a poke in the eye with his own *fourchette*.

Buoyed by . . . what is it now? . . . eight Michelin stars that carry him like wings from one restaurant debut to another,

Ducasse didn't mean to sound arrogant when he agreed to create the thrill of three-star dining in the freshly gussied-up cocoon that was once Les Célébrités in the Art Deco nostalgia of the Essex House. There would be only one sitting per night and a server for every customer. Veterans of the chef's growing army would drill local recruits in the Ducassian gospel: perfect products, precise cooking, proper service, and, *after* dessert, lollipops and at least three different flavors of caramels. (He is the Baskin-Robbins of caramels.) He never mentioned price. But rumors ricocheted. It hit the *Daily News*: dinner for two, $500. Type as big as V-J Day or Martians hovering over Times Square.

Well, we have always had this little problem with the French. Remember that first trip to Paris? How they made us feel like boobs. So no surprise: On opening day, the alligators slithered into Ducasse's gaudy rose-gold-black brocade banquettes. The porcupines tensed their quills as they nibbled the $160 prix fixe.

Opening week, a seasoned advance team is still wading through 2,700 reservation requests. With his usual just-descended-from-Mt. Sinai portentousness, Ducasse announces, "There will be no special treatment for the press. Only for *les clients* of Alain Ducasse/Paris and Louis XV in Monte Carlo." There are 1,750 in New York, he claims. "If they come only once a year, that's 600 tables." Aha, I am one of them. True, I had been conflicted about floating a second mortgage to finance my first dinner at the outrageously rococo-on-rococo Louis XV, $250 for two in 1988. But I loved the Marie Antoinette insouciance of his Provençal ditties and Italian borrowings in all that pomp. Loved the pigs' feet and leeks, the Pecorino ravioli in his coconut soup, the herb-flecked risotto with frogs' legs; loved the spit-roasted lamb served with a ragout of its innards.

I'd also paid my respects when Ducasse moved into the gloriously overwrought maisonette at the Hotel Le Parc vacated by the shocking retirement at 51 of Joel Robuchon. "Half-baked," I wrote of those five meals at Alain Ducasse/Paris in 1996. As for the jet-setting on his wearying eight-hour biweekly commute between Paris and Monaco, I wrote, "We've gone from Robu-chon to Robo-Chef." Even so, you might say I am a loyal client. I get my table on the second night.

We are tucked into our grand, circular VIP booth—there are only four, back to back—under a gold-leafed dome that broad-casts whispers from faraway tables. Instead of prudently hang-ing one's handbag on one's knee or nesting the precious Judith Leiber on one's lap as a reasonably paranoid New Yorker must, women are urged to recklessly leave their purses on a low uphol-stered stool, as we did without fear in Monaco. I ask for ice water, New York water, tap water. Eyes fly wide. This may be a first. But without a sneer, water is poured from a silver pitcher. (I've saved $20 or $30 already.)

The attempt to evoke Louis XV luxe (and justify Louis XV prices) feels a bit claustrophobic in such close quarters. A clash of colors and cushions, with a riotous mosaic of trumpets and saxophones by the clearly music-loathing sculptor Arman. So many captains and waiters and majors. So many cadets, ramrod-stiff, toting long rectangles of silver on one shoulder. So many classic uniforms. Yet the staff is surprisingly loose and engaging, not at all forbidding. And hooray, no one once utters the word "Enjoy." Voluptuous bouquets of roses stand at the entrance and above our heads, a few already wilting, but none on the table. And the plates created just for New York are somber stoneware. For a moment I read ADNY etched on the knife as *anno Domini*. With an exaggerated flourish, two small cone-covered dishes are placed on the table. The cones, cup size A from a fifties Maiden-form bra, are set at an angle so the waiter can identify the but-ters. "This is sweet," he says, pointing. "And this is salt." Getting it backwards. And the butter is so warm, we send it back.

A cadet halts at our table, swivels, presents arms. The waiter removes the single dish from the long silver tray. "The chef sends you an *amuse-bouche* to tease your taste." We stare at a plate of small brown wafers. "Rye tuiles to set the theme. Sweet, salt, citric, and bitter—sun-dried tomato, Parmesan, lemon zest, and cracked pepper." I taste. I let one melt in my mouth. I taste another just to be sure. It's not even a big nothing. It's a small embarrassing nothing. "Maybe it's supposed to be the host," suggests one of my guests. "The body of our Lord Ducasse."

No serious critic would judge a kitchen's cooking the second night. But even we, four obsessed foodniks confounded by Michelin's obeisance to Ducasse, are shocked. Chicken wings and frogs' legs "in green and white," a joke. Santa Barbara prawns muffled in thick mucilage on muddy citrus purée. The simperingly bland salmon and overcooked halibut. Our Stepford servers are so relentlessly programmed, they tremble in fear of the master's wrath because my mate, the Road Food Warrior, won't let them slice his steak. Pièce de boeuf de l'Arizona grillée is hardly the feisty prime we take for granted. You're talking New York, buster. Don't try to fool a steak man.

Still, a luscious scallop with a topknot of Iranian caviar in a pool of slightly bitter greens impresses. A teacup of haunting sea-urchin royale is jealously shared. I'm enchanted by a wondrously melting globe of sweetbreads. The sommelier's chivalrous selection of a delicious $82 Concha y Toro Cabernet from Chile (as the red-wax-sealed wine card lists it). The caramels. "Take more," says the waiter. "We have to eat everything you leave." We chuckle over the choice of twenty pens presented on leather to sign the check. "Choose your weapons," the waiter cries. I total it $860 for four with my sleek Cartier ballpoint, a respectable discount on the rumored $1,000. Each couple is given a farewell goody bag with a yeasty almond-crusted brioche Riviera wrapped in tissue, perfect for breakfast. Two meals for the price of one.

I never believed Ducasse would really come to New York. Not even Robo-Chef could juggle three ambitious houses so far apart. He was already spending half his time aloft on the tedious commute between Monaco and Paris, with an occasional helicopter spin to check out his inn at Moustiers. And several critics blasted him for his chutzpa (French for audacity). He is more fax machine than poet, wrote one.

But the starched and stuffy Michelin gave Ducasse his double three-star epaulets anyway. One year later, at the age of 41, Ducasse crowed, "Michelin has accepted that it's possible for a chef to do something besides get fat behind his stove." No wonder he thinks he is the chosen one. Critics all over the world now hail his celebration of a lettuce leaf as the mark of a second coming (or first if that's your position). "We are like a machine," Ducasse likes to boast. The machine is ambidextrous. Between authoring (more or less) a parade of cookbooks, Ducasse opened a surf-and-turf joint called Bar & Boeuf in Monte Carlo, and three months later it had Michelin's "macaroon." As the consultant at Il Cortile, an Italian spot in Paris, he can claim yet another star.

He startled Parisians with macaroni and cheese, chicken wings, and bubble-gum ice cream at Spoon Food & Wine, then exported it to the Seychelles and to Ian Schrager's Sanderson Hotel in London, where it quickly became a canteen for the usual boldface names. Bergdorf and Le Printemps peddle his Objets: Saveurs kitchen equipment and tableware. Even eskimos in wired igloos can explore the world of Ducasse on his Website. Restaurant critic Gilles Pudlowski, looking at what makes Alain run in *Le Point*, calls him *Ducasse le boulimique*—"perpetually unsatisfied." Having survived the plane crash that killed four companions in 1984, "he fights himself, trying to astound the world."

Now he cannot sit still. Mr. Spoons wiggles and twitches and muses. We are having breakfast at Petrossian. Wonderful croissants. He might do a Spoon in Dubai. "Fabulous city, have you been?" He loves the Basque country. He is thinking of what to do next in New York. Maybe an inn. "I love the Inn in Little Washington, Virginia." Alain Ducasse/Paris, transplanted to the Plaza Athénée, reopens in September. A new restaurant, 59 Avenue Raymond Poincaré, devoted to fruits, vegetables, lobster, and beef, takes its place at Le Parc. "You are the first to know," he confides, as if he were giving me an emerald. (And he's already dispatched an aide to buy one of those painted cows on our sidewalks to graze outside the door of the new gambit.)

"You are the talk of New York, Alain," I begin. He grins. He is almost adorable when he smiles, actually sexy. "Everyone wants to know who is my *cabinet de P.R.* Who does my *publicité*? I do not have a *cabinet de P.R.* I am only a *petit artisan. Petit petit petit.*" He lowers his hand toward the carpet, thumb and index finger less than half an inch apart. "I am a *petit artisan* in a *petit* restaurant in a giant city." He sits there, his leg bouncing a little, picking his nails, which seem to be bitten. "Have you read my books? Well, I will send them this afternoon. If you read the books, you will know the real me."

On Tuesday, July 10, I call to book a table anonymously for lunch the next day. Very humble. The reservationist studies her schedule, murmuring, "Ah . . . mmm . . ." Infinitely polite, she sounds amazed but pleased to find a table for two tomorrow at noon. Though we've been warned the room is booked for eight and a half months, there can be empty tables, especially at lunch. No-shows. (From now on, the house will charge a $150 deposit on your credit card when you reserve.)

I arrive in time to catch a uniformed courier delivering baby carrots. The bronze whimsies of Parisian sculptor Folon have arrived, too. In the entrance, an urban man in a fedora, split down the middle. I chew on that symbolism till we're at table, with our own Folon mini—a man with the Empire State Building for his head. Suddenly a figure in white leaps into the room. It looks like Jim Carrey. But no, it's Ducasse, advertising his presence, greeting an Asian couple in French. Is this the Ducasse who never goes into the dining room? He swivels and smiles. Aha. Fooled you, didn't I? Kisses my left air. Kisses the right. "Is it really you?" I ask. "Or is it your evil twin brother?" He smiles. He understands some English, but not everything.

Then he's gone, like a brief apparition. And in his place are those nebulous rye tuiles again, offered like rare collectibles. But the bread seems fresher, and once again the young Belgian sommelier knows his lines, quickly offering a glass of the inexpensive Cabernet I liked last time when I reject his $30 glass of Pinot Noir as "too expensive." A drop spills. The waiter rushes over with a linen napkin to hide the scandal. And then another chef's *amuse-gueule*. Small and delicate bites of lobster en gelée with intense lemon cream, salted with more of that fabulous caviar, and for the first time I'm seeing stars, maybe even rainbows.

Granted, butterfly pasta with bits of ham and Parmesan is a yawn, and the pathetic roulade of sole reminds me of childhood at Longchamps. By mistake, the waiter brings Santa Barbara prawns—a chance to note that they're remarkably livelier this time. Now I am asked to choose a knife for my squab from the dozen or more arrayed in a leather case. I feel like an idiot . . . if there's a best knife for squab, surely Ducasse should choose it.

"Give me a nice feminine knife, please," I say. There's no time to brood. Two perfect ovals of exquisitely rare squab arrive and I'm soaring again. I ask for a reprise of the tart and citric apricot compote topped with melting bitter-almond ice cream I fell for at that first shaky dinner. Dismissing my guest's pedestrian soufflé, I go for its partner, a refreshingly tangy tropical fruit on custard spiked with a faintly bitter splash of coco-Malibu liqueur. Then from the rolling goody cart: cherry claufouti, nougat, and too many caramels. Now I see a faint light at the end of this tunnel. I sense the kitchen finding its edge. I'm eager to return.

New York has gone berserk. By week three, we are consumed with rage against this monomaniacal intruder who thinks we will line up to pay $1,000 or more for a clever riff on the tomato that is not as thrilling as Jean-Georges's or Daniel Boulud's at half the price. We sneer at his $50 foie gras in a pepper bouillon and the $74 fillet of striped bass and suddenly find Alfred Portale's supernal roasted lamb chops a bargain at $36. Nonetheless, we join the line, scheming for a table. Could our grasping, aggressively insecure burg have given hotter press to Elvis if he'd been discovered dishing up fried eggs at the Essex? *W* predicted a feeding frenzy in June, surely feeding it. Ducasse was charm personified in Charlie Rose's hands. Then the *Times* critic chimed in with a "sneak preview" he said was not a review but read like a personal ad seeking someone with a reservation at Ducasse to invite him along. I guess that's a welcome of sorts to our town. What's so unthinkable about a $500 dinner? the chef wanted to know. Great products cost money. "When you go to see the Knicks to sit on the floor, it's very expensive, $500," he told the *Times*. "*C'est fou, c'est extraordinaire*, but it's a wonderful moment."

And in fact, the kitchen at the Essex House is demanding products that no one else in New York asks for, says his devoted supplier, Ariane Daguin of D'Artagnan. "Alain wants the foie gras wrapped in parchment, delivered on ice, not vacuum-packed. The most expensive squabs, strangled. Organic chickens air-chilled with the feet on. I had to get special permission from the FDA. It's costing him double the usual price. They are the most focused, the most demanding."

My friend Elizabeth calls in triumph. Her connection in Paris has pulled a few strings. We have a table at 8:45 tomorrow. The Road Food Warrior, having sworn never to return, decides to join us. ("I like that crack about the Knicks. Whoever fed him that line was clever.") We've got yet another VIP booth. The four of us feel rich and glamorous already. The crowd tonight is neither hip nor beautiful nor brand-name, but the chat is amusing. "Did you hear So-and-so was charged with killing his wife and children?" we overhear a woman ask. A man responds: "They are getting less and less tolerant about that kind of thing these days." Hoping to shed the absentee-chef charge, Ducasse now swoops into the dining room once or twice a night—Escoffier only knows where he goes in between. Tonight he's a blur of white moving past my line of vision until he's sure I've noticed. A gift from the kitchen, silvery Iranian caviar piled on a perfect round of potato in buttery potato purée, is instantly disarming.

There is still much much genuflecting over those ditzy rye discs, but we're caught up in the thrill of yet another *amuse-bouche*, tomato four ways: intense molten slices on creamy salad greens in a pungent tomato vinaigrette, with a saucer of satiny tomato sorbet on green-tomato preserve. Flushed from the sommelier's warm and rounded $32 Malbec from Argentina, we giggle over the possible uses of the odd gynecological-looking implement a waiter has left for Elizabeth. It's an asparagus lifter, we learn, so she need not dirty her fingers eating the crab croquette that comes with the pea soup—for the first time, transcendent. Dishes I'm tasting for the second or third time are all tuned up a notch. The vegetable lasagna. Long, thin slices of lobster with a kicky ginger-tinged salsa. Exquisitely poached foie gras with apple confit and raw apples slivered razor-thin on a truffle slicer at the table. The thick salmon again, perfectly cooked, firm and expertly seasoned. I'm knocked out by the pow of its spooned-on condiment, caramelized sweet pepper and onion. The halibut is still overcooked, but its haunting sea-urchin custard and a crunch of seaweed salad are fair recompense. Even a breast of chicken, invariably abused and boring, shows mastery at the stove. I can't stop eating the voluptuous macaroni in cream and cheese that comes with the chicken. And the sautéed grenadin of veal with a chunk of steamed veal breast wins over our table's fussiest carnivore.

We're all quite high now, on both the theater of the absurd and the first intimations of authentic three-star indulgence. We trip through a portion of truffle-doused goat cheese, an exquisite salad of just-born leaves, and desserts (how courageous, no crème brûlée). Then sorbets, chocolates on a silver compote, little macaroons, and the candyman with his rolling treat cart, doling out pear-shaped essence of pear in a gel, pistachio caramels, cookies, and yet more pastry. (Another laugh for the silly fountain-pen shtick.) I'm in a waltz now with Fred Astaire. I'm cuter than Ginger, sexier than Rita, more graceful than Cyd. The only blip is the check: $663.73 before the tip. "What's wrong with us?" cries the Road Food Warrior. "It's not enough. It's embarrassing."

Do I really want to believe the chef is personally squirting basil-oil polka dots on my plate? Must the chef of an eminent restaurant be in the kitchen every night? On Tuesday, July 25, at 8:25 p.m., I stop by to see Jean-Georges in his big telltale open kitchen. He's at Vong in London. Daniel Boulud is vacationing in Lyons. At Daniel, his *chef de cuisine*, Alex Lee, is driving a huge crew to feed a full house and 150 in the private-party room. At Le Bernardin, Eric Ripert is vacationing, too. "We try to be sure one of us is always here," says owner Maguy LeCoze. I follow manager Walter Krajnc through the kitchen of Danube into the kitchen of the Bouley Bakery on the trail of David Bouley—"He was here just a few minutes ago." "I'm looking for Nobu," I tell the woman at the podium. "I was looking for him myself today," she says. "He's in Tokyo." Only Gotham Bar and Grill's Alfred Portale, deeply tanned from Hampton weekends, is in his kitchen. "You caught me cooking," he says. "We're working on new dishes for the summer menu. I work behind the line every night I'm here, four nights a week, five days."

Next day the all-stars check in. "I am 95 percent of the time in the kitchen, 300 days of the year," Boulud tells me. "I'm only gone two weeks. I have to follow my daughter's school schedule. I trust my staff very much." From London, Jean-Georges Vongerichten assures me he is in his kitchen every night when he is in New York. "If you want your meal to be 100 percent Jean-Georges, I could only have six seats and do everything myself."

Bouley calls. "I was away cooking a dinner someone won at a benefit," he tells me. "But normally I'm like a tennis ball between the two kitchens. It's only 37 steps. I spend 80 percent of my time doing spontaneous tasting dinners for regulars during the service, actually cooking." Eric Ripert on the line. "I'm never away more than two weeks at a time. I don't cook during service, anyway. I expedite. I don't see how you can control both the kitchen and the dining room if you're cooking."

"I have a very modern way of thinking," Ducasse likes to say. "The chef is there to lead the team and not just to sit behind the piano." So let's give him his frenetic wandering. After all, AD/NY is closed weekends, ideal for dashing off to open his latest Spoon in Tokyo. Maybe we are grown-up enough, we fussy New York eaters, that we don't need either Ducasse or Jim Carrey jetéing through the dining room. I have eaten two lunches and three dinners at Alain Ducasse/New York, and his presence doesn't seem to matter. Remembering the euphoria of that one dinner, I recall my mate observing: "I get what it's about now. An evening of indulgence. Where you won't mind paying $500 because you're not coming if you can't afford it." Many New Yorkers may be less demanding, but for me the food must be seriously good.

And it isn't. In that last lunch, even the holy tuiles are a mess, with bits of melted Parmesan flying. Without whatever gave the tomato cocktail its sublime aura a few nights earlier, it is fussy, a foolish stretch that may remind you that the tomato is a fruit, but it lacks even a slice of fresh tomato. Prawns à la royale is simpering baby food. The special raw scallops have a crude taste unmitigated even by caviar. And now the $66 breast of chicken tastes no better than any other delivered minus its feet. This $76 veal chop is not as good as many I can name in New York, certainly not twice as good. The chocolate, "hot and strong in taste, iced with coffee crystals," is not the swamp it was on first tasting, but it's lost the ice, and the caramelized brioche cubes are a reach. At dinner that same night, the spaghettini is actually less sodden but still much ado about nothing. The frog's legs have no redeeming social value. The gossamer sweetbreads would be so much better discovered inside a crunch of crust.

I'm not really amused being forced to choose my knife or my pen just so the house can show off how many it's assembled. I'm annoyed. It's an intrusion and it's vulgar. Were Ducasse to try that gimmick in Paris, I think they'd roll him through town to the guillotine. It doesn't really matter much if I say the $500 dinner for two is obscene when our neighbors don't get enough to eat. I think $500 Knick tickets are obscene, too (by the way, Alain, they're $1,500 on the floor), not to mention $1,200 handbags (I bought mine at a sample sale and feel wanton enough). So on questions of what's worth what, maybe I can't be trusted. In certain circles now, nothing succeeds like excess.

But the kitchen desperately needs to be brilliant, and soon. These recipes he claims to create in his head . . . they are too intellectual, too contrived. Narcissus is in love with his own gimmicks. The food has no emotion. If the emperor is naked, we will drape him in a tablecloth to give him time to get his ermine back from the Laundromat. Open to anything? Yes, we are. But in the end, we're not so easily fooled.

Today's Special

by David Sedaris
from *Me Talk Pretty One Day*

David Sedaris's brand of humor may be a little skewed, but *Me Talk Pretty One Day* sailed handily onto the best-seller lists this year. In this essay, he hits comic pay dirt by training his absurdist wit on a deserving subject: food-fashion victims.

I t is his birthday, and Hugh and I are seated in a New York restaurant, awaiting the arrival of our fifteen-word entrées. He looks very nice, dressed in the suit and sweater that have always belonged to him. As for me, I own only my shoes, pants, shirt, and tie. My jacket belongs to the restaurant and was offered as a loan by the maître d', who apparently thought I would feel more comfortable dressed to lead a high-school marching band.

I'm worrying the thick gold braids decorating my sleeves when the waiter presents us with what he calls "a little some-

thing to amuse the palette." Roughly the size and color of a
Band-Aid, the amusement floats on a shallow, muddy puddle of
sauce and is topped with a sprig of greenery.

"And this would be . . . what, exactly?" Hugh asks.

"This," the waiter announces, "is our raw Atlantic fish served
in a dark chocolate gravy garnished with fresh mint."

"Not again," I say. "Can't you guys come up with something a
little less conventional?"

"Love your jacket," the waiter whispers.

As a rule, I'm no great fan of eating out in New York restaurants. It's hard to love a place that's outlawed smoking but finds
it perfectly acceptable to serve raw fish in a bath of chocolate.
There are no normal restaurants left, at least in our neighborhood. The diners have all been taken over by precious little
bistros boasting a menu of indigenous American cuisine. They
call these meals "traditional," yet they're rarely the American
dishes I remember. The patty melt has been pushed aside in
favor of the herb-encrusted medallions of baby artichoke hearts,
which never leave me thinking, Oh, right, those! I wonder if
they're as good as the ones my mom used to make.

Part of the problem is that we live in the wrong part of town.
SoHo is not a macaroni salad kind of place. This is where the
world's brightest young talents come to braise carmelized racks
of corn-fed songbirds or offer up their famous knuckle of flash-
seared crappie served with a collar of chided ginger and cor-
nered by a tribe of kiln-roasted Chilean toadstools, teased with a
warm spray of clarified musk oil. Even when they promise something simple, they've got to tart it up—the meatloaf has been
poached in seawater, or there are figs in the tuna salad. If cooking is an art, I think we're in our Dada phase.

I've never thought of myself as a particularly finicky eater,
but it's hard to be a good sport when each dish seems to include
no fewer than a dozen ingredients, one of which I'm bound to
dislike. I'd order the skirt steak with a medley of suffocated
peaches, but I'm put off by the aspirin sauce. The sea scallops

look good until I'm told they're served in a broth of malt liquor and mummified litchi nuts. What I really want is a cigarette, and I'm always searching the menu in the hope that some courageous young chef has finally recognized tobacco as a vegetable. Bake it, steam it, grill it, or stuff it into littleneck clams, I just need something familiar that I can hold on to.

When the waiter brings our entrées, I have no idea which plate might be mine. In yesterday's restaurants it was possible both to visualize and to recognize your meal. There were always subtle differences, but for the most part, a lamb chop tended to maintain its basic shape. That is to say that it looked choplike. It had a handle made of bone and a teardrop of meat hugged by a thin rind of fat. Apparently, though, that was too predictable. Order the modern lamb chop, and it's likely to look no different than your companion's order of shackled pompano. The current food is always arranged into a senseless, vertical tower. No longer content to recline, it now reaches for the sky, much like the high-rise buildings lining our city streets. It's as if the plates were valuable parcels of land and the chef had purchased one small lot and unlimited air rights. Hugh's saffron linguini resembles a miniature turban, topped with architectural spires of shrimp. It stands there in the center while the rest of the vast, empty plate looks though it's been leased out as a possible parking lot. I had ordered the steak, which, bowing to the same minimalist fashion, is served without the bone, the thin slices of beef stacked to resemble a funeral pyre. The potatoes I'd been expecting have apparently either been clarified to an essence or were used to stoke the grill.

"Maybe," Hugh says, "they're inside your tower of meat."

This is what we have been reduced to. Hugh blows the yucca pollen off his blackened shrimp while I push back the sleeves of my borrowed sport coat and search the meat tower for my promised potatoes.

"There they are, right there." Hugh uses his fork to point out what could easily be mistaken for five cavity-riddled molars. The dark spots must be my vegetable.

Because I am both a glutton and a masochist, my standard complaint, "That was so bad," is always followed by "And there was so little of it!"

Our plates are cleared, and we are presented with dessert menus. I learn that spiced ham is no longer considered just a luncheon meat and that even back issues of *Smithsonian* can be turned into sorbets.

"I just couldn't," I say to the waiter when he recommends the white chocolate and wild loganberry couscous.

"If we're counting calories, I could have the chef serve it without the crème fraîche."

"No," I say. "Really, I just couldn't."

We ask for the check, explaining that we have a movie to catch. It's only a ten-minute walk to the theater, but I'm antsy because I'd like to get something to eat before the show. They'll have loads of food at the concession stand, but I don't believe in mixing meat with my movies. Luckily there's a hot dog cart not too far out of our way.

Friends always say, "How can you eat those? I read in the paper that they're made from hog's lips."

"And . . . ?"

"And hearts and eyelids."

That, to my mind, is only three ingredients and constitutes a refreshing change of pace. I order mine with nothing but mustard, and am thrilled to watch the vendor present my hot dog in a horizontal position. So simple and timeless that I can recognize it, immediately, as food.

First Bite

by Patric Kuh

from *The Last Days of*
Haute Cuisine

In his fascinating culinary history,
Patric Kuh—himself a classically
trained chef and restaurant critic
for *Los Angeles Magazine*—
reveals how the country's evolv-
ing gourmet fashions mirrored
seismic shifts in American culture.

J ust off the Avenue de l'Opéra in Paris, not far from the neighborhood known as Les Grands Boulevards, in the tiny Place
Gaillon, is the Restaurant Drouant. It is painted appropriately
enough the same dove-gray as a boulevardier's spats, and in
the same spirit the entire building is rakishly well maintained.
The first-floor windows have potted carnations, the corner mold-
ing reads "Drouant 1880," and the oyster displays are backed up
against the outside walls, shielded from the passing traffic by a
bank of sculpted shrubs. It is a few minutes' walk from here to the
Palais Garnier opera house and only a slightly longer stroll to the
Comédie Française and the colonnaded gallery of the Palais Royal.

It is, however, a long way from here to a reclaimed landfill in the borough of Queens, New York, though that is where this quintessential *Belle Époque* restaurant may have left its most lasting mark. It was from Drouant and its sister restaurant, the nearby Café de Paris, that a group of restaurant workers would embark to open the restaurant at the French Pavilion at the 1939 World's Fair. The fair was held within sight of the Manhattan skyline, on a piece of land that *Life* magazine, even as it tried to promote the fair, could only describe as "a desolate, swampy, stinking expanse called Flushing Meadow." The French Pavilion was meant to communicate something finer, a certain idea of France—and in a very Parisian way, it did. The second-floor balcony of the restaurant looked across the Lagoon of Nations with all the elegant entitlement of the terrace of Fouquet's on the Champs-Élysées, as if its every fluttering parasol were announcing to the country that the French had arrived.

The president of the fair, Grover A. Whalen, wrote that it "was built and dedicated to the people." Brotherly spirit was in the air and the theme that the entire fair was centered around was nothing less than "The World of Tomorrow." In the real world of tomorrow, Hitler would be invading Poland on September 1 of that year; but in the world of tomorrow the way the organizers meant it, everyone would have a GE toaster, a Chevy in the driveway, and AT&T long distance. Subtlest of all the promotional devices was the concept of audience interaction. The hard sell would have introduced a jarring note within the communal spirit of the fair and so, instead of simply showing a product as one did in a showroom, corporations showed Americans how the products worked. Thus, a market segment became "an audience," a sales floor became "a diorama," and a pitch "a demonstration."

At General Motors's "Futurama" exhibit, fairgoers could gaze at Norman Bel Geddes's design for a city surrounded by fourteen-lane highways that somehow managed to be both car-filled and fast-moving. Meanwhile, AT&T provided a balcony where three hundred people at a time could listen in on one lucky person's free long-distance conversation. GE brought its audience in by having engineers put five million volts of electricity through a hot dog to see if it would cook. (It wouldn't; it simply tasted burned.) Among international participants, the English may have failed to understand the subtlety of the interactive method when they brought the Magna Carta, an object that could not be bought. The French did not make that same mistake. They did not bring Gobelin tapestries or the *Mona Lisa*; they brought a restaurant that could seat four hundred, Le Pavillon de France.

The team of men who would work at this restaurant had been put together in France like specialists for a heist. The chef had been chef at the Hôtel de Paris in Monte Carlo; the sous-chef had worked at La Coupole in Montparnasse. Even a minor fish cook like Pierre Franey had been well trained in the kitchens of Drouant. The front of the house was taken care of by Monsieur Drouant himself, while the day-to-day operation was run by the maître d'hôtel of the Café de Paris, unknown as yet but soon to be mythical in the American restaurant world, Henri Soulé. Picked by Monsieur Drouant, backed by the French government, transported by the ocean liner that was the pride of the French Line, the *Normandie,* they disembarked at Pier 88 in the spring of 1939 and took their first steps in America across the still-cobblestoned Twelfth Avenue.

May 9, 1939—two days after President Roosevelt officially opened the fair—was a busy day at the Flushing fairgrounds. At the AT&T Pavilion, with three hundred people listening in, a member of the crowd, Carl Joss, Jr., put through a call to a certain Mrs. Alberts in St. Cloud Minnesota. ("Hello, is this Mrs. Alberts?" *The New York Times* reported the conversation as starting. "This is Carl. I got a lucky number at the World's Fair so I'm able to make this call free.")

"What's that?"

Carl Joss, Jr., undoubtedly used up his three free minutes explaining to Mrs. Alberts how it came to be that the American Telephone and Telegraph Company was giving away free phone time. Meanwhile, Mayor La Guardia, appearing unannounced at the Italian Pavilion, made a plea in two languages for world peace. Some of the attendees failed to understand either one of them and replied by shouting "Viva Mussolini!" and bursting into the Fascist hymn "Giovinezza."

At the French Pavilion, the restaurant opened with a gala meal. Served to Mr. and Mrs. Grover A. Whalen, the French ambassador, Count René Doynel de Saint-Quentin, other dignitaries, and 275 guests was the following menu:

> *Double Consommé de Vineur*
> *Paillettes Dorées*
> *Homard Pavilion de France*
> *Riz Pilau*
> *Noisettes de Prés-Salé Ambassadrice*
> *Chapon Fin à la Gelée d'Estragon*
> *Coeur de Laitue Princesse*
> *Fraises Sati*
> *Frivolités Parisiennes*
> *Café*

A meal that the *Times* translated in the next day's edition as "Chicken consommé with twisted cheese sticks, broiled lobster with cream sauce served over rice, saddle of lamb with potato balls and stuffed artichokes, cold capon with aspic, and asparagus with French dressing served on lettuce leaves, strawberries with ice cream and whipped cream, with petit fours and coffee."

As lacking as the translation is, it does communicate the exoticness with which French food was perceived at the time (and, more subtly, the fact that the dishes were unheard-of by most readers), but the article does not claim that such food was actually unavailable in New York because, in fact, it already was. Perhaps not at the wholly American restaurants like the Stork Club or the "21" Club, but certainly at a select few French-influenced restaurants. Escoffier himself had opened the kitchens of the Pierre Hotel in 1930; and at the Ritz-Carlton Hotel, the famed chef Louis Diat not only created soups like vichyssoise but also dishes named after Hollywood stars, such as Chicken Gloria Swanson. At the Colony, on Sixty-first Street near Madison Avenue, the favorite restaurant of New York society—the polished owner, Gene Cavallero (who in the circuitous genealogies of the restaurant business would employ as a young captain Sirio Maccioni, who would go on to open Le Cirque) could, with the help of his French chef, also have produced such a meal. But he probably would not have had it translated, the understanding of the time being that if you needed to have it translated, you probably couldn't afford it.

At the Colony, the ladies' bathroom was famously filled with yapping lapdogs, and the dining room a sea of tables of ladies in hats with their fur coats draped over the back of their chairs. Here, the sense of clubbiness was so pronounced that the author of the restaurant's history, Iles Brody—described by his publisher as "informal, witty and urbane"—saw fit to describe the scene when someone who did not belong dared to venture in. "When perchance an unfamiliar face appears in the doorway of the dining room, all conversation within stops, forks on their way to lovely lips pause in midair, and you, newcomer, find yourself the focus of beautiful and inquisitive eyes of patricians." Anyone with a taste for twisted cheese sticks who would be uncomfortable being the focus of all this patrician attention was out of luck.

The restaurant of the French Pavilion would change that. The day after the opening gala, the average fairgoer arrived. In the first month of operation, the restaurant served 18,401 meals. In the second month, that number increased to 26,510. This was a restaurant very much in the spirit of the fair. The experience offered was not that of some wonder of technology but of dining in a French restaurant. Here, the restaurant itself was the diorama, eating was the audience participation, and, most prophetic of all, gastronomy was the product.

Grover A. Whalen may have cared about "the people" but Henri

Soulé had only ever cared about the *right* people. In this regard, the configuration of the dining room at the French Pavilion could not have pleased him. Every table spread out over the five semicircular tiers looked out across the Lagoon of Nations toward the massive statue of a heroic worker that crowned the Soviet building. It wasn't that the view bothered him, it was that every table had the same view. No table, therefore, was better than any other one, thus denying him the opportunity to show preference to a customer and to display the true artistry of the classic French maître d' that is not a dainty show of carving but rather the expertly delivered snub. This was an area of expertise in which Henri Soulé had had the very best training that France could provide.

A portly five-foot-five-inch native of a hamlet near Bayonne in the French Basque country, Soulé followed the classic waiter's career path, going through all the stops at a very high speed. First as an apprentice at the Hôtel Continental in Biarritz, continuing up in Paris as a waiter at the Hôtel Mirabeau on the Rue de la Paix; he was a twenty-three-year-old captain at Claridge's on the Champs-Élysées and eventually assistant maître d' at the *Michelin* three-star Café de Paris. This last restaurant was managed by the famed restaurateur Luis Barraya, brother-in-law of Jean Drouant, who also managed the Pavilion d'Armenonville and the Pré Catelan in the elegant Bois de Boulogne (and, yes, Fouquet's). It is a list of names that is definitive of a level of elegance that certain French restaurants excel at and for which, ironically, they use an English word to describe—they call it *le standing*.

It was directly across from the St. Regis that Henri Soulé—after working the 1939 season in Flushing, then returning to France to join a machine-gun company in the French army before being sent back to Flushing as manager of Le Pavilion de France for the 1940 season (by order of the French prime minister)—opened his New York restaurant. He shortened the name to Le Pavilion, put up Paget murals of the chestnut trees of the Champs-Élysées, and on October 15, 1941, opened for business. He invited the Vander-bilts, the Cabots, the Rockefellers, and the Kennedys for that first evening. He served them a set menu of caviar, *sole bonne femme, poulet braisé au champagne*, cheese, and dessert. And when it was over, he went upstairs to his changing room where he kept the tuxedos he wore for dinner and the blue suits, white shirts, and Macclesfield ties he would wear for lunch. He thought of all the people, including his wife, who because of the war could not be with him and he cried.

But let's not leave Soulé like this. Let's fast-forward several years to the glorious period of postwar New York, a city that Jan Mor-ris, quoting John Cheever, describes as filled with "river light." It is in that light, on a bracingly cold winter's day, that we stand at 5 East Fifty-fifth Street before the restaurant's awning. Its three lines read:

5
Henri Soulé
Le Pavilion

Because it is a ground-floor restaurant, there is no possibility of a sweeping staircase for customers to make la grande descente. Con-sequently, the front door becomes the focal point of the restau-rant, and just as on all great ocean liners where the best tables were always the ones closest to the staircase, at Le Pavilion, the best tables are those closest to the door. Soulé has seven tables right at the entrance. He calls it "la Royale," the waiters call it "the blue-blood station." It is filled with the now mainly forgotten titans of Café Society: the Comtesse Camargo, who gave legendary parties at her estate in Cuba, Dubonnet, the Duchess of Windsor, Colonel Benes, and Cole Porter. But let's deny ourselves, for now, the expe-rience of being the recipients of Henri Soulé's sizing-up should we venture in the front door and instead move just a few steps to the right to a more battered door from behind which the slightly insane sounds of a lunchtime service going at full speed emanate. It is the service entrance and let us instead pull this door open.

Here, there is a stairwell; the steps are dark with a compacted coat of grease left by deliverymen's work boots. We descend. The first people we see are two New York police patrolmen, in from the cold, warming themselves with big bowls of pot-au-feu that they rest on stacked cases of leeks. We pass them and, as we approach the kitchen, the noise level and sense of tension increase. Many of the menu items are cooked au gratin, under the salamanders. Because the only way to keep the salamanders hot enough to perform the gratin but not so hot that they will curdle the sauce is to intermittently throw water underneath it, the cooks are essentially working in a steam bath. These are men many of whom came over to work at the World's Fair, who are in America but not quite here. They may catch the IRT to Brooklyn every night after pulling their daily double shifts, but they still send their white bonnets back to France with friends who work on the French Line to have them pressed by nuns who, because of their own veils, are experts in pressing pleats into starched cotton.

We go up the busy stairwell that leads to the dining room, following a waiter carrying a silver serving dish with a rack of lamb surrounded by a bouquetière of tiny perfectly turned vegetables, and we slip inside just as the swinging door closes behind us. At the Royale, Cole Porter is still beaming at the recent memory of seeing the entire score of "Begin the Beguine" laid out in truffle notes on the surface of eighty eggs in aspic that were served at one of his private parties. Meanwhile, at his table, Joe Kennedy is tucking into his favorite order of veal chops Orloff, a dish that as proof that le standing could survive two world wars had been served by Escoffier himself to the ship-fixated kaiser aboard the Imperator in 1913. Soulé is happy also. The dining room is filled with the right people and everything is going well. As the waiter puts the lamb dish down on the gueridon, or small table, from where it would be served, the customers who have ordered it look up in admiration. Soulé beams in a very French way. He is going to show them how it is done. He shoots his cuffs to better show off the cuff links that are a gift from the Duke and Duchess of Windsor (or, historically, from the grandson of the man whose appendicitis attack caused César Ritz to have a nervous breakdown) and begins to carve. Outside on Fifty-fifth Street, two strangely contented-looking patrolmen walk straight past all the double-parked limousines, both feeling the warm glow of a sensation wholly new to them—the taste of French food.

Pocketful of Dough

by Bruce Feiler
from *Gourmet*

This piece by Bruce Feiler generated a storm of readers' letters in *Gourmet*. Yes, it makes controversial allegations about the restaurant world's "dirty little secret," but beyond that, it's a hilarious story about prowling the Manhattan dining scene.

I am nervous, truly nervous. As the taxi bounces southward through the trendier neighborhoods of Manhattan—Flatiron, the Village, SoHo—I keep imagining the possible retorts of some incensed maître d':

"What kind of establishment do you think this is?"

"How dare you insult me!"

"You think you can get in with *that*?"

It's just after 8 p.m. on a balmy summer Saturday and I'm heading toward one of New York's most overbooked restaurants, Balthazar, where celebrities regularly go to be celebrated and where lay diners like me call a month in advance to try and secure a reservation. I don't have a reservation. I don't have a connection. I don't have a secret phone number. The only things I have are a $20, a $50, and a $100 bill, neatly folded in my pocket.

I've never bribed my way into a restaurant. I've never slipped a C-note or greased a palm. In truth, I've never even considered it. I've *assumed,* of course, that people do such things. I've seen my share of Cary Grant movies. I've *heard*—and wondered whether such old-fangled gestures would work in the high-stakes, high-hype world of New York City restaurants. For everyday diners in Manhattan, cracking the waiting list at Nobu is said to be harder than getting courtside tickets for the Knicks. But is that true?

Curious, I hatched a plan. I would go to some of the hardest-to-penetrate restaurants in New York armed with little more than an empty stomach, an iron-clad willingness to be humiliated, and a fistful of dough. Most people (including the editors of this magazine) assumed I would get turned down at half the places on my list. "You'll never get into Daniel," said one. "Union Square Cafe?!" said another. "Forget it."

My plan was to show up between 8:15 and 8:30 on varying nights of the week. I would go with a different companion each night. I would try to get a reservation by telephone that afternoon and go only if I were turned down. And I would carry a twenty and a fifty in my left pocket, and a hundred in my right pocket. I did have an incentive: I could eat at any place I could success-fully finagle my way into.

Balthazar, on this night, does not look promising. A few peo-ple are lolling around in the foyer when my girlfriend and I step inside the door. I glance at the maître d's podium and panic: There's more than one person standing behind it. To whom should I give the money? I approach haltingly and ask if they have a table for two. The man and woman appraise my appear-ance—black trousers, gray button-down Italian shirt, buckle shoes—and the woman looks at the man. He is obviously the person in power. "Perhaps we can seat you in about 20 minutes," he says in a manner that suggests it will be closer to an hour. We retreat to the bar.

Seconds later the woman departs and the man is left alone. This is my moment, I decide. I reach for the twenty and positively bolt toward the podium. I crane my left arm around the side. "I hope you can fit us in," I mumble, and slip the bill into his hand. I am sweating; my heart is racing. "Oh. Thank you," he says. "Don't worry."

Two minutes pass—*two minutes!*—and the woman approaches. "We can seat you now," she says, and leads us to a corner booth. "This is one of our best tables," she adds. Suddenly I'm Frank Sinatra. I'm King of the Strip. I exude aftershave and savoir faire. Call it the fedora effect. My girlfriend looks at me in a way she hasn't since I surprised her by uncharacteristically demolishing a friend on the tennis court.

In talking to people about slipping money, I found a clear split: People of my father's generation seemed comfortable with the idea, knew the rules, believed it was part of the price of going out. People under 40, by contrast, thought it distasteful, degrading, and showy. (The restaurants seemed to agree with the latter. When asked for their policies at the completion of this project, responses ranged from "It's disgusting" to "The maître d' will be fired if he is caught accepting money for a table." A couple of the restaurants had no policy for or against.)

A few days later, I walked into Nobu, the Mecca of nouveau Japanese chic, with a female friend. A couple in front of us, wearing golf clothes, were just being turned away. I asked for a table. Again the two people behind the podium (both women) surveyed our appearance—black from head to toe. "Actually, we do have a table," one said at last. "It's not one of our better tables. It's by the kitchen."

"May I see it?" I said.

The woman led me to the table and I asked politely if she had something else. "Hmmm," she said, looking around. As she did, I reached into my pocket, pulled out two twenties and a ten, and moved them toward her hand. She continued—"I'm afraid there's nothing"—when suddenly she felt the bills in her hand, claimed them, and announced cheerily: "Just a moment, I'll go and check."

Several minutes later she returned, holding the bills in her hand. "You might want to take your money back," she said. "There really isn't anything we can do." Then she added, "In the future, if you want a reservation, call me," and gave me her name. Just like that, I had bypassed the masses yearning to break in. I had become an insider. And it hadn't cost me a dime, merely the willingness to indicate that I would tip for service.

I had already learned a number of lessons. First: Go. You'd be surprised at what you get just by showing up. Second: Dress decently. Third, and most important: Don't be ashamed. They're not, and neither should you be.

Soon I ventured uptown. I was wearing a jacket; my friend, pumps and pearls. We entered the hallowed seafood manor of Le Bernardin, where I spotted a few empty tables. "Could you wait 20 minutes in the lounge?" the maître d' asked. Seconds later, with new confidence, I slipped a fifty toward his hand and said, "Is there any way you could speed that up?" The man felt the money, then pushed it back into my hand. "Sorry," he said, "there really is nothing I can do."

Four minutes later, though, we were seated at a table for two by the window. Moreover, the maître d' came to our table several times to ask if everything was satisfactory. At the end of the evening, not because I had planned it but entirely because I *felt* like it, I gave him $30. He graciously accepted.

Outside, I realized I had just witnessed the gold standard. The maître d' turned down the money when it was a bribe, gave us the service anyway, then accepted the money as a well-earned tip.

If Le Bernardin offered the gold standard, I quickly encountered the opposite, at Jean-Georges, a citadel of New French elegance. Once again, though the restaurant was fully booked, we were offered a table in the formal dining room and asked to wait 15 minutes in the bar. After ordering drinks, I stepped over to the gentleman in charge, eased a fifty into his hand, and whispered, "This is a really important night for me." He took the money and slipped it into his pocket. Fifteen minutes passed, with no sign of him, and no table. Another 15 minutes passed, still no sign. Finally, one of his deputies escorted us to a table.

For the first time, I felt slightly oily. Here we were offered a table with no hint of money, then someone took my money and didn't deliver on his original promise. Worse, he didn't even apologize for what was probably a routine delay. Money slipped to a maître d', I was coming to believe, is a quick way of establishing a relationship, of becoming a valued customer. When no relationship developed, I felt I had been taken advantage of. I was a stooge, not a player.

Still, I was growing fearless.

There were 50 people lingering in the foyer of Sparks Steak House, a bastion of male power, when I entered at 8:15 with a male friend. We were told it would be 9:45 before we could be seated. I asked to be put on the list.

Given the size of the crowd and the length of the wait, I decided to reach for my right pocket. I waited until the man behind the podium was alone (Rule No. 6) and rested my left hand lightly on his back. Suddenly, I was Fred Astaire and he was Ginger Rogers. He knew *exactly* what to do. He pivoted toward me and turned his right hand from face down to face up, giving me a target. I slipped the bill into his hand and said again, "This is a really important night for me."

He disappeared briefly, then 45 *seconds* later, he reappeared at my elbow. "Right this way," he announced, and led us to a table. I had jumped a 50-person line and saved myself an hour-and-a-half wait. Forget Frank Sinatra. I was now James Bond.

Increasingly, I was struck by how much impact the experience was having on me. Surmounting this challenge night after
night was actually giving me a certain self-assurance, a feeling of
having grown up. Some might find this disillusioning: *"You
mean life is not first-come, first-served?"* I found I had a different
reaction: *"You mean all it takes to crack one of New York's most
daunting thresholds is fifty bucks?"* Even if I chose not to do it on
a regular basis, just knowing how doable it is brought the whole
puffery of New York restaurants into perspective. Bribing, it
turns out, has as much effect on the briber as it does on the
bribee.

A few nights later, the effect of this newfound glow became
clear. I walked into Le Cirque 2000, the gilt-edged establishment
on the East Side. "Sorry," I was told. "We don't have a table
tonight." No problem, I thought. I took a step back and tried to
identify the person in power. Seconds later, a gentleman in a
tuxedo approached. "We were wondering if you had a table for
two?" I said, clutching a bill in my pocket . . . but *not handing it
over.* He bowed. "Your table is ready," he said, and led us into the
dining room.

This was a new benchmark: I had bluffed my way in. Just by
being *prepared* to bribe, I had achieved my goal. Was there some
change in my appearance? Was I swaggering a bit or walking a
little taller? Perhaps. A couple of days later, I bluffed my way
into Aureole.

Despite my luck, I knew I had saved the hardest places for last.
Union Square Cafe has, according to the *Zagat Survey,* been New
York's "most popular restaurant for four years running."

"You'll be eating at McDonald's tonight," a friend said.

When I arrived at 8:30, the gentleman in charge said, "We
can seat you in an hour." I told him my name, took a few steps
back, waited for him to step away, then approached and slipped
him a $50 bill. "This is a very important night for me," I whis-
pered, and waited for the rebuff. To my surprise, the man

seemed positively giddy. "No problem, sir," he said, clenching the bill with boyish abandon. "I'll check right now." Ten minutes later we were shown to a corner table in the back. The deed had been done with such effortlessness, such quotidian blaséness, that my friend was nonplussed. "It feels so normal," she said.

By this point, with the quick addition of Daniel, where $50 got me bumped up from the lounge to the dining room in 30 seconds, I had demystified the act. I had learned a new skill. I had gained ten pounds. And I seemed to be breeding followers: One friend called for advice on how to "tip" her super; another friend announced she had slipped a twenty to a clerk at the Charlotte airport. Also, people were bribing *me* to take them out to dinner.

But it turned out I still faced my biggest hurdle.

"You must try Alain Ducasse," declared my editor. At first, I thought this was a cruel joke. The press was buzzing about the new restaurant from France's maestrochef that boasts a $2 million interior, a $160 tasting menu, and a bill for four approaching $1,500. Although the phone lines weren't yet open, the word on the street was that the 65 seats a night were already booked for six months, with a 2,700-person waiting list. According to *The New York Times*, "Ordinary diners have less than a snowball's chance of landing a table at Ducasse."

I was clearly in another league of exclusivity. Lay eaters wouldn't dream of trying to enter a restaurant where if you order verbena tea they bring the *plant* to your table and a white-gloved waiter snips the leaves with silver shears.

Still, I had no choice.

It was just after 8 p.m. on a Monday when I entered the ornate foyer. With gold columns, shiny black walls, and eccentric art, the room seemed one part Paris, one part Vegas, one part Decline of the Roman Empire. Within seconds, a French gentleman approached. I bowed.

"I was wondering if you might have a cancellation."

"Oh, no, sir. We are fully booked."

I slid a $100 bill toward his hand. He was overcome with the look I had expected all along: complete and utter horror. "No, no, monsieur. You don't understand!" he exclaimed. "We only have 16 tables. There is absolutely no way!"

"In that case," I said, changing tacks, "I was wondering if you might have a cancellation later in the week." As he moved behind the podium, I reached for my business card (which lists no affiliation) and tucked the $100 bill *underneath* my card. I handed both to him, adding, "I am here all week." He accepted them, and pressed the card onto a small leather folder with his index finger. He was shaking at this point, and I realized I was calmer than he was—a switch.

He then took a piece of paper and asked me my name (even though it was on my card), the size of my party, and my telephone number. "How about lunch?" he said.

"I would prefer dinner."

"Okay," he said. "I'll call you."

We shook hands, and I left. The following day, every time the phone rang, my heart leapt. The end of the day came, however: no call. The next day, 42 hours after I had walked into the restaurant, the telephone rang. It was a woman from Alain Ducasse. "We have a table for four tonight," she said. "Can you find three guests to join you?" I asked if I could make a few calls. She said yes and gave me the private number. A few minutes later I called back and accepted.

For as little as $100—that's $25 *each* for a meal that would ultimately cost close to $375 per head—I had jumped what was rumored to be a 2,700-person waiting list and gotten into the hardest restaurant in the world that week. Also, I had shot the moon. And I had done it by following a set of rules so old-fashioned that my grandmother could have written them: Dress properly, act dignified, be polite, smile. And spend a little extra for good service—it will pay you back in droves.

Forget Frank Sinatra. Forget James Bond. For the rest of that day, for the time it took me to call everyone I know, for the three hours and 45 minutes it took me to eat my 11-course meal, I was the lights on the top of the Chrysler Building. I was the smile on the Statue of Liberty. I was New York.

I was money.

The Döner Party

by Jeffrey Eugenides
from *Food & Wine*

There's a wonderful feverish energy to this restaurant-hopping narrative by novelist Jeffrey Eugenides (*The Virgin Suicides*). Hop on for the ride—and hold on tight.

I t is a cool March evening in Berlin. We are heading west on Bundesallee, a wide commercial street that might be in Cleveland. Actually, I'm not sure which way we're headed. But I don't let on. I'm the guide tonight. This was my idea.

The editors at *Food & Wine* seem to have a war-room map, studded with pins. Each pin represents a writer. They know where we all are. They know which exotic cuisines we might be eating. The Eugenides pin (just a thumbtack, really, not the royal-blue pushpin of Updike, not the flat-head nail of Mailer) impales Berlin. "He's over there on some kind of fellowship," one editor said at the morning story meeting. The next day, the invitation arrived. *Food & Wine* wanted me to write about my favorite food here in the new capital of the united Germany.

I accepted. My wife had been lobbying for an expensive dinner out. Here in Germany they have something called Social Democracy. Over in America we have something called the expense account. Self-employed novelists don't get one. This was my only chance.

I made a reservation at the hot new place Berliners are talking about. It was a restaurant in the Kreuzberg neighborhood called Le Cochon Bourgeois. "Good evening," I said, in my faulty German. "I am writing a restaurant review for a famous American magazine. It is also my birthday." For whatever reason, the service that night was fantastic. My glass was never empty. The waitress bent close to my ear to suggest a wine for each course. The Germans at our table dined on beef cheeks, which they claimed were the tenderest part of the beast. I had lamb, from a nonfacial area, while my wife had blood sausage, worth every bit of karmic debt. Finally, the entire staff, including the chef, brought out a cake and serenaded me with "Happy Birthday." Le Cochon Bourgeois was a great find. But I knew even then, as my candles sputtered out, that I had nothing interesting to say about it.

Tonight's different. Tonight I can feel the quickening in my blood that comes when a writer connects with his material. What are we doing driving around Berlin? We are on a mission: to seek out, in a single night, in a gastronomic marathon, the best fast food in Berlin.

THE DEFINITION OF DÖNER

People have the wrong idea about Berlin. They think it's gray, when it's actually green. They think it's tortured, when it's actually peaceful. And they think it's German, when it's actually, significantly, Turkish.

Decades ago, Turks began coming to Berlin as guest workers,

settling in Kreuzberg. Biblically disposed, they were fruitful; they multiplied. Today, if Kreuzberg were a city, it would be the fifth-largest Turkish city in the world. Nothing symbolizes this Turkish presence more than the ubiquitousness of döner here. It is said that the best döner to be had on earth is not in Istanbul but right here on the streets of Berlin. There are döner restaurants and döner fast-food stands and old GDR trailers selling döner out of rear windows. In general, Turkish döner resembles Greek gyro. Both revolve on spits. Both are made of geological layers of processed meat. Both are the shape of a tornado. But while gyro is usually made of lamb, döner is beef or, more commonly, veal. As a döner spins, dripping juices, the chef shaves off thin, slightly crusty pieces. These go into pita bread along with chopped tomatoes, onions, cabbage and spices. You can have either the traditional yogurt-and-garlic sauce or a red hot sauce. This being Germany, the hot sauce is not hot.

Along the avenue I watch the *Spiesse* turning in the windows of döner stands. Some skewers of meat look fat and happy, others emaciated and forlorn. The German *der Spiess*, meaning skewer or spit, gave rise to the slang term *spiessig*, meaning Philistine or, that favorite term among Europeans, petit bourgeois. What does it mean that I've chosen to write not about nouvelle German cuisine but about grilled meat? I can't think about this right now. I am mesmerized by all the spinning, glistening *Fleisch*.

I have standards, however. "Only places where we can sit down," I tell my friends. "I don't want to stand."

Why are we doing all this in one night? Simple. This isn't my car.

THE CAR

It is a 1962 Fiat. A classic car, as small, shapely and collectible as a Bakelite radio. The Berlin Wall went up in 1961; a year later the Italians made this automobile. Now the Wall is gone but the Fiat is still going. The dashboard has only three switches: windshield wipers, heat, vent.

"What adjectives are you going to use to describe the car?" the driver asks.

"Imperturbable," I answer. "The small red imperturbable Fiat."

The driver gives me a withering look. "It's Bordeaux," he says. "Red? I can't believe you're a writer."

My Cahorts

The person who says this to me is the painter Glen "The Educated Palate" Rubsamen. He is wearing a gray Austrian jacket made from boiled wool. It makes him look woodsy and genteel. Seeing him in profile now, I also think, not for the first time, how much Glen resembles the composer Philip Glass. He hates this fact, however, so I don't mention it.

In the backseat is the sculptor Rita McBride. Rita and Glen are married. This is a good thing as they are perfectly suited for each other. But let's not get too happy here: There is sadness in the air. Tonight is Rita and Glen's last night in Berlin. Our search for the best döner in the city is a farewell party.

I have asked Rita and The Palate along because they, unlike me, have taste. A few months ago, The Palate cooked me a meal I'll never forget. The main course was pork simmered in milk. It was some kind of sophisticated cut tied up in string, like a miniature edible harp. "They make this pork dish in only one village in Italy," The Palate said. "And in the next village over, a place called Cremona, they make this special mustard to serve with it."

"What mustard?" I said. On my plate next to the pork were only two pieces of candied fruit, a cherry and an orange.

"Try a little bit of that cherry with your pork," The Palate said, smiling.

I cut a slice of pork, a slice of cherry, and put them into my mouth. The cherry tasted like hot mustard!

With food, as with a paintbrush, The Palate is a magician. He is here tonight to tell me what it is I am eating.

THE ETERNAL MYSTERY OF DÖNER

Our first stop is a place called Habibi in the district of Schoneberg in West Berlin. This is The Palate's suggestion. There are tables inside with stools. I don't like stools. Does anybody like stools? Nevertheless, it qualifies.

As we're eating our döner, however, I notice something. "Hey, it says schwarma on the window. This isn't a döner place."

"It isn't?" says The Palate.

"I'm supposed to be writing about döners," I say, pointedly, to The Palate. Then I remember the car. "It's good, though. This schwarma. It's basically the same as a döner. And fresh-squeezed orange juice. Good choice. Though not strictly in my purview."

"We should ask how they make one of these things," The Palate says, changing the subject.

"Good idea," I say.

When we do, however, the man only answers, "We make it here."

"No," The Palate persists. "How do you make it?"

"Here. We make it here."

At our next stop, a bona fide döner stand, we try again. "Don't worry," the döner shaver says. "You don't have to make one. We make it for you."

"They don't want to tell us," Rita says.

ENLIGHTENMENT UNDER THE OVERPASS

As we hurtle down Yorckstrasse a few minutes later, heading east across the city, The Palate's nose twitches. "We have to try that place. That looks great."

I shake my head. "You have to stand."

"Unfortunately for you," The Palate informs me, "I'm driving." He pulls the Fiat into a parking lot.

The Imbis Hisar Spezial Döner glows whitely under the overpass of the elevated S-Bahn train. It's a lovely, desolate location. Soot-blackened walls rise across the street. Trains run past overhead. The surrounding land is open, junk-strewn, filled with the unexpected hope of crumbling places. In every city there are areas that exude, in a concentrated form, the basic ingredients of life there. The Imbis Hisar on Yorckstrasse is such a place. The evening sky is glowing a soft light blue. The smell of coal drifts in from the furnaces in the East. You can feel it here, all of it: Berlin's industrial beginnings, its dark fanatic history and its irrepressible open-field present. Food depends on where you eat it. The Palate can discern this spice from that spice; for me, location itself is a flavoring.

I don't mind standing to eat here on Yorckstrasse. *"Alles klar?"* the man at the counter says to me. This means, essentially, "Everything okay?" But, a student of German, I still get caught up in literal denotations. "All is clear?" the counterman seems to be saying to me—as if, along with my döner, he's handing me the secret to life.

We Discover the Secret

An hour later, after stopping at five other stands, none worth mentioning, after having döner with stale bread or too much salt, we arrive in the Zehlendorf neighborhood, at Divan.

"This place is nice," I say. "You can sit."

Since this is a German Turkish restaurant and not a strict Muslim one, we order three enormous beers. When our food arrives, it is enormous also. The Palate gets the Iskender Kebab, a mound of döner under a red sauce. I get the Divan Teller Spezial, which includes spicy kofta meatballs along with döner, roast chicken and *pommes frites*. Rita gets the Shish Yogurtlu, which is lamb with a spiced yogurt sauce. All of these dishes taste exactly the same.

When the waiter comes over, I try one last time. I explain that I'm writing an article for an American magazine. And then I ask, "How do you make döner?"

"You want to know how we make döner?" He grabs me by the arm and lifts me out of my seat. He drags me across the restaurant to a small, greasy document posted near the skewer itself.

"There are over fifty-five different companies in Berlin making just döner," he tells me. "There are all kinds. Our döner is seventy percent *Scheibenanteil* and thirty percent *Hackfleisch*. Some restaurants have only fifty-fifty. The more *Scheibenanteil*, the better. Here, seventy-thirty. Here is our card. The name on it is the owner's. Do not mention him in your article. Mention me, Türkay Aslan."

So that's the answer. Döner is part meat cuttings *(Scheibenanteil)* and part ground meat *(Hackfleisch)*, pressed together into a huge cone. On a napkin, I write down the name of the company that makes the döner. "I may have to visit one of these döner factories," I tell my friends.

"I can't drive you," says The Palate. "By then Rita and I will be in Ghent, a lovely medieval town known for its prunes."

DISASTER STRIKES

"I forgot to get a receipt!" I say as we get to the car. I run back to get one. When I return to the Fiat, Rita and The Palate are silent. We drive away. I look over at The Palate. His boiled-wool Austrian jacket still looks elegant. His recent haircut at the hands of a Rastafarian doesn't seem quite so unfortunate in the darkness of the Fiat's interior. But something seems to be wrong with The Palate. He is sitting funny. "No more!" he cries at last. "No more döners!"

He is clutching his stomach. I realize my mistake at once. Going back for the receipt has allowed The Palate and Rita to think about things, and they are now pulling out of our mission. It is time to rally the troops.

"We haven't even been to Kreuzberg yet," I say. "The heart of Turkish Berlin! Think of how many döners there are in Kreuzberg."

The Fiat lurches. Something is going on inside The Palate.

Maybe it's my fault. Maybe I should never have enlisted a man of such culinary refinement to sample so many roadside bags of meat. But then I have a brainstorm.

"Rice pudding!" I shout. "You have to have the rice pudding at Hasir. That will settle your stomach."

It is touch and go. Fortunately, Rita McBride votes against her husband, and The Palate steers our classic vehicle in a new direction. Lovely, spacious, sad old apartment buildings pass on either side. The Landwehr canal glints in the moonlight. The Fiat is very loud inside; also, air is coming in the window, making me cold. But we are headed east toward Kreuzberg.

DÖNER DECONSTRUCTED

On the way, I have time to think. The similarity of döner and gyros has a personal meaning for me. My paternal grandparents came from Asia Minor. They lived outside Bursa in what today is Turkey, part of a Greek minority under Ottoman rule. The relations between the Eugenideses and the Turks (including a girlfriend I had in my twenties) haven't always been especially warm. My grandmother, in fact, was nearly killed by Turkish soldiers and had to hide in a cave for almost a week in order to escape. Nevertheless, I don't think these hatreds should be kept going. The poison must be drawn off after a while. I feel the same way about Jewish friends who refuse to visit me here in Germany. Such thinking is primitive. It ascribes to living persons the guilt of the dead and invests the land itself—the soil, the trees—with a residue of evil. I don't know how my grandmother would feel about my frequenting Turkish restaurants in Berlin, but the fact is, I feel more at home, or at least less out of place, in a Turkish restaurant than I do in a German *Kneipe*.

The Turks in Germany, just like the Greeks in America, have had to market themselves. In order to sell a native cuisine, you have to translate it, and that, often as not, means kitsching it up. I'm thinking about this German word *spiessig* again. People of the spit. This is what Greeks in America and Turks in Berlin have had to become. Both döner and gyros are fabrications. Meat cuttings are pressed together to simulate the body of an animal roasting on a spit. People like to see Greeks and Turks in this way, as simple villagers, as slaughterers of goats. There's a direct line from the gyros spinning today in the Olympia Diner on Third Avenue in New York City to the pagan sacrifices described by Homer in the *Iliad*. The scent of roast lamb rises to Olympus, pleasing the gods. And Manhattanites.

This is one reason for the sympathy I feel here in Berlin for my supposed historical enemies. When I was young, my father used to take me to all the Greek-owned fast-food restaurants in Detroit. He was a mortgage banker, but he always knew the guys behind the counters or at the grills.

SAVED BY DESERT

If you visit only one döner restaurant in Berlin, it should be Hasir. There are four Hasirs, actually. One, on Nürnberger Strasse, has no döner and is upscale. The second, in Schoneberg, has a döner made of 100 percent *Scheibenanteil*. The third is in Spandau. All are good. My favorite, however, is the Hasirin Kreuzberg. The interior is tiled blue and white in abstract designs. There is a painted mural of the suspension bridge over the Bosphorus. The restaurant is full of Turkish Berliners, most of them ordering the Mercimeck Corbasi, which is a red-lentil soup. People stop in for döner to go or sit at one of the booths or tables inside. In summer, there are tables outside, close to the traffic.

All the main dishes at Hasir are good, especially the Acili Ter-biyeli Shish Kebab, which is shish kebab with garlic and veg-etables in an authentically hot sauce. With Rita and The Palate, I order only the desserts. The Sutlac, or rice pudding, is incred-ible. "This is the best rice pudding I've ever had," I say, "except for my grandmother's."

"The Kazandibi is also very good," says The Palate, already picking up the lingo, as he spoons in the sweet Turkish dessert.

"Try this," Rita says. She offers her husband some Tel Kadayif, an exotic pudding with walnuts, pomegranate, peach, grapes, raisins and syrup.

The Palate is eating and smiling. The crisis is averted. There is a good chance he will drive me home.

AUF WIEDERSEHEN

I have enjoyed my night immensely. I will miss Rita and Glen. As we leave, I take out the napkin where I've written the address of the döner factory. After looking at it a moment, I crumple it up and toss it into a trash can. I decide not to find out how döner is made. Some things in life should not be inquired into too deeply.

Paris Through Yam-Colored Glasses

by John T. Edge

from *Oxford American*

John T. Edge is The Man when it comes to Southern cooking—director of the Southern Foodways Alliance, proprietor of the website y'all.com, and monthly contributor to the *Oxford American* (Oxford as in Mississippi, please).

I did not set out for Paris in the best of moods. The idea that I would soon be trodding French soil in search of the best fried chicken in all of Paris—when seemingly every other *traiteur* on every single market street would be hocking those lovely, yellow-legged Bresse chickens stuffed with pungent Périgord truffles—well, let's just say it threw me into a sort of pre-prandial funk.

My previous week's reading matter did not help much. I had spent the better part of the past few days dipping in and out of A.J. Liebling's *Between Meals,* a masterful chronicle of one trencherman's culinary apprenticeship in Paris. Liebling was an adventurous eater, the kind of gourmand a truck driver can cozy up to. In the book's opening paragraph, he savages Proust and his damned little wafer, declaring a preference for small birds, stewed rabbit, and stuffed tripe, while musing that, "In light of what Proust wrote with so mild a stimulus, it is the world's loss that he did not have a heartier appetite." I could only imagine what Liebling would have had to say about my summons to Paris, my plan to eat good ol' country cooking when burbling terrines of sausage-studded cassoulet awaited.

My first day of eating began with great promise. Rapping at the entrance to Chez Haynes—open since 1949 and thus the oldest operating Southern-style restaurant in Paris—I found the door bolted and a sign indicating that, contrary to my reconnaissance work, dinner, not lunch, is the sole meal served. I consoled myself at a nearby bistro with a baker's dozen of butter-drenched *escargots à coquilles,* followed by a roasted leg of lamb served with delicate tarragon-perfumed *flageolets.* A demi of Crozes Hermitage to drink, a nice *mâche* salad to cleanse the palate, and a selection of Camembert and Cantal cheeses rounded out a fine first meal. But it was not what I was here for.

Retracing my steps, I became lost in the warren of switchback streets and dank alleyways that define the north Paris neighborhood known as Montmartre. Without a map, I tried in vain to get my bearings by the architectural confection of Sacré-Coeur, perched high atop the butte. Somehow I wound my way through canyons of mansard-crowned limestone and granite, ran a gauntlet of strip bars near the Place Pigalle (known to generations of U.S. servicemen as Pig Alley), and, as dusk descended upon the city, found myself, once again, smack dab in front of quite possibly the sole storefront in Paris boasting a log cabin facade: Chez Haynes. This time the door gave way.

Rumor has it that prior to founder Leroy Haynes's tenure, the birch-fronted boïte at 3 rue Caluzel housed a cabaret that catered in large part to a lesbian clientele. Indeed, the little grotto still exudes an overtly feminine feel, framed as it is by pairs of sinuous columns attributable to what might best be described as the Late Harem school of Turkish design. The rest of the interior—save for the scores of signed black-and-white photographs of the likes of Louis Armstrong and Sarah Vaughan—is movie-set French: ten or twelve tables scattered about a tile-floored room, each set in classic café style with red-checked cloths, squat wine glasses, and dull stainless flatware.

But now the restaurant appears to be in its dotage, the victim of a long and increasingly precipitous decline that began in 1986 with the death of Leroy Haynes, a stalwart of the postwar black expatriate community in Paris. His second wife, Maria, a woman of Portuguese ancestry, has carried on in his stead, but ten minutes into my visit with her, I knew that I'd arrived around fifteen years too late. When I asked her to bring me the best of what the kitchen has to offer, she returned with a platter of pallid vegetable turnovers. Though ham hocks and cabbage are still featured on the menu, along with red beans and rice, barbequed spare ribs, and a queer coleslaw laced with bits of pineapple and peach, her choice of pastries did not bode well for the future of Southern cookery in the City of Light.

Contrary to popular belief, Chez Haynes was not the first Southern-style restaurant in Paris. Indeed, Haynes and his wife arrived late on the scene. While Montmartre and Pigalle were the epicenters of black expatriate life between the World Wars, by the time Chez Haynes was in its prime, the focal point for Southern socializing had shifted to the Left Bank, where spots like Buttercup's Chicken Shack in Montparnasse and Tom's Barbeque near the Place Madeleine drew musicians and artists and writers by the score. Long gone were the days when Langston Hughes worked as a glorified *plongeur* at the swank Le Grand Duc on rue Pigalle, dishing up fried chicken to the demimonde.

By anyone's measure, Leroy Haynes's culinary career was sin-
gular. Within an hour of crossing the threshold of Chez Haynes I
had learned this much: A native of Clinton, Kentucky, he earned
an undergraduate degree from Morehouse College in 1938, followed two years later by a master's from Atlanta University. In
1941 he shipped out for active duty in the Pacific theater. Next
came a short stint in Germany. Rather than return home, he
applied to study at the Sorbonne on the G.I. Bill.

To earn extra money, Haynes took to bartending and waiting
tables. By 1949, along with his first wife—a young Frenchwoman
named Gaby, whom he would soon divorce—he scraped together
enough money to open a cubbyhole of a joint on the rue Manuel
in Pigalle, just a block from the restaurant's current location.
Their specialties: fried chicken, stewed chitlins, and barbequed
pigs' feet, conjured from Haynes's Kentucky childhood. The col-
lard greens were also highly touted, though, given the least prod-
ding, Leroy would reveal that they were not true collards but
branches de broccoli—the oversized, leathery outer leaves that
surround the tight green florettes—salvaged from the rubbish
heap by a kindly greengrocer.

The ersatz collards hooked me. Though I had arrived in Paris
intent upon conducting a grand tour of Southern cookery on the
continent, in short time I began ambling about the city trying to
piece together a portrait of Leroy Haynes. At the American
Library, set in the shadow of the Tour Eiffel, I combed the stacks
for trace sightings, chance recollections. In the novelist Chester
Himes's autobiography, *My Life of Absurdity*, I came upon a
description of Haynes in his prime: "Leroy was a spectacular figure, a huge black man weighing well over 250 pounds, with
biceps as big as my neck."

In Carlene Hatcher Polite's novel *Sister X and the Victims of
Foul Play* I read along as the character Abyssinia, in the midst of a
fight with her Parisian paramour, exclaims:

Man, don't you put your hands on me because if
you've got eyes, you can see I am in a big hurry. I've got

some eating to do. I'm so sick and tired of this sauce shit, till I don't know what to do. If I can just taste one thing again, before I die, that is not disguised with somebody's sauce. All I want is a plate of plain o' greens, boiled in plain o' water, some plain fried chicken, a hot biscuit or two, some corn on the cob, potato salad with celery, candied sweets, Cole slaw, [and] some of Haynes's hot sauce or chow chow.

I talked in fractured French and stilted English with Haynes's friends and colleagues. From a former bartender, I learned that Haynes had once operated a nudist colony in the South of France. From a waitress who served up his fried chicken for all of two weeks, I heard that, at an early age, Haynes left Kentucky for Chicago where—she swore—he worked as Al Capone's paperboy.

I spent a Friday afternoon perusing the stucco walls of the restaurant, tracing Haynes's sporadic movie career. For the most part he played bit roles in Eurotrash gangster flicks and French-fried versions of spaghetti westerns, though if a variety of signed proclamations and celebrity glossies are to be believed, Haynes counted David Niven, Brigitte Bardot, and Jackie Gleason among his admirers. The more I looked, the odder things got: Just beneath a signed portrait of Elizabeth Taylor and Richard Burton, I spied a blurry publicity still from the movie *Chitty Chitty Bang Bang*. Wasn't that Haynes, tricked out in a plaid leisure suit, standing tall on the rear bumper of the car?

On Saturday I spent a couple of hours thumbing through the yellowed pages of Haynes's old guest books. Rod Steiger liked his fried chicken. James Baldwin doted on his red beans and rice. Martin Luther King Jr. and his wife apparently paid a visit on their way to Sweden to pick up the Nobel Peace Prize. Stokely Carmichael signed his tribute to Haynes, *For the liberation of all oppressed people. Black power!* Three pages later, George C. Scott saluted Haynes's ribs.

Late in my trip I journeyed to the suburbs of southern Paris where, in conversation with Michel Fabre, biographer of Haynes's fellow expatriate Richard Wright, I learned that, in the early 1950s, Haynes and Wright were involved in a group known as the French-American Fellowship, and when Wright's adaptation of Louis Sapin's play *Daddy Goodness* debuted in 1959, burly Leroy Haynes played the lead role. What's more, Fabre told me that Albert Camus was a regular at Chez Haynes in 1955, when he staged an adaptation of Faulkner's *Requiem for a Nun* at a nearby theater.

Like an English pub in Calcutta or a German beer garden in Dubuque, Chez Haynes traded in remembrances of things past. It's out-of-the-way location fueled the mystique. "Naturally a Paris boulevard is just about the last place to ever think of singing the blues, and so the black exile does the next best thing," wrote Ollie Harrington in his essay collection, *Why I Left America:*

> He takes the Metro to the foothills of Montmartre where he will find Leroy Haynes, himself an exile, who will fix any brother or sister with generous helpings of chitlins with collard greens, red beans and rice, and even corn bread! Haynes with his restaurant has struggled valiantly with this problem of nostalgia and in the process has come up with a variety of chili-based condiments. The most famous of these are called Big Brother and Little Sister.

This notion of nostalgia was a profound one for the black men and women of Leroy Haynes's generation, who made their way to Paris not to be in close proximity to the grandeurs of the Louvre but with the express purpose of escaping Jim Crow.

Life in Paris promised freedom. "[B]eing in Paris is a matter of air," the writer James Baldwin told a *Newsweek* reporter in 1964. "I can take a deep, long breath before going back under water for the long and painful count."

While Baldwin's exile was intermittent, others, like Leroy Haynes and Richard Wright, chose permanent exile. The choice was purposeful, political. Each time Wright crossed the threshold of Chez Haynes, he would fix his friend with a mock-serious expression and call out, "Leroy, when are you going home?" To which the restaurateur would reply, "Have they built a bridge?"

Yet spend enough time away from home and any good Southerner will soon be pining for collards and kinship. For those lucky few in Paris, Leroy Haynes was the man to see for a mess of greens doused with a glugg of Big Brother, served with a crumbly tile of corn bread on the side.

Over the course of a week spent wandering about the city, I returned often to Chez Haynes, not so much for the food—though I do still harbor a strange craving for a dish the menu lists as "Ma Sutton's Fried Chicken" which was, in essence, a nicely browned quarter bird, doused in a sticky sauce tasting of equal parts lard and honey. Instead I came to pay homage to Leroy Haynes. I came to hear the mellifluous drawl of my people, black and white.

One Sunday night I sat down to supper with a couple of Savannah, Georgia, natives at the tail end of a mad cross-continental dash. Over bowls of hoppin' John, we talked of how we loved grits and loathed gnats. The next day I shared a beer with a man from South Carolina who claimed to have taught Leroy Haynes how to skin a catfish. Late one Friday night I slipped in the front door of the restaurant just before closing to listen to the last set of a chanteuse named Electra, who sang a sultry rendition of "Summertime."

When I wasn't at Chez Haynes, I was eating my way across Paris. At a bistro near the Bastille, I tasted wild hare in a sauce of red wine and redder blood. At a grand restaurant across from the Palais Royal, I sipped champagne and slurped delicate Breton oysters. And at a wine bar near my hotel, I snacked on andouille sausage that looked like it had been sliced from a link of bologna imprinted on the bias with the rings of an ancient sequoia, and tasted as if it had spent a week or two in close proximity to a mess of chitlins.

Though I was tempted, I did not wholly forsake my native victuals. Out in the chic thirteenth arrondissement, at Percy's Place, a jewel box *salon de thé* plastered with ads for Mammy brand oranges and Aunty brand okra, I ate fried chicken wings dusted with curry, and a jambalaya that tasted like a cross between Cajun étoufée and Texas chili. And at the newly opened soul outpost Bojangles, set just down the hill from Chez Haynes, I traded news of home with proprietors Bennie Luke (the onetime star of the stage and screen versions of *La Cage Aux Folles*) and Sharon Morgan over bowls of pumpkin soup and quaking platters of pork chops and baked chicken and dressing, black-eyed peas and candied yams.

And then, quite unexpectedly, my culinary peregrinations came to a shuddering halt when, two nights before I was scheduled to leave for home, I woke with a start, my stomach clenched tight and churning. Most adventurous eaters know the telltale signs: food poisoning, no doubt about it. To this day, however, I am unsure as to whether I was done in by a bad piece of chicken at dinner or a surfeit of *foie gras, confit de canard,* and *boudin noir* at lunch.

After a restless sleep in a nest of clammy sheets, I climbed from my sickbed, unsteady on my feet, unsure of whether it was day or night. I needed something solid in my gut, something substantial. Haynes was closed, and the thought of eating anything even remotely French sent my stomach catapulting and caterwauling again. So I succumbed to small defeat. I dragged my weary bones to a McDonald's on Boulevard de Clichy, a few doors down from the Moulin Rouge, where I wolfed down a cheeseburger and a small order of fries. It would be my last meal in Paris. Five hours later I boarded a plane for home.

Desperately Seeking Ceviche

by Calvin Trillin

from *Gourmet*

To read Calvin Trillin's food writing (try his book *Alice, Let's Eat*), you'd think this is a man who takes absolutely nothing seriously except his appetite. Told with his trademark martini-dry wit, this is a picaresque tale of a gastronomic junket to Ecuador and Peru.

O n a steamy June afternoon seven or eight years ago, I was standing just off a curb in midtown Manhattan, trying unsuccessfully to get a cab to La Guardia Airport. I found myself having thoughts about the city that would not have pleased the Convention & Visitors Bureau—thoughts about the weather, thoughts about the structural flaws of the New York taxi industry. Then a Lincoln town car appeared in front of me. The uniformed driver lowered the window, and I was hit with frigid air. "Where you going?" he said.

"La Guardia," I said.

"Twenty-five dollars."

"Deal."

I got in. The driver identified himself as José. As we made it over the bridge and hit the Grand Central Parkway, he told me that he was from Ecuador, a country I had visited a few months before. I told him how much I'd enjoyed Ecuador—the gorgeous mountains, the markets, and, most of all, the *ceviche*.

Ceviche in Ecuador, I said, is to American *ceviche* what the seafood cocktails of Veracruz—oysters, shrimp, snails, octopus, crab, avocado, onions, and coriander chopped in front of your eyes into a liquid that in a just world would be what Bloody Mary mix tastes like—are to those balsa-wood and ketchup combinations that people in country-club dining rooms get when they order the shrimp-cocktail appetizer.

Ecuadorean *ceviche* starts out with fresh fish cured by being marinated in lemon juice and enlivened by whatever else the chef has thought to add. It's liquid, like a bowl of tangy cold soup. Roasted corn kernels (flicked off Andean corn, whose kernels are sometimes the size of broad beans) are served on the side, to be tossed in for both flavor and crunch. Some restaurants offer not only roasted corn kernels but popcorn. Yes, popcorn—what less fortunate humans eat at the movies!

"You like that *ceviche*?" José asked. He sounded pleased but mildly surprised, like an artist who has just heard effusive praise of a painting that is actually one of his earlier works.

"I love that *ceviche*, José," I said. "I would probably kill for that *ceviche*."

"When's your plane?" José asked.

"Oh, I've got time," I said.

Instantly, he swerved off the Grand Central, and we were driving along a commercial street in Queens. Most of the signs on the stores were in Spanish. Some were in Chinese or Korean. In five minutes, we turned onto a side street, in front of a restaurant called Islas Galapagos.

We got two orders of *ceviche*. We cleaned our bowls. Then we got back into the car and drove to La Guardia. "This is a great city, José," I said as I hauled my baggage out of the icy splendor of his town car. "A little hot sometimes, but a great city."

On the other hand, the sort of New Yorker who's confident that even a stroke of good fortune can be complained about might point out that I had to go all the way to Queens to find Ecuadorean *ceviche*. I live in lower Manhattan, and at the time I met José, I'd almost never had a *ceviche* close to home. In New York I had never even seen roasted corn kernels—what Ecuadoreans sometimes call *tostados* and Peruvians call *cancha*. (They are neither roasted nor toasted, of course, but panfried, then salted, so that they're crunchy on the outside and soft, almost powdery, on the inside.) A couple of *ceviches* I had in Manhattan actually came accompanied by commercial Cornnuts, which, being approximately the right size and color, serve as a substitute for *cancha* about as effectively as marshmallows, being approximately the right size and color, would serve as a substitute for diver scallops.

These days, *ceviche* is definitely available in Manhattan. Around the time of my La Guardia adventure, Douglas Rodriguez brought it into the mainstream at Patria, and he later installed an entire *ceviche* bar at Chicama, complete with popcorn. I've read about a Manhattan restaurant that offers a sort of *pour la table ceviche* appetizer for $50—a dish no visiting Ecuadorean would be able to eat, of course, since he would have fainted dead away upon learning the price.

Still, as the years passed, I thought more and more about a trip to serious *ceviche* country, which could mean, of course, almost anywhere in Latin America. When FBI agents tapped the prison phone calls of former Panamanian dictator Manuel Noriega, one conversation that made them suspect that he was employing a devilishly clever code concerned a *ceviche* recipe. *Ceviche* is so entrenched in Mexico that Rick Bayless, a scholar of Mexican food, has been serving it, usually made from marlin, since he opened Frontera Grill in Chicago 14 years ago. There is wide agreement, though, that the red-hot center of *ceviche* eating is around Ecuador and Peru—two countries that, after several decades, have more or less settled their border dispute but still argue about which one does the best job with marinated fish.

Last spring I decided I had to go to Ecuador and Peru to get a booster shot of the real article. A number of people asked me if I really intended to travel all that way just to eat *ceviche*. Not at all. In Peru, for instance, I was looking forward to sampling the stuffed pepper that many consider the signature dish of Arequipa, and I fully intended to have my share of Andean potatoes. I thought I might tuck away some *churros*—possibly some *churros* with chocolate on them. I still remembered a couple of the soups I'd had during my first trip to Ecuador while staying at a charming inn called Hacienda Cusin, near the great Andean market town of Otavalo, and I thought I might see about arranging a reprise. I was seriously considering guinea pig, which is such a strong regional specialty around Cuzco that the most famous 17th-century religious painting in the Cuzco cathedral shows it as what Jesus and his disciples are about to eat at the Last Supper. I also had visions of sitting in a comfortable hotel bar somewhere sipping Pisco sours while tossing down handfuls of *cancha* and expressing sympathy for travelers who were at that moment at other hotel bars all around the world trying to make do with mixed nuts. No, I assured the people questioning my trip, I wasn't going all that way just to eat *ceviche*. I like to think of myself as a broad-gauged person.

My older daughter, Abigail, who lives in San Francisco, agreed to meet me in Peru, and my wife, Alice, said she'd link up with us in Quito. When I dropped into Chicama to ask Douglas Rodriguez for some tips about where to eat down there, he said he'd prefer to show us himself, and we arranged to meet him and his wife and his publisher and the *ceviche*-bar chef from Chicama in Guayaquil for a couple of days of sampling. We had become the *ceviche* gang.

• • •

"Would it be fair to say that you're wimping out on the guinea pig?" Abigail asked.

We were in a restaurant in Cuzco. At the table next to us, there was a woman who had the appearance of a classic gringa—a very pale American of the type that the people of Cuzco sometimes refer to as a *cruda*, meaning, literally, "uncooked." She looked like the sort of tourist who might ask the waiter if there was anything available from a can, but we had just seen her presented with an entire roasted guinea pig, head and all. Abigail had spoken just as the waiter took a picture of the guinea pig and then carried it back to the kitchen to be dismembered. As the carcass passed our table, it occurred to me that Louisiana, which is trying to encourage people to eat nutria, might find it advantageous to join forces with Peru to form a Rodent Marketing Board.

I reminded Abigail that trout was also a specialty of the area, and I had ordered trout *ceviche*—a bold move into freshwater *ceviche* that I considered the equivalent of going to Wisconsin and ordering, say, walleye sashimi. I'd also had *ceviche* in Arequipa, squeezing a sea-bass version in between stuffed-pepper stops, and it was already clear to me that Peruvians and Ecuadoreans had different notions of what authentic *ceviche* is. In Peru *ceviche* is not something soupy that comes in a bowl; it would not ordinarily include additives like tomatoes. It is, essentially, chunks of fish (or shrimp or some combination of shellfish) and spices and shredded onions—served on a plate, eaten with a fork, and flanked by a couple of thick wedges of potato or corn. I would imagine that Peruvians consider their version of *ceviche* stately and Ecuadoreans consider it dull.

Abigail and I had a lot of it. In the Lima shorefront neighborhood of Chorrillos, we visited a couple of spots that had a dozen or two *cevicherias* side by side in a single ramshackle shed. And at Costa Verde, one of the vast and somewhat overblown Lima restaurants built out into the Pacific, a waiter wearing a tuxedo served us Ceviche Don Raúl, a scallop, shrimp, and mushroom mixture that, according to the menu, was a contender for culinary honors at the World Exposition in Seville in 1992.

About an hour south of Lima, in Pucusana, a fishing village that is also the site of some flashy vacation houses, we came across a neatly dressed young man behind a cart of the sort hotdog vendors use in New York. He was wearing a baseball cap and an exceedingly white T-shirt. He had set up shop just a few yards from the market shed where the local fishermen brought in their catch. A couple of umbrellas shaded the cart, and a half dozen plastic stools had been placed on one side for customers. A sign announced that the young man was a specialist in instant *ceviche*. After a customer had ordered, the instant *ceviche* specialist went to work, using a stainless-steel kitchen bowl as a sort of wok. He squeezed a few hyperacidic little lemons onto the fish, then added chopped-up celery and garlic and peppers and a little water and shredded onions. He stirred and cut with practiced motions, at one point flicking a bit of the sauce on the back of his hand so he could check the balance of spices with a quick taste. The entire *ceviche*-making process couldn't have taken more than 30 or 40 seconds. After he'd placed my *ceviche* on a plate, he hesitated for a moment, and then tossed onto the side of the plate a handful of *cancha*. Abigail seemed to catch the relief on my face. I think at that moment we may both have faced up to the possibility that what I had been dreaming of for seven or eight years was not *ceviche* but panfried corn kernels.

Not that I had any complaints about the *ceviche*. The one dished out by the specialist in instant *ceviche* was first-rate, and so was the one I had across the street, in a restaurant called Bahia-Turistica, an hour later. I was having trouble keeping my focus, though, because other dishes crowded in on the *ceviches* like so much tasty static. This problem was particularly acute at Costanera 700, a Lima seafood restaurant whose proprietor, Humberto Sato, is spoken of by *ceviche* hounds like Douglas Rodriguez in tones approaching reverence. Sato named his restaurant after its address—a service to customers, since there is no sign. Like a lot of serious seafood restaurants in Lima—or serious purveyors of Arequipena specialties in Arequipa, for that matter—Costanera 700 is open only for the midday meal. It's in a line of buildings on the water's edge of the less-than-uplifting Lima neighborhood of San Miguel. Its main dining room, while not unpleasant, suggests a smallish airplane hangar. Our cab-driver had a difficult time finding Costanera 700 and was not convinced we had made it even after we'd arrived. The drivers of important politicians and businessmen apparently have no such problem; they're familiar with the route.

Humberto Sato turned out to be a preternaturally calm man of Japanese ancestry who speaks about fish in the way a master furniture-maker might discuss fruitwoods. His menu offered five sorts of *ceviche*. Abigail and I ordered Ceviche Costanera, which is made with olive oil, and Ceviche La Paz, a Peruvian coastal *ceviche* that takes on a yellowish color from the peppers used to season it. The *ceviches* were perfect: The tastes of the fish and the marinades and the spices blended together with great subtlety. We figured that before we went on to the *tiradito*—a Peruvian form of *ceviche* in which the fish is in slices, as in sashimi, instead of in chunks, and is usually served without onions—we'd vary the meal with shrimp served sizzling on an iron griddle. That dish can sometimes be no more than a garlic delivery system, but not in Sato's hands. Encouraged, we tried the *chita,* a fish I'd never heard of, cooked inside a cast of salt, which the waiter carefully cracked open, like an experienced orthopedist freeing up a mended ankle. Then we had rice with tiny shrimp. At that point, the *tiradito* was simply an impossibility. I comforted myself with the thought that we were about to go to Ecuador, where something like *tiradito* would probably be thought of as nothing more than a good start.

"Be careful, save room," Douglas Rodriguez said. "We're on our way to Mecca." He kept on eating as he spoke.

Led by an Ecuadorean friend of Rodriguez's named Humberto

Mata, we'd arrived at one of those multi-*cevicheria* buildings in Playas, a town an hour or so west of Guayaquil. Our eventual destination was the resort town of Salinas, where Douglas had predicted we'd have the best *ceviche* in Ecuador at a place he'd once visited called La Lojanita. The building in Playas was a large shed that had a thatched roof and used split-bamboo fences to carve out separate outdoor dining areas for a dozen or so *cevicherias* with names like Cevicheria Brisas del Mar and Cevicheria Viagra Marina—the latter an allusion, I assumed, to the widespread belief in that part of South America that *ceviche* is useful not only as a hangover cure but as a sexual tonic. ("Anything with that much acid in it can't actually be good for hangovers," I had been told by a resident of Lima, who was mum on the sexual-tonic issue.) The *cevicheria* we'd chosen was a corner establishment called Fuente del Sabor, or Source of Taste, and the food made Douglas's warning difficult to heed. After some fine black-clam *ceviche*, we had been served *patacones* (chunks of plantain pressed down into the frying pan with a wooden mallet until about the size of a cocktail-party crab cake), a spectacular seafood and rice combination, and a huge oyster that, after having been pried open with a hammer and chisel, had been covered with cheese and butter and mustard and cooked right on the flame of the range, with its enormous shell acting as the cooking vessel.

The *ceviche* gang was on its second day of eating. In Guayaquil, our haul had included a *ceviche* with so much tomato that it veered toward the fish cocktails of Veracruz and, in a simple but spectacular restaurant called Los Arbolitos, a sort of mixed-stew platter that included a tripe stew, a fish stew, a mixture of salt cod and onions, and, perched on top of the pile like a jolly hat on somebody wearing a dull brown uniform, a *ceviche*. We'd eaten fish in a peanut sauce that tasted almost like curry, plus a sort of onion soup with tuna. At a place called Churrin Churron, in a flashy shopping center that also had a Pizza Hut and a Dunkin' Donuts, we'd had a chocolate-filled *churro* that Abigail said was worth the trip.

We had also eaten *fanesca,* an astonishing fish and vegetable soup, nearly as thick as porridge, which is available in Ecuador only during Holy Week. In the Quito market, on the day after Palm Sunday, I'd noticed signs saying HOY FANESCA! By Tuesday I'd eaten it three times. As I worked on the rice and shellfish in Playas, I found myself wondering what good deed I might have done long ago that resulted in my landing in Ecuador by accident during Holy Week. In other words, I was trying to anticipate *ceviche* at La Lojanita while daydreaming about *fanesca* and shoveling in a shellfish and rice dish I couldn't seem to stop eating. "Save room," Douglas said again as he carved off another piece of the oyster. "Don't forget about Mecca."

La Lojanita turned out to be a couple of blocks inland from the Saunas beach, just past a *cevicheria* cluster called Cevichelandia. It was an open-air place, with permanent stools lined up next to a counter on two sides. Its sign was further proof that the Coca-Cola company had a lock on *cevicheria* signage in Ecuador and Peru. Douglas did the ordering, and I could hear him go down the list, almost like a chant: black clam, octopus, regular shrimp, shrimp in the manner normally used for *langostina* (which were unavailable), sea bass with the sort of mustard sauce usually accompanying crab (also unavailable), mixed. As we started to eat, I looked around and realized that much of the *ceviche* gang had fallen by the wayside. Douglas and his publisher, Phil Wood, and his *ceviche* chef, Adrian Leon, and I were the only ones left at the counter. In front of us I counted 20 bowls of *ceviche.* "Do you think you really have to taste every single one?" Alice asked from the sidelines. She spoke in the tone she uses when, after quick inspection of the outfit I've chosen for an evening out, she asks, "Is that the jacket you're going to wear?"

I did think I had to taste every single one; I couldn't let the side down. We grabbed spoons and started. Everyone remarked on the glories of the black clam. After Adrian tasted the second type of shrimp, I heard him mutter, "Russian dressing." I was trying to keep up with the rest of the gang, even though it did occur to me that Humberto Sato would probably describe most of what we were eating with whatever Spanish phrase translates roughly into "gussied up." Douglas praised the octopus but thought that, all in all, La Lojanita was not quite as good as it had been on his previous visit. It was possible that the proprietor had become distracted, he said, since the splendor of her *ceviche* had led to her being elected mayor of Salinas.

I woke up the next morning feeling a bit fragile. For some reason, I was imagining the Seville culinary competition Abigail and I had seen mentioned on Costa Verde's menu. I envisioned it as purely a *ceviche* contest. The judges appeared to be Sevillano gazpacho experts pressed into service, although there were also some of those stone-faced East Germans who always seem to be among those judging Olympic diving competitions. The instant-*ceviche* man was there, again in a baseball cap and a crisp white T-shirt, practicing his moves in the corner. Manuel Noriega paced back and forth, glowering at his competitors in an attempt to frighten them away. Rick Bayless walked in from Chicago carrying a huge marlin on a sling across his back, the way Indian women at the Otavalo market sometimes carry full-grown sheep. Off to the side, Humberto Sato, dressed in street clothes rather than his chef's whites, stood silently, having decided to withdraw because the fish were not up to his standards. Some health-food demonstrators who objected to the acid in *ceviche* were parading around with signs that said IF IT DOES THAT TO A SEA BASS, THINK OF WHAT IT'S DOING TO YOU! I wasn't planning to stay for the judging. I'd decided to take a day or two off from *ceviche* eating.

A couple of days later, we were back at Hacienda Cusin—the rare example of a place that has been restored into complete comfort with no accompanying glitz. I was sitting in one of the courtyards, having a chat about *fanesca* with the chef, Marco Yanez, who had provided us with a particularly splendid example on Good Friday. An explanation of its preparation makes *fanesca* sound like something that should appear on an absolutely accurate menu as Potage Labor Intensive. It must include 12 grains and beans, to represent the 12 apostles—each ingredient soaked and cooked and dried and peeled separately. The base, salt cod cooked in milk, is thickened with peanuts; naturally, it's mandatory to start with raw peanuts, then toast them, then peel them, then grind them. I could see why *fanesca* is eaten only during Holy Week: When some frantically slurping teenager calls out, "Mom, can we have this again next week?" it stands to reason that Mom, her fingers sore from peeling corn kernels and fava beans, would answer, "Talk to me in about a year, buster."

Fanesca must be, among other things, a restorative: With a couple of bowls of it under my belt, I was able to begin my next lunch by enthusiastically polishing off a shrimp *ceviche* and a hearts of palm *ceviche*. Even while I was eating the *ceviche*, though, I found myself calculating how many more *fanesca* opportunities I'd have before Easter Sunday. I couldn't help wondering if, assuming the labor-cost issue could be sorted out, some restaurant in New York—maybe even some restaurant in lower Manhattan—might be induced to put *fanesca* on its menu. In New York, of course, there'd be no reason to be overly strict about the custom of serving it only during Holy Week. When the ingredients were available, a sign on the restaurant would announce HOY FANESCA!

A
Copenhagen
Christmas

by Raphael Kadushin

from Gourmet

Wisconsin-based book editor Raphael Kadushin makes a great virtual travel companion: He sketches foreign settings with a poet's attention to detail, he easily makes friends with the locals, and he's always up for a good meal.

O utside, the Copenhagen afternoon had turned the steely Nordic blue that signals a coming snow squall, but inside Slotskaelderen Hos Gitte Kik, everything glowed yellow under the restaurant's hanging lights. Lining the long wooden counter in the front of the café were thick slices of fresh-baked bread wearing different toppings: pressed lamb; roast beef furled around grated horseradish; and an exploding fish-tank of Baltic shrimp and smoked salmon, the ingredients stacked up like a tower, so that the homely sandwich got transformed—literally—into very high art.

The real tour de force, though, was still in progress. "Danish smørrebrød sandwiches have always been as much a part of our landscape as the snow, sea and air," said Lene Just, Gitte Kik's manager and smørrebrød queen, as she smeared liver paste over fresh bread. "Some people prefer this one over all others."

"Which people?" I asked. Flicking back her blond braid like a drumroll, Just surveyed the schoolchildren and businessmen clustered by her counter. Then she balanced onion on top of salted beef on top of the liver paste, and decided to confide.

"Well, the King of Sweden for one. I didn't give him any privileges, though, when he stopped by last month. He still had to come up to my counter to order his favorite calf's liver sandwich, just like anyone else."

Only in Copenhagen would visiting royalty trade the fois gras for liver on rye. It was a typical Danish story and there was a word to describe it. The word, which I had heard again and again when I first came to town as a boy, was *hygge,* and it was the same word that people used to describe what they liked most about Christmas.

"It means 'cozy, homey, snug, warm," ' Just told me. But she didn't have to translate. What hygge meant was all around us: the lights glowing against the bruised afternoon dusk; the rows of Danish comfort food; the memory of the king who swept through, trailing a note of fairytale whimsy, yet who still got treated like part of the extended family.

You don't have to hunker down at Gitte Kik to savor the spirit that fuels Copenhagen's Christmas, and that was part of the reason I had returned. I also had a mission in mind. My most vivid memory of that first boyhood trip to Denmark centered squarely on the candy-colored town houses lining Nyhavn canal, and a neighboring pastry shop where I ate the cake I couldn't forget: a frothy cloud of cream studded with nougat that instantly got imprinted on my taste buds. Where did I sample what became the measure of every dessert to follow? My parents couldn't remember the name of the shop, and I only had my wistful palate to guide me.

It didn't matter. Reliving my own best Christmas past would prove easy enough in Denmark's capital city, even if I didn't find the spot where I cut my first sweet tooth. That's because a hunger for winter coziness seems built into the city's DNA—especially at Christmas—and so does a kind of regression. The result is an eight-hundred-year-old city that never fully grew up itself.

I saw that the minute I stepped outside. The bus drivers shooting down Hans Christian Andersen Boulevard, named after the town's favorite son, were wearing Santa caps. The public statues—apparently approved by some ministry of fairy tales—depicted more dragons and mermaids than straight-faced states-men, and the Royal Life Guards marching in front of Amalienborg Palace looked like toy soldiers. Even Kongens Nytorv, the city's busiest square, had swapped serious business for sheer whimsy: Glazed with a sheet of ice, the plaza had been turned into a skat-ing rink. Quaint? Santa's workshop looked like Dante's Inferno by comparison.

Copenhagen's almost collective will to re-create a child's per-fect Christmas became clearest, however, when I set out for my first dinner in town, at Grårødre Torv 21 restaurant, in a mustard-yellow town house on a pastel-washed square. If I was trying to relocate my boyhood, owner-chef Torben Jensen had already reclaimed his, which was passed in the heart of Denmark's heart-land. That was obvious from the rooms filled with flickering candles and old family photos and the sprays of conifer in each window. The effect was as purely Scandinavian as sharing a bowl of lingonberries with Pippi Longstocking.

So was Jensen's most popular dish: a roast duck wrapped in crackling skin and framed by a bed of red cabbage and fat prunes. "I remember the smell of that duck cooking in the oven on Christmas Eve clay when I was a boy," said Jensen. Appar-ently all his diners did, too. Beside me a group of men wearing strap-on reindeer antlers—proof that you can regress a little *too* far back—watched with reverence as the golden bird was placed on their table.

I witnessed the same kind of devotion the next day when I had lunch at Fregatten Sct. Georg III. Anchored in a lake at Tivoli Gardens, Copenhagen's elegant amusement park, the floating restaurant is a replica of an eighteenth-century Danish frigate, and it takes its theme very seriously. It boasts high masts, cabins doubling as dining rooms, and yo-matey waiters decked out in striped pirate shirts.

But there is nothing stagy about owner-chef Rasmus Bo Bojesen's passion for his food. For him, reclaiming the taste of childhood means rescuing a whole culinary tradition.

"I trained in France and Tokyo, but I always remembered the flavors of my grandparents' farm west of Copenhagen, where we spent summers picking asparagus and strawberries," he said. "Eventually what excited me as a chef wasn't truffles and caviar but rye bread and herring. When I returned home for good, I realized what other Danes were discovering: Why copy French or Japanese style when we have our own proud food traditions?"

The point was hard to argue as Bojesen's roll call of classics began to crowd the table. Herring with a creamy curry made clear why the fish—which Danes variously fry, boil and marinate—swims to the top of the food chain here. A silky smoked eel wore a lattice of leeks, and fork-tender pork was crowned by a thick, crispy skin. This is the kind of clean cooking that distills Nordic flavors to their essence.

The traditional Christmas dessert, though, broke loose with a touch of flamboyance. Bojesen's imperial almond rice pudding, dressed with a hot cherry sauce and pillowed with whipped cream, appeared as white as a Baltic snowdrift. For a moment I thought I'd found my way back to my first Copenhagen dessert—but the nougat was missing. At least the culinary flashback proved complete for Bojesen: "I can picture my grandmother sitting up in heaven, eating her raspberries and cream, and smiling down on us." He grinned as he swallowed a spoonful.

At Tivoli Gardens, the throngs of young Danes didn't need to claim their inner child; they were clearly enjoying their first youth. After lunch, I scanned the scene from the top of the garden's Chinese pagoda. Famous as the world's most genteel summer amusement park since it premiered in 1843, Tivoli began reopening for the month of December in 1994, and promptly became the heart of Copenhagen's holiday season.

It was easy to see why. Crowding the park's epic Christmas market were rows of garland-draped pastel cottages selling seasonal specialties: peppermint sticks, *gløgg*, fur hats, marionettes, waffles laced with apples, buttery sweet rolls that put the Danish back into danish. But only a few customers were buying. Bundled in neon-bright parkas, waves of children were busier skating around Tivoli's rink and bobbing on an heirloom carousel.

This tribute to playfulness—sprawling across the kind of prime downtown real estate that harder-headed cities would have reserved for office blocks—seemed purely expressive of Copenhagen. Yet as Christmas neared, I realized that the city didn't really need its holiday trimmings or amusement parks; its permanent landscape was enough of a fantasyland. Castles still outnumber skyscrapers in Copenhagen, and the most photogenic palace was moated Rosenborg. Shooting up in the middle of a downtown intersection, surrounded by a twenty-first-century traffic jam, its turrets and towers seemed stuck in their own immutable dream time.

Yet it would be a mistake to consider Copenhagen some storybook suburb of Tivoli Gardens. The city's abiding whimsy also feeds a cutting-edge sensibility that has turned Denmark's capital into one of Europe's new style centers. That is most evident along the city's pedestrian Strøget street where streamlined Danish Modern housewares offer chic Christmas shopping—and in the local bumper crop of next-generation restaurants. Minimalist, globe-trotting kitchens like Capo, Olsen and Konrad swap the boiled herring for squid ceviche and showcase high-concept dining rooms that feel more hip-hop than hygge.

At Schultz, where the new wave crests, the traditional ceiling beams have given way to a poured-concrete dining room, and trendsetters are fittingly draped in fun furs. The crowning touch is a wanderlust menu that sails far beyond Baltic shores. On the night I stopped by, grilled scallops dotted a creamy risotto dressed with lime sauce. Sea bass was laid over two hollowed-out celery roots gorged with foie gras, and my wedge of cheesecake came laced with licorice.

"Good?" asked chef Allan Schultz, a pumped-up young man with a shaved head who had cooked in Los Angeles and had brought back his own dialect—a yo-man kind of Dane-glish. "Like all the younger chefs here, I'm trying for a new sense of adventure, because we want to put Copenhagen on the map," he said. "And we are. This place is on fire, man."

His surfer-dude excitement, though, couldn't mask the fact that Schultz would probably be happiest hanging ten with the Little Mermaid. "I love it here," the chef said. "I may explore different influences, but I always Scandinavianize them and use Danish products: goose, prunes, cabbage, apples, pork, mushrooms. Your foie gras is stuffed in celery root because that's a kitchen staple; I created the licorice cheesecake because no one eats more licorice than the Danes. Copenhagen is open to the world now, but walk outside in winter and it still feels like a friendly ice village. That's what I live for."

So do most of his contemporaries. A short walk away, at Kong Hans, chef Thomas Rode Andersen brings the landmark kitchen's Michelin-starred haute cuisine down to earth, gently, with a newly patriotic menu that salutes both Escoffier and Aunt Inge, and fittingly so. Kong Hans is housed in a historic building where Hans Christian Andersen once wrote, and it looks over the city's corkscrew church towers and ice-glazed harbor. While the legendary writer probably wouldn't recognize his namesake's foie gras marinated in kirsch, he would instantly know my duck. Robed in a sauce of red wine, cinnamon, ginger and honey, it tasted like the soul of a Danish Christmas.

But it was Kommandanten, where I went for my last dinner, that evoked Copenhagen's truest holiday flavor. Circling the town one more time, on the afternoon before Christmas Eve, I felt primed for a final celebration. Everything I passed looked like a seasonal signpost: the white lights strung between the carriage lanterns of Nyhavn; the families lining up to hear the Copenhagen Boys Choir at Our Lady's Church; the crowds jamming the Royal Copenhagen Porcelain shop, where the showroom tables were set with flower-strewn Flora Danica plates.

When I opened the door of Kommandanten's seventeenth-century town house, I knew I'd reached a sort of yuletide epicenter. Punctuating the dining room, which could have been jointly designed by Isak Dinesen and Edward Scissorhands, were iron chairs stretched out into neo-Gothic thrones, and old plank floors leading past blue-trimmed windows.

The menu kept the fantasy going. "Try these," said manager Lars Nielsen, serving a lobster folded into a pastry shell, and oysters wrapped in Chablis-marinated salmon. And things only got better, with chef Mikkel Maarbjerg's truffle sauce ladled over tenderloin of veal; a prune and plum terrine; and a huge macaroon stuffed with hazelnut puree that momentarily eclipsed my first Danish sweet.

"We do a mix of classic and contemporary cooking," Nielsen said, "but the Christmas dinner I cook for my family is purely old-fashioned. It has to be. I have three children who believe Santa is coming, and I want to make sure I pass all the traditions on to them. That means they each get a single present every night in December. We bring our ice skates to church. And tomorrow, on Christmas Eve, we will all link hands, sing carols and dance around the real tree we cut ourselves and decorated with real candles. I want them to have the kind of Christmas I had myself."

That, in the end, may be the key to a Danish holiday: Reclaiming their own childhood by passing it on, Danes make sure the dancing circle holds and the legacy stays intact, perfumed by a roasting duck. The proof of their success was everywhere as I walked back to my hotel, surrounded by a whole city holding impromptu lessons in hygge and ensuring that the next generation won't give in, quite yet, to a virtual Xmas dot.com.

On Kongens Nytorv a man in a tuxedo was leading his wobbly toddler across the ice. At an antique shop behind the Nyhavn, a girl was handing her baby brother a leather-bound storybook. And on a street off the Stroget, as the streetlights lit up for an endless Nordic night of dreaming, I passed a pastry shop called La Glace, where all of Copenhagen's grandmothers seemed to be pouring out cups of hot chocolate. I quickly returned, pulled by a mounting sense of déjà vu.

"We close in fifteen minutes," a waitress told me as she served me a piece of the café's signature sportsman's cake, but that was plenty of time. Swallowing a dense cloud of whipped cream and crumbled nougat, I closed my eyes and knew in an instant what I had found. It a tasted just as good as I remembered.

Food
Fights

Fresh from
the Pod

by Derek Cooper
from *Snail Eggs and
Samphire*

As I sat on a park bench in New
York reading this collection by
U.K. food journalist Derek Cooper,
a visiting Brit interrupted me to
rave about Cooper's influence at
home. As a consumer watchdog
and tireless promoter of local
foodstuffs, Cooper has (unfortunately) no American counterpart.

I will be with you before curfew," wrote Pitt one summer day
despatching a messenger from Westminster to his friend
William Wilberforce in Wimbledon, "and expect an early
meal of peas and strawberries." It is the taste of those early,
green, succulent peas, their freshness from the pod, that we,
with all our resources and our high technology, have almost lost.

There is nothing to compare with them. Certainly not the
dried pea nor the canned pea surfeited with sugar, nor the green
blue dyed marrowfat bullet tasting of sulphur and the chemistry
lab. Nor, alas, the frozen pea; least of all perhaps the frozen pea
which raises visual expectations it never satisfies.

It looks good, it retains its shape and texture, it is tender in the mouth. Unfortunately the pea the frozen food industry chose for mass planting and harvesting in the flatlands of Lincolnshire and Humberside has great commercial advantages but no taste at all. None. And even when in desperation the marketing men added an artificial hint of mint (NEW, NEW, NEW!) it couldn't redeem that bland forkful of inoffensive nothingness.

Had they only taken the delicious garden pea and frozen that, then all would have been well. But they needed a freezer pea— a species which would grow well, crop well and be disease resistant. In the producing of the Wonder Pea the plant geneticists bred the flavour out of it. A whole generation has now been reared on this neutral cultivar, a generation which has never shelled a fresh pea in its life and has come to believe that the specious frozen pea is what peadom is all about. The acreage under fresh garden peas has fallen dramatically. In the part of the world where I live you can no longer buy peas in the pod. Soon I predict they will be a universal rarity like quinces, persimmons, samphire, mulberries and Jerusalem artichokes.

The bland freezer pea which sends no stimulating messages to the tastebuds is a classic example of the way in which commercial imperatives manipulate raw materials so that eating becomes an exercise in marketing, not in joy and pleasure. Soon there will be, I'm told, a designer freezing strawberry that won't disintegrate into a mushy watery mess when it thaws. It will look like a picture book strawberry and photograph superbly for the TV commercials. But what about its flavour? Will the New Strawberry like the New Pea be just another mouthful of nothing? And how long will it be before the only strawberries available will be the frozen variety?

Already technology has mutated even the simplest foods so that the taste is smothered or replaced by the far from natural. It is becoming increasingly difficult to find fresh milk in public places; its place has been usurped by little plastic tubs of metallic-tasting UHT "milk" or sachets of chemical powders which 'whiten' tea or coffee. Potatoes are mixed into a tasteless and frothy mash from powder; ice cream has the soapy taste of palm oil; fish is battered and crumbed, beef is burgerized, steaks become additive-rich steaklettes, chickens are nuggetized, veal is chopped into choplettes. Raw materials are massaged and minced and steamed and pasteurized and extended with ersatz bulkers. And because the end result is characterless, flavours are sprayed on and artificial colours are added to create a spurious authenticity.

These new value-added foods, debased with salt and sucrose, are nasty but never cheap. Frequently the advertising budget costs more than the raw materials so you end up buying an edible equivalent of the Emperor's clothes—rubbish masquerading as a desirable and scrumptious treat. The vinegar-flavoured crisp is not a contradiction in terms: it is the logical and inevitable end result of the sterile philosophy of over-processing.

And what isn't over-processed and over-refined and bombarded with synthetic fragrances is by a process of unnatural selection gradually robbed of all taste. A perfect partner to the frozen pea is the cosmetic carrot, a designer product if ever there was one—lovely to look at but flavourless on the palate. And for all I know the plant breeding research stations are even now developing all manner of handsome turnips, raspberries, plums and apples which will pack well, travel well and have a profitably long shelf life. And once again taste will be of little importance.

Time perhaps that we formed a Society for the Preservation of Taste. There are plenty of bodies preserving trees, disused mineshafts, trams and ospreys. Help the poor pea, that's what I say. Help milk, potatoes, kale and carrots. Before it's too late.

I'm convinced that if there is a strong and insistent demand for food that actually has real taste then there will be market gardeners and farmers who would get great pleasure out of satisfying that demand. But we must play our part. Badger the greengrocer, bend the ear of the superstore manager, get them enthused too. If we just take what is handed out then the handouts will become progressively more bland. It's up to us.

Organic? Why Has It Become a Dirty Word?

by
Tamasin Day Lewis

from *The London Telegraph*

As a columnist for London's *Telegraph* newspaper, Tamasin Day Lewis raises disturbing questions about the organic food industry in Britain—questions increasingly echoed by disillusioned consumers in the States as well.

I suppose it had to happen. Sooner or later, "organic" was going to become a dirty word. What started as a fragile plant watered by a few hardy eco-warriors is now the stuff of big business, buy-outs and cynical marketing. A symbol that implies purity, good husbandry and wholesomeness, a move away from the processed and supra-refined, has become something we must question, whose integrity and quality is not guaranteed and which does not deliver what it originally stood for, namely great flavour and unimpeachable standards.

But let us begin at the beginning, in the halcyon days when

health-food shops were still considered the province of the brown-rice-and-sandals brigade, and standing at the radical end were the macrobiotics, sprouting mung beans and alfalfa. Those of us who played some part in this small scale resistance to the emerging packaged-and-processed culture, usually by adhering to whole grain, less meat, vertiginous levels of fibre and the questionable delights of the lentil bake, were gradually vindicated. Organics went mainstream.

The small growers, rearers and dairies that had survived the supermarket revolution and kept good food and good taste alive against the odds looked as if they would be able to consolidate their position and reach a larger, better-educated public, hungry for quality rather than cut-price factory fodder. Only it hasn't quite worked out like that.

The crises in the food industry, E coli, salmonella, BSE and genetic modification—blessed though they be to the organic movement—have started panic elsewhere. The government and the supermarket giants have had to respond to the public's growing mistrust of the rotten state of industrial food production, and "traceability" and "provenance" have become the new-generation buzz words. Crudely, the small producers who have brought about a renaissance in food over the past 20 years are all threatened by buy-outs.

Rachel's Dairy, known for its integrity and sublime organic yogurts, has been bought by Horizon, a huge US food consortium. To expand the business, it is having to import organic milk from abroad, a practice known as "food roiling": fundamentally against traditional organic principles—that promote the use of locally produced ingredients—I would have thought. As far as I know, there are only two small, independent, entirely organic dairies left, September Farm and Manor Farm. Whole Earth and Meridian have both been bought, as has Rocombe Farm, the best of the organic ice cream makers, by Yeo Valley.

I suspect a small business has to remain very small to survive these days and operate at farmers' market level, because the investment needed to produce volume and quality is more than most private individuals can muster, unless they've got very deep pockets or have retired from the City.

The problem is that people have entered the market whose desire is to saturate it and they've got huge marketing budgets that will inevitably undercut the smaller companies. The new, large-scale organic products that you see in your supermarket are an entirely cynical marketing exercise. The Enjoy Organics label is owned by Rank Hovis McDougall. Seeds of Change is owned by Mars. These are companies that have the financial clout, the contacts, the infrastructure and, unlike the small independents, can afford to lose money while they develop the product.

Commercially made organic food is not commensurate with quality. You lose the care, the traceability, all the things you believed were intrinsic to the organic manifesto. The giants start whittling away at the corners, because quality is not their prime objective. I'm not saying that the organicness is the problem; more that it's the cynical abuse of something people have worked hard at because they believe in it, and which is now being exploited purely for financial gain.

Look what has happened at Iceland. It is renegotiating the contracts it gave to its organic growers in the wake of its recent share crisis. The growers had to gear up to take on the contracts, some even converting to organic on the strength of the contract. Other supermarkets give contracts up to five years and think nothing of renegotiating them after six months. Where does that leave the small, organic supplier, who is, by then, captive?

Many of the labels are selling you a dream, something beautiful that you can trust, with rustic paper, pretty pictures and eco-packaging. Consumers are lulled into not reading the label, by the word "organic" emblazoned across the product. Yet why do you think that organic, mass-produced convenience food should taste any better than the nonorganic equivalent? The answer is because of brilliant marketing.

So, read the label. Tesco's organic shepherd's pie contains only

17 per cent meat—Argentinian beef. The potato—well, it's organic, so of course, it must be good. In fact, it is "organic rehy-drated flaked potato." That's an organic equivalent to Smash to you and me, reconstituted potato starch with a slimy texture not unlike wallpaper paste.

The meat, as in organic, mass-produced sausages, has proba-bly been passed through a grinder and could consist of gristle, ears, skin and all the extremities you can imagine. I asked Char-lotte at Swaddles Green Organic Farm what percentage of meat she uses in her shepherd's pies. "Sixty per cent," she replied. "The supermarket ones are full of water. And they don't taste of anything because the meat's too young and they don't hang it. Hanging costs money and takes up space. You'd be better off going to a decent organic butcher than buying organic super-market meat. The supermarkets are using the organic label to sell heavily processed foods.

'Denhay, Eastbrook Farm and Duchy Originals all use sodium nitrite in their bacon cure, albeit in small quantities, which is absurd," she adds. "You cook it, so you're not going to die of botulism."

The Soil Association allows them to carry the organic label, despite the fact that as far back as 1978 government scientists on the Food Advisory Committee said sodium nitrate and nitrite should be eliminated as soon as practicable, because when com-bined, in large quantities, with some chemicals in food, they form nitrosamines, one of the most carcinogenic substances known to scientists. Yet Swaddles Green makes delicious bacon and sausages without these additives.

There is a huge difference in standards between one organic chicken and another, too. The Soil Association allows a maxi-mum flock size of 500 birds in movable arks, so they perma-nently have fresh grazing. Organic farmers and growers allow a flock size of 4,500 birds in static sheds with flap-up sides. Organic doesn't wholly mean organic, either; the Soil Association allows up to 20 per cent of the chickens' diet to be nonorganic.

The ubiquitous jars of pasta sauces bearing the organic label are similarly lacklustre. They have clearly not been cooked long enough for the water content to evaporate and the flavour to intensify. And why not charge people for water? It's something our food industry has perfected, although what we are best at in this country is packaging; dressing things up with words and fancy outsides, while not bothering too much with what's inside the packet.

There is organic and organic, and my money will stay with the small, specialist producer. The shepherd's pie, I'll make at home. enough water to barely cover. Bake for 45 minutes before turning the potatoes over and cook for a further 45 minutes. They should be cooked through, but I have known them to take a trifle longer. Serve alongside the fish with plenty of the oily, lemony juices.

The Raw Deal

articles by Debra DeSalvo and Robert Sietsema

from *The Village Voice*

These two companion articles from the *Village Voice* offer up the paradox of any trendy movement. The enthusiasts Debra DeSalvo profiles are persuasive promoters of the raw food way of life—but restaurant reviewer Robert Sietsema comes at it from a different angle.

Eat It Raw!
by Debra DeSalvo

Yo! Any vegetarians in the house?" hollers Stic.man of hip-hop's radical duo Dead Prez. A roar and dozens of fists rise up in CBGB, which is packed. It's 3 a.m. and the young, mostly Latino crowd has been hanging all night for a showcase of politically conscious Latin bands booked by Ricanstruction. Despite the late hour, the air is strangely smoke-free.

"Any vegans?!" More shouts from the crowd. "All right!" Stic nods enthusiastically, dreads bouncing as he hops back and forth.

"What about the raw foodists? Any raw foodists in the house?" A few whoops and hands shoot up, waving wildly. "Yeah!" Stic shouts. "That's the shit!" as Dead Prez slam into "Be Healthy," from their Loud debut album, *Let's Get Free*.

"Be Healthy" exhorts would-be revolutionaries to forgo fried chicken for juiced greens. They should play it at New York's newest raw food restaurant, Quintessence. "It's a political act to eat raw foods, because major corporations are poisoning people with over-processed, denatured food," says Dan Hoyt.

Hoyt and his wife, Tolentin Chan, both 37, opened Quintessence in December above his former recording studio on East 10th Street. A sandy-haired Midwesterner with twinkling ice-blue eyes, Hoyt first reduced his space to rubble 16 years ago, cutting a hole in the floor and installing Vital Music in the basement. He recorded scads of East Village rockers, from Alice Donut to Clowns for Progress. In 1997 he tore the place apart and reemerged with the Lab, which specialized in custom sound design.

Meanwhile, Chan was doing some rewiring of her own. A technical designer at DKNY, Chan had asthma and caught frequent colds. When a colleague raved about the effects of a raw food "cleanse," Chan visited her counselor, David Jubb, a self-described "specialist in colloidal biology" with a Ph.D. from NYU, who's been eating raw for 27 years. He guided her through "nutritional fasts" consisting of smoothies, blended soups, and juices. Today Chan, a slender woman with bright black eyes, gorgeous skin, and a quick, slightly mischievous smile, recalls, "My health improved tremendously. Now I'm 100 percent raw and my asthma is completely gone. I never get sick, and my energy is really high."

Inspired, Hoyt saw Jubb too. "The results from fasting are really drastic, so it's very motivating," Hoyt says. "I lived with hay fever, food allergies, but when these problems go away and you learn more about eating this way, it seems so logical."

The raw food diet consists of fresh fruits, vegetables, and sprouted seeds, nuts, grains, and legumes. "Sprouted grain loses its enzyme inhibitors and releases more nutrients," explains Jubb. Raw foodists obtain most of their calories from monounsaturated fats like avocado, young coconut, and olive and flax oils, instead of cooked grains and beans. Protein and minerals come from leafy greens, spirulina, bee pollen, seeds, and nuts.

"People assume raw food is hard to digest," Hoyt notes, "but when you cook food you destroy enzymes and must use your own to digest it. Raw food digests itself. You don't even have to eat it—if you blend a tomato and leave it overnight, it'll be 90 percent digested by the morning. Cooking was invented to prevent foods from breaking down overnight."

"When you eat cooked vegetarian food, you lose the life force raw food has," says Chan. "Vegetarians are calm and relaxed, but they don't always look energized, don't have that vibrant, glowing quality. That's the difference between a raw foodist and a vegetarian."

Chan and Hoyt began attending classes and lectures around town. "People were into the nutrition, but they weren't making the greatest tasting—or looking—food," Hoyt says, laughing. "We were making really good food at home."

So he gutted his space once again and, with Chan, created Quintessence. They opened in bitter weather, but lines soon formed out the door. "I thought there were a few hundred rawists in the city, but there are at least a few thousand!"

Neighbors are drawn in by the restaurant's calm beauty and gourmet menu. "People think eating raw is gonna be like chewing on weeds," Hoyt says, "but raw food is very vibrant. We use lots of spices and sauces. The flavors are very strong and clean."

These days Quintessence has regular customers from the tristate area and beyond. "Six kids drove 16 hours from Iowa to get here after they found us on the Internet!" Hoyt exclaims.

Competitive triathlete Mathew Mercur, 26, another customer,

is convinced that eating raw enhances his athletic performance. "I was nervous to try it," Mercur admits, "but now I'm 90 percent raw and I love it! I never get sick, I can train more, and I recover faster." Mercur, who won the U.S. triathlon series championship for his age class and is training for the 2004 Olympic trials, says he benefits from the concentrated nutrition provided by juicing and loading up on raw fats. "I find fats a better source of long-term fuel than cooked carbs, which weigh me down."

As for protein, Mercur says, "When you eat a steak, you have to break it down to amino acids. But leafy greens, nuts, and seeds are packed with amino acids and minerals your body can use to build protein right away."

Until recently, the main resources for someone like Mercur were classes and coaching provided by High Vibe, the city's only store devoted to raw foods, and lectures and counseling by Jubb and his ex-wife, Annie.

Jubb, raised on an island between mainland Australia and Tasmania, was influenced by his Nepalese grandfather, "who understood that our choice of food was affecting the earth." Jubb loves the East Village because "there are more people interested in this lifestyle here than in any other place in the country. There's a critical mass of consciousness building that's going to affect the entire earth."

Dagger, who owns High Vibe, also senses an accelerating interest in raw food among New Yorkers. "We get new people in here every day, and now with Quintessence, more people are getting together and communicating. Things are rolling." Like Hoyt, Dagger transformed his former creative space—"my art studio, my darkroom"—into his business. He describes his inviting basement, with its cavelike white stucco walls and strings of white icicle lights, as "the East Village gone Southwest—a sanctuary, a place for people to hang out."

A laid-back artist-photographer-musician with tattoos running up both arms, Dagger got into raw foods because "I had done so many drugs and I just felt so bad. But I always tried to eat right. I started riding my bike like crazy and eating a lot of watermelon. I felt compelled to eat tons of it. I found out later that it's very alkalinizing, and drugs make you very acidic." Although he credits eating live foods with his vibrant health and ability to function on four to five hours of sleep, Dagger says he's "not in favor of zealotism. Do you feel good? That's the only thing that should influence your decision."

Paul Nison, who's developing a restaurant called Eden above the Hygeia Center on East 23rd Street, agrees. Nison was diagnosed with ulcerative colitis and told diet had nothing to do with it. Desperate, he experimented with raw foods and his symptoms disappeared. "I was told that by 30 I'd be lucky to have my intestines and I'd probably have cancer. I'll be 30 this year, and I did a 117-mile bike race, and haven't gone back to my doctor."

Jubb student Narda Narvããez, a physical therapist, founded the Natural Wellness School at Hygeia in February. "I started the school to help the community," she says. "Food is so connected with family and comfort that you need a new family to support this." Narvããez, looking for a new space, intends to bring in a variety of health practitioners. She's starting a database of clients who have recovered from serious illness using raw foods "because we need documentation and research."

Jyni Holland, a registered dietitian at NYU Medical Center, wants to see such research, as "there are no scientific studies showing an advantage to eating raw broccoli instead of cooked broccoli." Holland also contests claims that raw foods provide greater enzymatic activity, because "the minute you pull a plum off the tree, you've separated it from its life force and it begins to break itself down. I don't want to put this diet down without knowing more," she adds, "but if you have an immune system compromised by chemo or severe AIDS, we recommend a 'no raw food' diet to protect against bacterial infections. I would also be concerned about adequate caloric intake, and adequate protein, B12, calcium, and zinc."

Holistic physician Dr. Ronald Hoffman notes that "some people do really well on the raw food diet, yet some do abysmally. I do put some cancer patients on a raw food diet, as it is marvelous for detoxifying. We usually use it for two to three months." Lots of fats will "alleviate some of the potential problems with this diet. I give high doses of coconut oil to patients with immune problems, for example, as studies show it to be extremely helpful. Also, if you have ulcerative colitis or celiac disease, using only sprouted starches can help."

Hoffman favors metabolic typing, a blood-test-based method of determining appropriate diets. "We are finding that some people must have meat, while for others it's not metabolically suitable. My hunch is that the people doing well on raw food would be shown by metabolic typing to be in the latter category." He cautions that "people use food like a personal statement—too much of that is going around. It's best to avoid arrogance . . . or using food as an emblem of virtue. The macrobiotic people destroyed their movement with arrogance."

Eliot Tokar, a practitioner of traditional Asian medicine, agrees. "A raw food diet is a very strong yin diet; most people can benefit when it's used for a limited period. It's in danger of becoming a fad, however, with people thinking it can be applied in any situation and be beneficial. This may be because the diet can cause very rapid change and can make you hyper and spacey."

While building Quintessence, Chan and Hoyt flew to San Francisco to work at Juliano Brotman's Organica, a popular raw food restaurant. "Juliano was so helpful," recalls Hoyt. "He gave us names of suppliers, showed us recipes. This is kind of a movement, so if you know something you share it. It's a supportive community—everybody's networking. We love that people come to the restaurant and actually talk to people at other tables. That's what it's all about."

Feelings: Woe, Woe, Woe
by Robert Sietsema

Midway through a second meal at Quintessence, one of my regulars bitched, "You know, this is one of the worst things I've ever tasted." She was referring to the nori rolls ($9), and I had to agree. The seaweed wrappers were sodden—as if the rolls had been sitting around—and the filling of sprouts, sunflower seeds, avocado, and puréeed vegetables had an acrid flavor that quickly became a chemical-tasting afterburn. Without the mellowing effect of heat, strong flavors like onion, ginger, garlic, and radish can become overpowering. The pasta Italian ($11) was a disaster too, though the dish made a pretty picture on the plate. Dressed with a decent cheeseless pesto, the "pasta" of shredded raw squash tasted like so much hay, and it took a strong will to plow through it.

It's a very California idea: a café that serves organic vegetables, fruits, and grains—all painstakingly prepared, and untouched by the heat of the stove. But uncooked doesn't mean unprocessed—in fact, this new cuisine depends upon a phalanx of food processors, blenders, sprouters, cold presses, and dehydrators, which are often employed to turn familiar ingredients into unappetizing mush. Corollary is an odd compulsion to create simulacra like veggie burgers (nearly inedible) and ravioli wrapped with raw turnip (not bad). Sadly, while the Greenmarket may abound this week in delicious sugar-snap peas, miniature Tristar strawberries, and the season's first sweet corn, you'll find none of these unadulterated raw pleasures at Quintessence.

But there are good things on the menu too. The soups ($5), in particular, can be wonderful. A special of cucumber-dill is powerfully herby and tart, while regular offering "peter's pot"—gyrating little wads of tomato and avocado—possesses a rich and spicy flavor that compares favorably with gazpacho. The desserts are also good bets. A wedge of coconut cream pie is light and airy, with a crushed-nut crust and a squiggle of carob syrup—though I suspect it's as high in saturated fat as crème brûlée. The beverage called apple pie ($4), an organic cider blended with something that creates a brown scum on the surface, really does make you dream of pie. But skip the "electrolyte lemonade" ($3.50), for which the waiter made extravagant health claims. Milky and weird tasting, it prompted another friend to quip, "Hey, they've reinvented soap." Chemically and aesthetically, he was right.

My real complaint about Quintessence, though, is that it's more about religion than food. The front page of the menu proclaims all sorts of nutty-sounding things you're expected to agree with: "Weakened over the centuries by eating altered and artificial foods, we have lost much of our potential as a higher being"; "There is much supporting the fact that those who eat only raw food live free of illness and disease, their mind becomes sharp and negative emotions disappear." I'll keep my negative feelings, thanks, including the one that the food at Quintessence isn't very good.

The Trouble with Fries

by Malcolm Gladwell
from *The New Yorker*

One of today's most insightful cultural investigators, Malcolm Gladwell (*The Tipping Point*) has a way of getting to the nub of every issue he researches. The ascendancy of fast food in modern American culture is one that cried out for his sharp-eyed scrutiny.

In 1954, a man named Ray Kroc, who made his living selling the five-spindle Multimixer milkshake machine, began hearing about a hamburger stand in San Bernardino, California. This particular restaurant, he was told, had no fewer than eight of his machines in operation, meaning that it could make forty shakes simultaneously. Kroc was astounded. He flew from Chicago to Los Angeles, and drove to San Bernardino, sixty miles away, where he found a small octagonal building on a corner lot. He sat in his car and watched as the workers showed up for the morning shift. They were in starched white shirts and paper hats, and moved with a purposeful discipline. As lunchtime approached, customers began streaming into the parking lot, lining up for bags of hamburgers. Kroc approached a strawberry blonde in a yellow convertible.

"How often do you come here?" he asked.

"Anytime I am in the neighborhood," she replied, and, Kroc would say later, "it was not her sex appeal but the obvious relish with which she devoured the hamburger that made my pulse begin to hammer with excitement." He came back the next morning, and this time set up inside the kitchen, watching the griddle man, the food preparers, and, above all, the French-fry operation, because it was the French fries that truly captured his imagination. They were made from top-quality oblong Idaho russets, eight ounces apiece, deep-fried to a golden brown, and salted with a shaker that, as he put it, kept going like a Salvation Army girl's tambourine. They were crispy on the outside and buttery soft on the inside, and that day Kroc had a vision of a chain of restaurants, just like the one in San Bernardino, selling golden fries from one end of the country to the other. He asked the two brothers who owned the hamburger stand if he could buy their franchise rights. They said yes. Their names were Mac and Dick McDonald.

Ray Kroc was the great visionary of American fast food, the one who brought the lessons of the manufacturing world to the restaurant business. Before the fifties, it was impossible, in most American towns, to buy fries of consistent quality. Ray Kroc was the man who changed that. "The french fry," he once wrote, "would become almost sacrosanct for me, its preparation a ritual to be followed religiously." A potato that has too great a percentage of water—and potatoes, even the standard Idaho russet burbank, vary widely in their water content—will come out soggy at the end of the frying process. It was Kroc, back in the fifties, who sent out field men, armed with hydrometers, to make sure that all his suppliers were producing potatoes in the optimal solids range of twenty to twenty-three per cent. Freshly harvested potatoes, furthermore, are rich in sugars, and if you slice them up and deep-fry them the sugars will caramelize and brown the outside of the fry long before the inside is cooked. To make a crisp French fry, a potato has to be stored at a warm temperature for several weeks in order to convert those sugars to starch. Here Kroc led the way as well, mastering the art of "curing" potatoes by storing them under a giant fan in the basement of his first restaurant, outside Chicago.

Perhaps his most enduring achievement, though, was the so-called potato computer—developed for McDonald's by a former electrical engineer for Motorola named Louis Martino—which precisely calibrated the optimal cooking time for a batch of fries. (The key: when a batch of cold raw potatoes is dumped into a vat of cooking oil, the temperature of the fat will drop and then slowly rise. Once the oil has risen three degrees, the fries are ready.) Previously, making high-quality French fries had been an art. The potato computer, the hydrometer, and the curing bins made it a science. By the time Kroc was finished, he had figured out how to turn potatoes into an inexpensive snack that would always be hot, salty, flavorful, and crisp, no matter where or when you bought it.

This was the first fast-food revolution—the mass production of food that had reliable mass appeal. But today, as the McDonald's franchise approaches its fiftieth anniversary, it is clear that fast food needs a second revolution. As many Americans now die every year from obesity-related illnesses—heart disease and complications of diabetes—as from smoking, and the fast-food toll grows heavier every year. In the fine new book *Fast Food Nation,* the journalist Eric Schlosser writes of McDonald's and Burger King in the tone usually reserved for chemical companies, sweatshops, and arms dealers, and, as shocking as that seems at first, it is perfectly appropriate. Ray Kroc's French fries are killing us. Can fast food be fixed?

• • •

Fast-food French fries are made from baking potato like an Idaho russet, or any other variety that is mealy, or starchy, rather than waxy. The potatoes are harvested, cured, washed, peeled, sliced, and then blanched—cooked enough so that the insides have a fluffy texture but not so much that the fry gets soft and breaks. Blanching is followed by drying, and drying by a thirty-second deep fry, to give the potatoes a crisp shell. Then the fries are frozen until the moment of service, when they are deep-fried again, this time for somewhere around three minutes. Depending on the fast-food chain involved, there are other steps interspersed in this process. McDonald's fries, for example, are briefly dipped in a sugar solution, which gives them their golden-brown color; Burger King fries are dipped in a starch batter, which is what gives those fries their distinctive hard shell and audible crunch. But the result is similar. The potato that is first harvested in the field is roughly eighty per cent water. The process of creating a French fry consists, essentially, of removing as much of that water as possible— through blanching, drying, and deep-frying—and replacing it with fat.

Elisabeth Rozin, in her book *The Primal Cheeseburger,* points out that the idea of enriching carbohydrates with fat is nothing new. It's a standard part of the cuisine of almost every culture. Bread is buttered; macaroni comes with cheese; dumplings are fried; potatoes are scalloped, baked with milk and cheese, cooked in the dripping of roasting meat, mixed with mayonnaise in a salad, or pan-fried in butterfat as latkes. But, as Rozin argues, deep-frying is in many ways the ideal method of adding fat to carbohydrates. If you put butter on a mashed potato, for instance, the result is texturally unexciting: it simply creates a mush. Pan-frying results in uneven browning and crispness. But when a potato is deep-fried the heat of the oil turns the water inside the potato into steam, which causes the hard granules of starch inside the potato to swell and soften: that's why the inside of the fry is fluffy and light.

At the same time, the outward migration of the steam limits the amount of oil that seeps into the interior, preventing the fry from getting greasy and concentrating the oil on the surface, where it turns the outer layer of the potato brown and crisp. "What we have with the french fry," Rozin writes, "is a near perfect enactment of the enriching of a starch food with oil or fat."

This is the trouble with the French fry. The fact that it is cooked in fat makes it unhealthy. But the contrast that deep-frying creates between its interior and its exterior—between the golden shell and the pillowy whiteness beneath—is what makes it so irresistible. The average American now eats a staggering thirty pounds of French fries a year, up from four pounds when Ray Kroc was first figuring out how to mass-produce a crisp fry. Meanwhile, fries themselves have become less healthful. Ray Kroc, in the early days of McDonald's, was a fan of a hot-dog stand on the North Side of Chicago called Sam's, which used what was then called the Chicago method of cooking fries. Sam's cooked its fries in animal fat, and Kroc followed suit, prescribing for his franchises a specially formulated beef tallow called Formula 47 (in reference to the forty-seven-cent McDonald's "All-American meal" of the era: fifteen-cent hamburger, twelve-cent fries, twenty-cent shake). Among aficionados, there is general agreement that those early McDonald's fries were the finest mass-market fries ever made: the beef tallow gave them an unsurpassed rich, buttery taste. But in 1990, in the face of public concern about the health risks of cholesterol in animal-based cooking oil, McDonald's and the other major fast-food houses switched to vegetable oil. That wasn't an improvement, however. In the course of making vegetable oil suitable for deep frying, it is subjected to a chemical process called hydrogenation, which creates a new substance called a trans unsaturated fat. In the hierarchy of fats, polyunsaturated fats—the kind found in regular vegetable oils—are the good kind; they lower your cholesterol. Saturated fats are the bad kind. But trans fats are worse: they wreak havoc with the body's ability to regulate cholesterol. According to a recent study involving some eighty thousand women, for every five-per-cent increase in the amount of saturated fats that a woman consumes, her risk of heart disease increases by seventeen per cent. But only a two-per-cent increase in trans fats will increase her heart-disease risk by ninety-three per cent. Walter Willett, an epidemiologist at Harvard—who helped design the study—estimates that the consumption of trans fats in the United States probably causes about thirty thousand premature deaths a year.

McDonald's and the other fast-food houses aren't the only purveyors of trans fats, of course; trans fats are in crackers and potato chips and cookies and any number of other processed foods. Still, a lot of us get a great deal of our trans fats from French fries, and to read the medical evidence on trans fats is to wonder at the odd selectivity of the outrage that consumers and the legal profession direct at corporate behavior. McDonald's and Burger King and Wendy's have switched to a product, without disclosing its risks, that may cost human lives. What is the difference between this and the kind of thing over which consumers sue companies every day?

The French-fry problem ought to have a simple solution: cook fries in oil that isn't so dangerous. Oils that are rich in monounsaturated fats, like canola oil, aren't nearly as bad for you as saturated fats, and are generally stable enough for deep-frying. It's also possible to "fix" animal fats so that they aren't so problematic. For example, K. C. Hayes, a nutritionist at Brandeis University, has helped develop an oil called Appetize. It's largely beef tallow, which gives it a big taste advantage over vegetable shortening, and makes it stable enough for deep-frying. But it has been processed to remove the cholesterol, and has been blended with pure corn oil, in a combination that Hayes says removes much of the heart-disease risk.

Perhaps the most elegant solution would be for McDonald's

and the other chains to cook their fries in something like Olestra, a fat substitute developed by Procter & Gamble. Ordinary fats are built out of a molecular structure known as a triglyceride: it's a microscopic tree, with a trunk made of glycerol and three branches made of fatty acids. Our bodies can't absorb triglycerides, so in the digestive process each of the branches is broken off by enzymes and absorbed separately. In the production of Olestra, the glycerol trunk of a fat is replaced with a sugar, which has room for not three but eight fatty acids. And our enzymes are unable to break down a fat tree with eight branches—so the Olestra molecule can't be absorbed by the body at all. "Olestra" is as much a process as a compound: you can create an "Olestra" version of any given fat. Potato chips, for instance, tend to be fried in cottonseed oil, because of its distinctively clean taste. Frito-Lay's no-fat Wow! chips are made with an Olestra version of cottonseed oil, which behaves just like regular cottonseed oil except that it's never digested. A regular serving of potato chips has a hundred and fifty calories, ninety of which are fat calories from the cooking oil. A serving of Wow! chips has seventy-five calories and no fat. If Procter & Gamble were to seek F.D.A. approval for the use of Olestra in commercial deep-frying (which it has not yet done), it could make an Olestra version of the old McDonald's Formula 47, which would deliver every nuance of the old buttery, meaty tallow at a fraction of the calories.

Olestra, it must be said, does have some drawbacks—in particular, a reputation for what is delicately called "gastrointestinal distress." The F.D.A. has required all Olestra products to carry a somewhat daunting label saying that they may cause "cramping and loose stools." Not surprisingly, sales have been disappointing, and Olestra has never won the full acceptance of the nutrition community. Most of this concern, however, appears to be overstated. Procter & Gamble has done randomized, double-blind studies—one of which involved more than three thousand people over six weeks—and found that people

eating typical amounts of Olestra-based chips don't have significantly more gastrointestinal problems than people eating
normal chips. Diarrhea is such a common problem in America—nearly a third of adults have at least one episode each
month—that even F.D.A. regulators now appear to be convinced that in many of the complaints they received Olestra
was unfairly blamed for a problem that was probably caused
by something else. The agency has promised Procter & Gamble
that the warning label will be reviewed.

Perhaps the best way to put the Olestra controversy into
perspective is to compare it to fibre. Fibre is vegetable matter
that goes right through you: it's not absorbed by the gastrointestinal tract. Nutritionists tell us to eat it because it helps us
lose weight and it lowers cholesterol—even though if you eat
too many baked beans or too many bowls of oat bran you will
suffer the consequences. Do we put warning labels on boxes of
oat bran? No, because the benefits of fibre clearly outweigh its
drawbacks. Research has suggested that Olestra, like fibre,
helps people lose weight and lowers cholesterol; too much
Olestra, like too much fibre, may cause problems. (Actually, too
much Olestra may not be as troublesome as too much bran.
According to Procter & Gamble, eating a large amount of
Olestra—forty grams—causes no more problems than eating a
small bowl—twenty grams—of wheat bran.) If we had Olestra
fries, then, they shouldn't be eaten for breakfast, lunch, and
dinner. In fact, fast-food houses probably shouldn't use hun-
dred-per-cent Olestra; they should cook their fries in a blend,
using the Olestra to displace the most dangerous trans and saturated fats. But these are minor details. The point is that it is
entirely possible, right now, to make a delicious French fry
that does not carry with it a death sentence. A French fry can
be much more than a delivery vehicle for fat.

Is it really that simple, though? Consider the cautionary tale of
the efforts of a group of food scientists at Auburn University,

in Alabama, more than a decade ago to come up with a better hamburger. The Auburn team wanted to create a leaner beef that tasted as good as regular ground beef. They couldn't just remove the fat, because that would leave the meat dry and mealy. They wanted to replace the fat. "If you look at ground beef, it contains moisture, fat, and protein," says Dale Huffman, one of the scientists who spearheaded the Auburn project. "Protein is relatively constant in all beef, at about twenty per cent. The traditional McDonald's ground beef is around twenty per cent fat. The remainder is water. So you have an inverse ratio of water and fat. If you reduce fat, you need to increase water." The goal of the Auburn scientists was to cut about two-thirds of the fat from normal ground beef, which meant that they needed to find something to add to the beef that would hold an equivalent amount of water—and continue to retain that water even as the beef was being grilled. Their choice? Seaweed, or, more precisely, carrageenan. "It's been in use for centuries," Huffman explains. "It's the stuff that keeps the suspension in chocolate milk—otherwise the chocolate would settle at the bottom. It has tremendous water-holding ability. There's a loose bond between the carrageenan and the moisture." They also selected some basic flavor enhancers, designed to make up for the lost fat "taste." The result was a beef patty that was roughly three-quarters water, twenty per cent protein, five per cent or so fat, and a quarter of a per cent seaweed. They called it AU Lean.

It didn't take the Auburn scientists long to realize that they had created something special. They installed a test kitchen in their laboratory, got hold of a McDonald's grill, and began doing blind taste comparisons of AU Lean burgers and traditional twenty-per-cent-fat burgers. Time after time, the AU Lean burgers won. Next, they took their invention into the field. They recruited a hundred families and supplied them with three kinds of ground beef for home cooking over consecutive three-week intervals—regular "market" ground beef with twenty per cent fat, ground beef with five per cent fat, and AU Lean. The families were asked to rate the different kinds of beef, without knowing which was which. Again, the AU Lean won hands down—trumping the other two on "likability" "tenderness," "flavorfulness," and "juiciness."

What the Auburn team showed was that, even though people love the taste and feel of fat—and naturally gravitate toward high-fat food—they can be fooled into thinking that there is a lot of fat in something when there isn't. Adam Drewnowski, a nutritionist at the University of Washington, has found a similar effect with cookies. He did blind taste tests of normal and reduced-calorie brownies, biscotti, and chocolate-chip, oatmeal, and peanut-butter cookies. If you cut the sugar content of any of those cookies by twenty-five per cent, he found, people like the cookies much less. But if you cut the fat by twenty-five per cent they barely notice. "People are very finely attuned to how much sugar there is in a liquid or a solid," Drewnowski says. "For fat, there's no sensory break point. Fat comes in so many guises and so many textures it is very difficult to perceive how much is there." This doesn't mean we are oblivious of fat levels, of course. Huffman says that when his group tried to lower the fat in AU Lean below five per cent, people didn't like it anymore. But, within the relatively broad range of between five and twenty-five per cent, you can add water and some flavoring and most people can't tell the difference.

What's more, people appear to be more sensitive to the volume of food they consume than to its calorie content. Barbara Rolls, a nutritionist at Penn State, has demonstrated this principle with satiety studies. She feeds one group of people a high-volume snack and another group a low-volume snack. Even though the two snacks have the same calorie count, she finds that people who eat the high-volume snack feel more satisfied. "People tend to eat a constant weight or volume of food in a given day, not a constant portion of calories," she says.

Eating AU Lean, in short, isn't going to leave you with a craving for more calories; you'll feel just as full.

For anyone looking to improve the quality of fast food, all this is heartening news. It means that you should be able to put low-fat cheese and low-fat mayonnaise in a Big Mac without anyone's complaining. It also means that there's no particular reason to use twenty-per-cent-fat ground beef in a fast-food burger. In 1990, using just this argument, the Auburn team suggested to McDonald's that it make a Big Mac out of AU Lean. Shortly thereafter, McDonald's came out with the McLean Deluxe. Other fast-food houses scrambled to follow suit. Nutritionists were delighted. And fast food appeared on the verge of a revolution.

Only, it wasn't. The McLean was a flop, and four years later it was off the market. What happened? Part of the problem appears to have been that McDonald's rushed the burger to market before many of the production kinks had been worked out. More important, though, was the psychological handicap the burger faced. People liked AU Lean in blind taste tests because they didn't know it was AU Lean; they were fooled into thinking it was regular ground beef. But nobody was fooled when it came to the McLean Deluxe. It was sold as the healthy choice—and who goes to McDonald's for health food?

Leann Birch, a developmental psychologist at Penn State, has looked at the impact of these sorts of expectations on children. In one experiment, she took a large group of kids and fed them a big lunch. Then she turned them loose in a room with lots of junk food. "What we see is that some kids eat almost nothing," she says. "But other kids really chow down, and one of the things that predicts how much they eat is the extent to which parents have restricted their access to high-fat, high-sugar food in the past: the more the kids have been restricted, the more they eat." Birch explains the results two ways. First, restricting food makes kids think not in terms of their own hunger but in terms of the presence and absence of food. As she puts it, "The kid is essentially saying, 'If the food's here I better get it while I can, whether or not I'm hungry.' We see these five-year-old kids eating as much as four hundred calories." Birch's second finding, though, is more important. Because the children on restricted diets had been told that junk food was bad for them, they clearly thought that it had to taste good. When it comes to junk food, we seem to follow an implicit script that powerfully biases the way we feel about food. We like fries not in spite of the fact that they're unhealthy but because of it.

That is sobering news for those interested in improving the American diet. For years, the nutrition movement in this country has made transparency one of its principal goals: it has assumed that the best way to help people improve their diets is to tell them precisely what's in their food, to label certain foods good and certain foods bad. But transparency can backfire, because sometimes nothing is more deadly for our taste buds than the knowledge that what we are eating is good for us. McDonald's should never have called its new offering the McLean Deluxe, in other words. They should have called it the Burger Supreme or the Monster Burger, and then buried the news about reduced calories and fat in the tiniest type on the remotest corner of their Web site. And if we were to cook fries in some high-tech, healthful cooking oil—whether Olestrized beef tallow or something else with a minimum of trans and saturated fats—the worst thing we could do would be to market them as healthy fries. They will not taste nearly as good if we do. They have to be marketed as better fries, as Classic Fries, as fries that bring back the rich tallowy taste of the original McDonald's.

What, after all, was Ray Kroc's biggest triumph? A case could be made for the field men with their hydrometers, or the potato-curing techniques, or the potato computer, which turned the making of French fries from an art into a science. But we should not forget Ronald McDonald, the clown who made the McDonald's name irresistible to legions of small children. Kroc understood that taste comprises not merely the food on our plate but also the associations and assumptions and prejudices we bring to the table—that half the battle in making kids happy with their meal was calling what they were eating a Happy Meal. The marketing of healthful fast food will require the same degree of subtlety and sophistication. The nutrition movement keeps looking for a crusader—someone who will bring about better public education and tougher government regulations. But we need much more than that. We need another Ray Kroc.

Personal
Tastes

The
Inkblot
Test

by Robb Walsh

from *The Houston Press*

Robb Walsh's discursive restaurant reviews in *The Houston Press* go beyond a mere yea-or-nay ranking—he shares with his readers who he is and what he likes to eat. This particular piece is not only a personal manifesto, it's a rumination on the art of reviewing itself.

There are eight customers in the Triple A Restaurant at 10:30 in the morning; all of them are men, and four sport comb-overs. The wood-grain Formica on the tables and the orange vinyl on the chairs are a little worn. There is a picture of a 1935 high school football team hanging on one wall. My waitress is named Betty; she grew up in the Heights and has been working at Triple A for 18 years.

I am interested in a menu item that occupies almost half the page: "Two Farm Fresh Eggs (Any Style) with. . . ." The "with" options include a pork chop, a breakfast steak, chicken-fried steak with cream gravy and bacon or ham or choice of sausage. The sausage choices constitute another sublist. All of the above include grits or country-style potatoes and toast or biscuits. Betty describes the three kinds of sausage available: The home-made pan-style is a free-form patty that's been spiced up hot; the country sausage is a big link like kielbasa; and the little links are the regular kind. I order two eggs with chicken-fried steak and hash browns and biscuits. And I get a side order of that homemade sausage, just out of curiosity.

"How do you want your eggs?" Betty asks.

"Over easy and greasy," I smile.

"It's going to take a while," she says. "We batter the chicken-fried steak from scratch; it's not the frozen kind."

Neither are the crunchy potatoes; they are big pieces of fresh spuds fried crisp. The eggs are just right. The chicken-fried steak is piping hot with a wrinkly brown crust and a peppery tan cream gravy on the side. The biscuits are average. The biggest problem with Triple A's breakfast is the vehicle on which it is served: The oval platters are too small for the por-tions. I end up eating from three plates. I split my biscuits on the right-hand plate and pour a little cream gravy on them, while I eat the eggs, potatoes and chicken-fried steak from the middle plate. From the left, I sample the homemade sausage, which is extremely spicy and fried extra-brown.

Betty is gabbing with the other waitresses, and it takes a lot of gesturing to get my coffee refilled. But it's a sunny day out-side, and from the window by my booth I can see the farmer's market next door. I also see an old black shoe-shine man work-ing on Triple A's front porch. His customer is sitting against the wall, so I can't see his face, just his brown brogues. The shoe-shine man is spreading the polish with his fingers. I linger over my coffee until 11:20 and leave just as the lunch rush begins.

If the scene above were an inkblot test, how would you char-acterize it? Inviting? Depressing? Boring? Charming?

Before you answer, consider the following inkblot:

At 11 in the morning, almost all the tables are occupied at Century Diner on the corner of Main Street and Texas Avenue. There are some young, hip guys lingering over books and magazines, and a lot of downtown business folks in nice clothes eating lunch.

The vinyl booths by the window are two-tone, pastel green and off-white. The tables are covered with brand-new Formica in a bright pattern of circles and shapes, a design that was called "modern" 40 years ago. The waiters wear black-and-white bowling shirts with slogans such as "Something Superior for Your Interior" on the back. The menu is sprinkled with little nuggets about old diner lingo, such as the fact that "Adam and Eve on a raft" once meant ham and eggs on toast.

But ham and eggs on toast is not on the menu. Instead, the place offers a contemporary take on diner food, including "The Total New Yorker," a bagel with Nova Scotia salmon and cream cheese, and "The Health Kick," an egg-white omelet. Although two eggs with ham, bacon or sausage aren't offered, the menu does feature "Eggs N' Hash," two eggs with hash browns and New York-style corned-beef hash.

My waiter is a young guy with dyed black hair. He's too busy to chat, so I don't get his name. I order two eggs. They don't have hash browns at lunch, so I settle for french fries. The waiter doesn't know what the breakfast meats are, but he checks. I order the sausage and a side of biscuits and gravy.

"How do you want your eggs?" he asks.

"Over easy and greasy," I smile.

Coffee comes in a little stainless-steel Thermos, which is a nice touch. It reminds me of the little glass "hottle" you used to get at coffee shops in the 1960s. The eggs are just right. The french fries are excellent. The link sausage is just what you'd expect. The biscuits are huge, and the gravy has lots of bacon pieces in it. Unfortunately, it has been spooned over the top of unsplit biscuits. I try to break them up to soak up some of the gravy.

At a table just across the divide from mine, two men and a woman in conservative business suits are gossiping about somebody's chances in some election. The conversation is spirited, and the woman's eyes sparkle as she laughs at one of the men's observations. I can't hear what he said, but it must have been pretty funny. I pour myself some more coffee and copy down this quote from the big shiny menu: " 'The character of a diner builds up the way grime does.'—Douglas Yorke."

My own reactions to these diner-shaped inkblots are not hard to predict. Breakfast at Triple A puts me in a warm and wonderful mood. And the retro-chic at Century Diner feels phony. But I'm pretty much alone in this opinion.

One friend calls the breakfast at Triple A "a heart attack on a plate." Another finds the dark wood paneling, worn-out furniture and fat old guys with comb-overs "depressing." And she thinks the Century's decor and waiters' costumes are "precious."

What does the inkblot test tell you?

The same restaurant can feel entirely different to you and me. I can walk into a truck stop alone and feel right at home. But a beautiful young woman walking in by herself might feel differently. My mother is obsessive about cleanliness; she'd rather eat at McDonald's than at a place with character if there's the threat of grime. And then there are deeper prejudices.

When I moved to Austin from Connecticut to start school at UT, I was 17 years old, 2,000 miles away from my parents, and high on my newfound freedom. I drove my motorcycle all over town discovering funky places to eat. I loved little luncheonettes run by crazy old ladies, drugstore soda fountains and old urban institutions like the Southern Dinette on East 11th Street in the heart of the black east side.

Why did I love these places? It wasn't always about the food. I was also seeking a level of comfort. As a newcomer, I was fascinated by the characters in these old places and by the vestiges of a disappearing Texas. As a long-haired geek from the East, I was scared of the rednecks and fraternity boys who prowled the trendy campus hangouts. Maybe I ate in eccentric dives and places on the wrong side of the tracks because I felt like an outcast myself.

Sometimes friends who grew up in Texas, people who are concerned with healthy diets and whose families struggled with poverty in their childhood, don't find these funky joints nearly as endearing as I do. In another's eyes, these places are outdated, high-cholesterol slop houses, full not of colorful characters but of boring old farts. I understand these biases, and I want to be honest about my own.

It's still not always about the food with me. Sometimes I think a review needs to stick closely to the subject at hand. But in other cases, I'm more interested in food as a reflection of culture, and so it is with this case. There are some differences in the food at Triple A and Century Diner. But having breakfast at an old diner one morning and a new retro diner the next brings up intriguing questions.

Like, do you prefer sanitized imitations of old institutions to grimy old institutions themselves? And why does a retro-chic diner in the oldest part of Houston get its history lessons (and breakfast dishes) from New York? Does the architectural preservation downtown make any sense absent some cultural preservation?

Several letters to the editor lately have complained about my ramblings—that my restaurant reviews are too personal and not focused enough on food like those of my predecessors. To this charge I proudly plead guilty. Alternative weeklies have been at the forefront of developing fresh approaches to food writing in America. Instead of the conventional "soufflé to die for" fluff, these reviews take readers on first-person excursions into the politics, sociology and anthropology of food. And I am delighted to champion this style in Space City.

When I began reviewing at the *Austin Chronicle* in 1991, fellow critic Ed Ward and I both were influenced by the very personal narratives of food writer John Thorne. It was Thorne who pointed out in print that Paula Wolfert's ridiculously complex recipes took authentic ethnic dishes out of their cultural contexts and turned them into gourmet status symbols. He also published a long series of pieces, all written from the counter of the same New England diner in his newsletter, *Simple Cooking*.

Thorne's own inspiration was a restaurant reviewer for the *Boston Phoenix* named Mark Zanger, who reviewed under the pseudonym Robert Nadeau, beginning in the late 1970s. "He was teaching himself eating and drinking and simultaneously wondering out loud what he should be making of it, gnawing away at all pat assumptions. He taught me that "honesty means nothing if there's no real risk to it, no genuine self-examination," wrote Thorne.

Lofty aspirations for a restaurant reviewer, no doubt, but at least it's a worthy goal. In that spirit, I offer you this nonreview. And I invite you to visit Triple A and Century Diner and do some genuine self-examination of your own. Which one serves a better breakfast? Which one makes you more comfortable?

Into the Mouths of Babes

by William Grimes

from *The New York Times*

Being an objective restaurant reviewer is one thing, but in this Diner's Journal essay, *New York Times* critic William Grimes drops the mantle to get a little tetchy about a culinary trend that, in his opinion, has overstayed its welcome.

There is a specter haunting American cuisine. It comes in many guises. It bears many names. If it were human, it would have a terrible time getting a date, for it is bland, boring and overweight. Yet, with the ease of a practiced Don Juan, it seduces chefs, restaurateurs and, especially, culinary journalists. I speak of comfort food.

It is everywhere. It's a fad that turned into a trend that now threatens to become an unassailable institution, a mashed-potato mountain so large that a hundred backhoes working around the clock could not make a dent in it. Its warm, smothering embrace now extends to nearly every kind of restaurant, from downtown hot spots to ambitious culinary temples that can't resist the playful urge to sneak in a little slob food for dramatic effect.

At a time when the cuisines of the world are pouring into New York, and American chefs have risen to heights undreamed of merely 20 years ago, it is impossible to avoid culinary clunkers like franks and beans, pot pies, rice pudding, macaroni and cheese, and meatloaf.

Some restaurants, like Hudson Cafeteria, devote a special section of their menu to comfort food. Others make do with a single dish, often giving it an unexpected spin. At District, for example, the pot pie is filled with lobster instead of chicken or turkey. In the ultimate retrograde gesture, Ike, a downtown restaurant, will heat up Swanson TV dinners for $6. I thought Salisbury steak was nothing more than a bad memory. Now, it's back.

The actual food is not what bothers me. There's a place—a small place—for insipid old favorites, just as there is for beach novels and syrupy pop songs. But the all-out effort to raise the status of comfort food is a sentimental fraud, swaddled in a thick layer of pretense and nostalgia, a very bad combination.

Worst of all is the name itself, a damp, sticky, therapy-derived, feel-good term that should be resisted, like elevator music and television evangelists and holidays created by greeting-card companies. It contains, within its squishy-soft soul, a multitude of disturbing assumptions about Americans and what they really want to eat.

"Comfort food" first appeared in print in 1977, according to the Oxford English Dictionary, in the *Washington Post Magazine*. The reference was to grits. By the 1980's, the term and the concept had taken off, gaining a second life with the stock market crash of 1987, when many restaurants took their $30 pastas off the menu and replaced them with mashed potatoes, which took on the status of a leading indicator.

Cultural analysts had a field day. Stock market warriors, now weak and defenseless, were desperate for soothing foods, they argued. The reasoning was seductive. It's now received wisdom that complex, turbulent times demand simple "taste experiences." Adults, under pressure, crave the foods of their childhood. That's why you can find milk and cookies on the menu at Moomba, along with pretend Popsicles at Sea Grill and lollipops at Alain Ducasse.

It's no accident that the rise of comfort food coincides with the demographics of the baby boom. Just as the children of postwar America were starting to have their own children, they became seized with an intense nostalgia for the cultural signs and symbols that surrounded them m the 1950's.

Who can blame them? The 1950's were an era of peace, stability and low inflation. But it was also a time of bad food. In fact, it was the worst time for food in American history. Whatever fragile culinary roots America had put down had been torn out by the industrialization of food production and packaging. Fine dining had been destroyed by Prohibition and put on hold by the Depression and war. The counter-reaction, symbolized by Alice Waters's innovations at Chez Panisse, lay a generation away.

Dazzled by the Eisenhower-era American kitchen on display in Moscow in 1956, Nikita Khrushchev missed a golden opportunity to turn the tables on Richard Nixon in their famous kitchen debate. Yes, America had the hardware. But what was coming out of those Amana Radar Ranges?

What came out is what we are now asked to cherish as comfort food. It should not be confused with good, simple food that is carefully prepared. In France this would be called la cuisine grandmère. It is the heart and soul of nearly all Italian cuisine.

Comfort food is not that. Nor is it the inventory of classic American dishes regional or otherwise—old favorites that reappear in everyone's dreams, like North Carolina barbecue, Maryland crab cakes or banana cream pie.

The stars of the comfort food parade tend to be profoundly regressive, the dishes that recall the tastes and textures of infancy. What do macaroni and cheese, rice pudding, and mashed potatoes have in common? Milk. And the soft texture that tooth-less mouths can handle. They're baby food.

Taken by itself, comfort food is harmless enough. But cheer-ing it on encourages cultural backsliding. In evolutionary terms, it has not been that long since American cuisine learned to walk upright. It's been a struggle to stay there, a constant fight against the national impulse to slouch down over a sirloin and a baked potato laden with sour cream. The current explosion of steak-houses is a counterblast against the proliferation of ambitious, sophisticated restaurants in the past decade, a big fat no to sea urchin custard, wasabi granité and microgreens.

Steak is fine. But throwing it on a grill is just about the least imaginative way to engage a piece of meat that the human mind can devise. Macaroni and cheese, no matter how well it is pre-pared, ranks very low on the food chain. Summon up the taste of the finest meatloaf you've ever eaten. Imagine something twice as good. Still not that good, is it?

Learning to eat is a kind of education. It rewards the adven-turous. It pays double dividends to thrill seekers who dare to taste a sea urchin; who do not flinch in the face of an andouil-lette; who, instead of sniffing and picking and probing when something odd turns up on the plate, dive right in, sending off sparks with their forks. We have a name for such people. We call them adults. And when they go out to a restaurant, they are not looking for solace, they're looking for a good meal.

The Best Bit

by Terry Durack
from *Hunger*

Brash, opinionated, and wickedly funny, Australian columnist Terry Durack has skewered his share of pretentious chefs and would-be gourmets, but he also gets a kick out of his own foolishness—and he always seems eager to tuck into the next meal.

House special!" announced the Japanese restaurateur with pride, bearing a giant ceramic bowl in which lay half a giant fish head awash in light soupy juices. It was as if I had never tasted fish before. It tasted not only of the sea, but as if it were still in it; delicate yet forceful, single-minded yet complex. My chopsticks thrashed around the bowl like piranha, careful to strip off the rich, gelatinous cheek, and the juicy flesh around the severed neck.

The owner was horrified. Instead of taking away what was left in the bowl, he stared down at it in utter bewilderment.

"But you've left the best bit," he said. Best bit? All that was left was a little connective tissue, a few bones and one rather large eye. I entered my own private suspense movie. Cut from my appalled expression to MCU fish eye. Cut back to my face, but closer, then back to ECU fish eye; in which you could see the reflection of my appalled expression.

"Tastes just like oyster, only better," said the restaurateur. I picked up the eye in my chopsticks and placed it in my mouth. After about a hundred years, I swallowed, and discovered that it did indeed taste like an oyster. I never left the best bit again.

But how many best bits had I unknowingly left behind out of unwillingness or ignorance, until then?

I made a fool of myself over my very first Shanghai hairy crab in Hong Kong one winter. Having picked out the sweet, succulent, ginger-fragrant flesh, I put down my chopsticks. My host blushed for me, before pointing to the roe-laden head shell, explaining that it was the eggs that made the crab such a delicacy.

"Tastes just like scrambled eggs, only better," he said. And of course, he was right. He then pointed to my discarded prawn heads from a delightful dish of prawns steamed in their shells.

"But you've left the best bit" he said as he picked up one of the heads and sucked like a vacuum cleaner.

The trouble is, one culture's best bits is another culture's garbage. In Spain, pigs' ears are cooked in a delicious, addictive casserole with pigs' trotters and chorizo sausages. In other countries, you can't even buy a pig's ear, much less turn it into such a silk purse of a dish.

In Beijing, duck feet are boned and tossed in a salad with cucumbers and yellow mustard sauce, while in Guangzhou, steamed and braised chicken feet are the juiciest stars of the dim sum trolleys. In a Greek home, one is honoured to be served the head of the spit-roasted lamb, especially if it comes complete with tongue and brains. Nor would a Greek home throw out the stems and leaves of the beetroot, but simply treat them as a beautiful vegetable that requires a little steaming and a dressing of olive oil and lemon juice while still warm.

There are some best bits we are all very well aware of, like the curl of orange coral on a sea scallop, the fatty tail of a grill-scorched lamb chop, and the luscious bone marrow in osso buco. I always try the rind of a white mould cheese such as gratte-paille or brie de Meaux. If not ammoniacal, it gives me the wonderfully peculiar feeling of biting into cumulus clouds.

Even inedible rinds, such as the boot leather rind of a Parmigiano Reggiano is never wasted in Italy, but cleaned up and tossed into the makings of a minestrone soup, where it softens over the long cooking and leaves its ineffably fine flavour.

Determined never to leave the best bit, I now curiously eye off any old fish tail, potato peelings or leftover egg shells, just in case I'm missing out. My finest moment came at the end of a dish of deer penis, an entire platter of something that I'm sure even the deer would consider their best bits. Left on the plate was a perfect little sea horse, about the length of my little finger.

"You left the best bit," I said to my fellow diners, as I popped it in my mouth and crunched. They looked aghast.

"That was the garnish," they cried. "Ah," I said, recovering immediately, "tastes just like decoration, only better."

Rome Again

by Colman Andrews

from *Saveur*

One of the founding forces behind *Saveur* magazine, Colman Andrews writes about all sorts of food with the easy grace of a bon vivant. But there's something special about this piece, suffused with nostalgia for a special time in his life.

'm sitting in the warm afternoon light at Sabatini, on the piazza Santa Maria in Trastevere, one of the prettiest old squares in Rome, lunching with friends. We've just demolished a platter of carciofi alla giudia (artichokes in the Roman-Jewish style, deep-fried golden-brown and splayed open like blowsy peonies) and then one of deep-fried tiny scampi and calamari rings and are now working our way through portions of spaghetti alle vongole (with clams, in a mildly spicy garlic sauce) on our way to the thick-sauced Roman version of stewed oxtail, coda di bue vaccinara. We're on our third bottle of frascati.

The year is 1974, and I'm thinking that, although I'm a ripe old 29 and a veteran of many a restaurant table, I have never before experienced such an abundance of guilelessly good food, or taken such sheer guiltless pleasure in the act of eating.

Imagine an earlier time, a simpler time, an unimaginable time. A time when not one American in ten thousand had ever heard of, much less tasted—much less made a commonplace of— bruschetta or porcini or radicchio or rucola (the bitter green we insist on calling *arugula,* a term apparently derived from a dialect name for it). A time when olives in America were mostly uniform black ovoids with the center punched out, and mush- rooms were mostly small and white and chalky, or maybe little brownish-gray eraser bits that came in cans. A time when nobody ate pasta—just spaghetti or macaroni—and when sophisticated Italian dining meant "shrimp scampi" or veal parmigiana pursued by zabaglione.

This, difficult though it may be to recall, was the United States of not yet gastronomically savvy America in the early 1970s, when I started traveling regularly to Rome—at first just to visit my friend Karen, an American who had gone off to live there to learn the language of her paternal grandparents, and later, more and more, just because I'd fallen in love with the place, not least for how it fed me.

It's not an exaggeration to say that, over long hours at count- less Roman tables with Karen and her amiable Ferrari-dealer boyfriend, Gianfranco, and other friends of theirs, I discovered Italian food—the real thing, unencumbered by red-checked tablecloths and candles dripping onto straw-wrapped chianti bottles—and, more than that, discovered a style and a pace of eating that I have aspired to ever since: relaxed, appreciative, hedonistic, joyful.

I got to know Rome, at least casually, in every season in those days. I sweltered on the piazza Navona in July and fled for the day to Ansedonia on the coast for cool salt water and a hint of breeze; I spent Christmas one year on the Monte Mario, listening to every church bell in the city peal to commemorate the birth of Gesù Bambino, and then dodged furniture thrown out of windows (a both symbolic and practical expression of annual renewal) in Trastevere at the stroke of midnight on New Year's Eve. But my most vivid memories of the city, and especially of eating in the city, are autumnal.

In the fall, the light turns thick and golden, and the first roasted-chestnut sellers set up their carts on street corners, perfuming the air with savory smoke. Restaurant windows glow with heaps of meaty funghi porcini—the gigantic boletus called "little pig mushrooms" because of their size—and wild quail and pheasants hang from the ceilings in their faintly iridescent feathered glory, next to still-fragrant bouquets of drying late-summer herbs. At this time of year, too, the sturdy, irresistible pasta dishes for which Rome is known—spaghetti or penne alla carbonara (with eggs and pancetta, a recipe attributed to the wives of the charcoal makers who'd come down from Abruzzo to sell their wares in the city) or alla puttanesca ("whore's style", racy with tomatoes, garlic, black olives, anchovies, and capers) or all'arrabbiata ("angry", as expressed by the comparative violence of its heavy dose of red chile bits) or all'amatriciana (as prepared in the town of Amatrice, northeast of Rome, in a red chile-spiked tomato sauce scented with guanciale, or cured pork jowl)—begin to seem less like indulgences and more like seasonal imperatives.

Thus, when I started thinking about going back to Rome one last time before the end of the millennium—to revisit a city I hadn't seen for decades, experience again the dishes and the restaurants I'd loved, and maybe, out of intellectual curiosity, apply my considerably more developed tastes and culinary knowledge to the foods that had so impressed and helped shape me (all too literally, I fear) 25 years earlier—I knew I should go in autumn.

Planning my trip, I suddenly, over a distinctly non-Roman and not particularly joyful lunch one day in Manhattan, got a crazy, impractical, Roman sort of idea: What if I could not only revisit my old haunts but somehow revisit them with Karen and Gianfranco? Practically speaking, this was absurd: Karen has been married for years (to an American of great charm and generosity) and lives in California; Gianfranco still sells Ferraris in Rome but is himself wed, to a quiet, beautiful Ukrainian woman he met on a business trip to Moscow. But Karen and Gianfranco have kept in occasional touch over the years, and . . . well, I thought it might be worth a few phone calls. To my surprise, Karen and Gianfranco both loved the idea, Karen could get away for a week, and both spouses—rather remarkably, I thought—gave their dispensation. The next thing I knew, we were all there in Rome, planning our first meal together in a quarter of a century.

I'd had an image in my mind of the three of us beginning our week sitting in the garden overlooking the Tiber at Er Cucurucù, where we used to eat grilled slabs of smoked scamorza cheese and grilled quail and great tangles of raw greens illuminated with threads of shredded carrot, while gossiping about mutual friends and critiquing the latest Lucio Battisti record and beginning our discussions about where we should have dinner the following night. Alas, we learned that this old Roman institution had since closed. When Gianfranco started calling around, though, he found that every other one of our old favorites was still very much in existence.

We decided to begin at La Buca di Ripetta, near the piazza del Popolo and Karen's former apartment on the via Laurina, in the middle of an old neighborhood between the Tiber and the Villa Borghese whose streets are lined with venerable buildings in hues of terracotta pink and earthy gold. Walking through the door of La Buca—"The Hole" (as in hole-in-the-wall), which the Michelin guide describes succinctly if bilingually as a trattoria d'habitués, and where we used to spend hours upon hours forgetting that there was a world outside—was for me (and for

Karen, she later told me) like walking straight back across the years. Porcini were arrayed as they had always been on a platter near the door; the familiar aromas of long-cooked tomato sauce and roasting meat filled the air; the ladder-back chairs and whitenapped tables looked as if they hadn't been moved an inch since the late '70s. Even the waiters looked the same.

In fact, we learned that the original owners had sold it only six months earlier, and the new, young proprietors hadn't changed a thing, keeping even the old cooks and, yes, waiters—one of whom, Enzo Serantoni, informed us that he'd been there for 34 years and had almost certainly waited on us in the old days. And the food was as wonderful as ever. We started with a plate of silky, buttery san daniele prosciutto, then spied some fresh anchovies luxuriating in a marinara sauce, which we knew we had to have. Along with these, Serantoni brought us a plump orb of mozzarella di bufala, rich and nicely sour, seasoned with olive oil and salt and pepper. Then, of course, pastas: fettuccine with the sweet little clams called vongole veraci; more fettuccine with forest-scented slices of sautéed porcini; and then rigatoni all'amatriciana. This last was, in a sense, nothing special—just an adequate interpretation of a Roman basic—but as Karen and I dug into it, we both looked up and smiled; we were back in Rome, and the year was a matter of no consequence, as was fitting in what is, after all, the Eternal City.

In the days that followed, we walked all over Rome, pleased to find that in this age of multinational business and on-line living, the streets were still full of locals, walking, talking, gesticulating, playing. And we enjoyed one wonderful meal after another, having fun between the inevitable wistful moments. Wistfulness overtook us most poignantly when we lunched one day at Piccolo Mondo, off the celebrated Via Veneto. Piccolo Mondo was to Rome's "Dolce Vita" era of the '50 and '60s what Spago was to the Hollywood of the '80s and '90s: the celebrity essential, the nerve center, the institutional expression of a whole spirit of life. When Karen, Gianfranco, and I used to eat there, the photos that were haphazardly taped to the walls—of Cary Grant, Burt Lancaster, Audrey Hepburn, Brigitte Bardot with her German playboy husband Gunther Sachs, Esther Williams with Fernando Lamas, and, of course, scores of heart-breakingly beautiful and optimistic-looking young people who are now forgotten—were already cracked and curling. But the dining room was always a furiously bustling place, full of models and cinematographers and sleek Roman businessmen, all of whom seemed to know and like one another. And a wonderful round-faced, bald-pated waiter named Guido Paolessi used to make sure that we got a taste of everything everyone else was eating, in addition to our own already copious meals ("Some lasagne!" "A few more roasted potatoes!" "Taste the zuppa inglese!").

The restaurant—owned by the same family since 1954—looks much the same, though a pizza oven and a back room have been added and the photos are now neat under sheets of transparent plastic. And the food—including definitive bucatini all'amatriciana and juicy and flavorful roast baby lamb—is still better-than-average mainstream Roman. But Guido retired 15 years ago, and the modern-day equivalent of the old lunch crowd is probably now eating at McDonald's or at their desks. The place was almost empty, and the contrast with our memories of the bustle and spark that once animated it turned our meal sad.

But Rome ceaselessly renews itself, and that night we dined at another of our standards, Ambasciata d'Abruzzo—which sang with (Abruzzese-flavored) Roman verve and danced with warm light—attacking without mercy the huge basket of assorted mountain-style sausages presented the moment we sat down, then eating more fettuccine with porcini (it was the season, after all) and veal chops and drinking dusty, full-blooded montepulciano. And the next night we visited another Dolce Vita monument, Taverna Flavia (photos of Claudia Cardinale, Gina Lollobrigida, Doris Day, David Niven, et al., and more of those lost beauties), where a lifetime ago I tasted my first white truffles, shaved into the insalata Verushka (named for the stunning, larger-than-life model who used to appear topless in Vogue and whom I was thrilled beyond reason to see striding across the piazza di Spagna one day a few feet in front of me). We ordered that dish again—either the truffles were particularly wan or I've grown jaded—and then a big platter of delicious fried things (whole little long-stem purple artichokes, stuffed zucchini flowers, olives crusted with ground veal) before moving on to simple, impeccable meats: tiny piccatas of veal with lemon, a grilled veal paillard, and the small lamb chops called scottadito, "finger burner," because you're supposed to eat them with your hands.

Another day, we had lunch a few miles outside the city on the via Flaminia—one of those famous roads that lead to Rome—at a onetime country inn dating back to at least the 18th century, now called Casale, which is where I discovered antipasto, meaning that I discovered here that antipasto wasn't just an assortment of cold cuts and a few pickled vegetables. I might as well describe the array as I found it last October, because it was exactly the way I'd found it 25 years earlier: a large, three-level table jammed with plates and platters and bowls containing, yes, some pickled vegetables with strips of salami, but also marinated cipolline onions, three kinds of meat-and-rice-stuffed vegetables (onions, tomatoes, and bell peppers), lentil salad, butter beans in olive oil, borlotti beans in olive oil, fresh ricotta and fresh mozzarella di bufala (both anointed with olive oil and sprinkled with spicy red pepper flakes), marinated anchovies, grilled zucchini, marinated beets, several varieties of salami or hard sausage, several kinds of olives, and on and on.

Also on the table were big curls of raw homemade pasta, which we ordered variously sauced with porcini (of course), shrimp, and pumpkin flowers. Then came roast pork and lamb off the rotisserie, potatoes cooked in their dripping fat, and spinach first parboiled and then sautéed in olive oil with garlic and red pepper flakes. Fruit and parmigiano-reggiano were dessert; then came espresso and grappa, as the autumn afternoon grew slowly, almost imperceptibly, darker.

We decided to have our final Roman midday meal outside Rome, in the Castelli Romani, the hills a few miles southeast of the city, and specifically at Il Fico Vecchio in Grottaferrata, where more than once in the old days we'd lunched until dark. Il Fico, run by Claudio Ciocca, a handsome former member of the Fellini stock company with a snowy white ponytail, has grown casually prosperous over the years; its once simple tables are now set with overlapping white linens and hotel silver. The food is still Roman country fare at its best, though. We began with plates of antipasto, which in this case included miniature focaccia, fresh ricotta, roasted peppers and eggplant, broccoli salad, and prosciutto. The homemade pastas were arguably (and this is the kind of thing Karen, Gianfranco, and I have always delighted in arguing about) the best of our trip—pappardelle with bits of black truffle from the Umbrian town of Norcia, fettuccine with porcini, and earthy rigatoni alla pagliata, a uniquely and dauntingly Roman specialty of tube-shaped pasta tossed with similar-looking lengths of the intestines of suckling lambs. We moved on to a dish we used to dream about—Il Fico's pollo alla diavola, small chickens coated in black pepper, drenched in lemon juice, then blackened on the grill—served with little roasted potatoes, artichoke hearts in olive oil, and the crisp and curly chicory salad called puntarelle.

As we ate, I asked Karen how Rome felt to her after all this time. "I know it just sounds like a cliché," she answered, "but walking around my old neighborhood and eating at the same old places, I am amazed that so little has changed. There are some upscale boutiques where small markets used to be, and there are some newer things on the menus, but it's really mostly just like it was. These Romans haven't forgotten how to appreciate life. And the food . . . You know how you remember the way things tasted in the past, and then they're usually different when you try them again? Here everything is exactly as I remember it, from the fluffy espresso to the pasta to the ice cream. Italians understand that simple, true taste of things, but they don't seem to be able to export it. Nothing in America, even at the best Italian restaurants, tastes like it does here." Gianfranco, meanwhile, just smiled, as if to say, Hey, I do this every day, and nobody asked you guys to go back to America.

For my part, I was thinking about how we'd all changed, about how we're watching our weight (at least a little) and what we drink now, and thinking about calling home—instead of worrying about important things the way we used to, such as whether Roma would beat Juventus that night or whether the next day would be nice enough for us to eat outdoors. But I was also thinking about what we'd gained and lost in our gastronomy, and about how all the glossy new Italian restaurants in America, with their venison carpaccio and white-truffle-oiled pasta, come no closer to the real thing than the old ones that served spaghetti and meatballs and chicken marsala. And I was thinking that, though I had reached the age of 54, and despite it all, a long time had passed since I'd experienced such guilelessly good food—and such sheer guiltless pleasure in the act of eating.

The Town That Came to Dinner

by Gabrielle Hamilton

from *Saveur*

You might expect an accomplished chef/writer like Gabrielle Hamilton (her popular restaurant Prune is in New York's East Village) to write wonderfully about food; her account of a hometown community dinner, however, offers even more—it really reads like a short story.

A t 2 p.m. on the day of the Great American Spaghetti Supper in Lambertville, New Jersey, my hometown, I'm standing in the middle of Union Street, looking up. Clouds as dark as bruises hang overhead, and it sounds like wildcats and she-bears are pacing anxiously inside them. The tables where a thousand people will eat in a few hours still haven't been delivered; neither have the chairs or the burners, which we'll use to cook 250 pounds of pasta. Tableside. This huge outdoor party—our town's 150th birthday—is starting to look like the Great American Disappointment.

I cut down an alley behind Mitchell's Tavern, where we used to race bikes and eat shoplifted Kit Kat bars, and through the parking lot to St. John the Evangelist Catholic Church. I haven't lived here for 20 years, but that alley is as familiar as my own breath. On my way down the stairs to the church's basement cafeteria to see how the food prep is going, I pass my dad, Jim Hamilton, quietly sneaking out. "This whole thing was your idea, your inspiration, and you're splitting?" I mock-reprimand him. "Be careful down there," he replies, smiling. "It's all asses and elbows."

I descend to find those asses and elbows attached to a dozen beleaguered local restaurant people bent so far over banquet tables, feverishly assembling antipasto plates, that you can't see their heads. Helen Papa, who's 75 years old and caters all kinds of community events, steps out of the walk-in refrigerator and asks, "What're those eggs for? I got forty dozen eggs in there." She checks the menu. "Holy crow. Those eggs gotta be cooked." The problem—besides the fact that the tables haven't arrived and the rolling racks came from the rental company without trays and dinner's supposed to start in a few hours and it's about to rain wild beasts—is that hundreds of antipasto plates, egg-less, have already been taken out to the refrigerated truck. Nobody's sure exactly how many, though; they lost count a while ago.

Lambertville lies on the same stretch of the Delaware that George Washington so famously crossed on Christmas Eve in 1777 on his way to attack the British in Trenton, 17 miles south. The streets are tree-lined, and the houses close enough to each other for neighbors to talk from porch to porch. In the 1830s a canal was built here that made barge transportation possible; now, long after the advent of trains and trucks, it serves only to distinguish the landscape.

Our house was actually across the Delaware on the Pennsylvania side, in New Hope, but my tether to Lambertville is tight and strong. My grandfather, a country doctor, raised his family here. My father, who designed theater sets and lighting, had a shop here, where dusty, chain-smoking carpenters built mammoth sets to be trucked all over the country. He also opened, with my sister, Melissa (now director of the SAVEUR kitchen), a restaurant called Hamilton's Grill Room in Lambertville (it's still thriving 12 years later). My brothers rode minibikes here. And I took guitar lessons and a beating from a girl gang here.

When I was growing up, Lambertville was a tough town, with more grit and integrity than New Hope but less wealth. There were machine shops and lumberyards still, while New Hope had long since become a sort of dollhouse community of fudge kitchens, pewtersmiths, and Ye Olde Antiques Shoppes. The stuff a person actually needed—a dozen eggs, a package of undershirts—you had to get in Lambertville. We found our Buster Browns here, at Phil Pittore's shoe store—Phil was also mayor of the town at the time—and got new tires for our bikes at Mort's Sports Shop. We bought groceries at the Acme, where Donny Lewis, a man my dad's age who might have slipped through the cracks had he lived in a bigger city, would help load your bags into the trunk of your car.

But Lambertville, at 150, has changed. We still don't have fudge or scented candles, but Mort's is a cappuccino joint now, and the shoe store is a gallery. Art, Money, and Warm Frisée Salad have tucked themselves in right next to God, Family, and Country—and the two points of view don't always coexist comfortably. When you ask some of the old-timers what changes they've noticed in the past couple of decades, they usually just shrug and won't say anything more damning than "all the new people"—but I can't help wondering if they feel edged out of their own town. Or maybe it's just change itself that raises the bristles.

The idea for our dinner had been loitering—leaning up against a lamppost having a smoke—in the back of my dad's mind for years. A party. Outdoors, at one long, uninterrupted, well-dressed table. My sister had a similar image in her head, from a photograph she'd seen of a sit-down feast, of tables set end to end through the ancient, winding streets of an Italian city, connecting neighbor with neighbor. But it wasn't until Lambertville's sesquicentennial that they could both let the idea unfurl—all 1,000 seats of it.

Because my dad and my sister had been instrumental in planning so many other events in our town, they were charged with staging the birthday dinner. They shrewdly pulled together a well-balanced committee of brains and brawn and bean counters: restaurateurs, the fire chief, a public relations pro, trusted family members. We made lists and set up a phone tree. We ordered wineglasses etched with the anniversary logo and decided to serve spaghetti. Then we decided to serve penne instead because it's easier to dish up. For weeks there was a polite deadlock over how to cook the pasta: partially in advance, to be reheated; or just before dinner, on-site. Finally, Andrew Abruzzese—a restaurateur who's so charming it hurts and who grew up doing ravioli church suppers with his aunts—broke the deadlock by saying, "If anybody can convince me why I should cook it, haul it to the site weighing 1,000 pounds instead of 250 pounds when it was dry, reheat it, and then deliver an inferior-tasting product simply to save three minutes, then I'll do it." No one could.

Abruzzese made the tomato sauce, too, and got Vincent Giordano's market in Philadelphia to do thousands of tender meatballs. We tried to set a rain date, but Helen Papa, scrutinizing her pocket calendar, said, "I got to cook for a reunion, class of 1949, the next day and a family picnic after that, and then we're on the bus to Atlantic City." So we just decided it wouldn't rain.

Somewhere around five p.m. on this midsummer evening, the tables and chairs and burners finally arrive and a lively churning starts in the street as volunteers rush to arrange them. I find myself struggling to roll out reams of white butcher paper on the tables as early guests simultaneously try to decorate them (a prize will be given later for best table decor). A couple of kids buzz around in a golf cart distributing buckets of sauce and meatballs, boxes of kosher salt, and loaves of Italian bread, and the refrigerated truck inches up the street with a crew of waiters walking behind, doling out a thousand antipasto plates—not one missing its wedge of hard-boiled egg.

The table decorations are a horrible and wonderful array that reflects the unlikely but unquestionable harmony that is Lambertville. Carnations, dyed red, white, and blue and rigidly propped in kitschy plastic baskets, border plum-tomato cans spilling with bawdily gorgeous wildflowers. A simple, almost somber cluster of American flags sits serenely between a clothesline hung with boxer shorts and a group of revelers in wigs of yellow yarn that resemble spaghetti. In the midst of it all stands a stunning arrangement of branches formed into natural candelabras, set with votives and twined with clusters of red grapes, made by a famous Manhattan floral designer who has a weekend house nearby. Beautiful as it is, it has nothing to do with the Lambertville I know.

Like cream that becomes butter during the last turns of the paddle, our party comes together only in the final moments. Former firemen and nurses and schoolteachers, some with walkers and many with hearing aids, arrive at precisely 6:30 and quietly chew their way from antipasto to cookies in the time it takes the younger crowd, boisterously calling for more red wine, to find their seats. The food is fresh and delicious: The antipasto has good genoa salami, crunchy celery, dark briny olives. The penne is hot and cooked perfectly—yielding, but not mushy—and the sauce is vibrant with tomato flavor. People pass their plates back for more.

I'm gratified to see that even though many of the old stores are gone, the people who ran them aren't. All around me, former shop-owners are having dinner with the very people who have turned their places into galleries and antiques stores. And even though the Acme has disappeared, Donny Lewis is still here, his ticket proudly and firmly in hand. If the way you verify your past, I start to think, is by having some markers of it, and if all the places I used to know are gone, then where is my past—and where does that leave me? Choked up and very glad to see Donny Lewis, that's where. If he's here, then so is my Lambertville.

After dinner, we listen to a few speeches and a prayer for Phil Pittore's wife, who's had triple-bypass surgery. The decorating prize goes to a table with place mats made from historic photos of Lambertville. And then, as we're eating our slices of cake, the storm lets loose. Everyone runs for cover, and through the sheets of rain I see my dad short-cutting it down the alley I thought only I knew about. But the party continues down side streets, on porches, and under eaves, old-timers crouched next to newcomers. We drink the last of the red wine in the rain, eating soggy cake, reveling in our community.

Abstinence Makes the Taste Buds Grow Fonder

by David Leite

from *leitesculinaria.com*

Though most of David Leite's web site, leitesculinaria.com, features polished professional food writing, this essay stands out, not just for its humor but for its shrewd insight into the psyche of a food lover.

I have butterfat flowing through my veins, and I have the documents to prove it. The day before my 40th birthday the universe decided to torment me with a little game of Mess With Your Head. I was happily gathering information for this month's column about ice cream, perhaps God's greatest gift to mankind after elastic waistbands and *Entertainment Weekly*. While dipping away in batches of homemade heaven (research, of course), the phone rang.

"David, it's Dr. Rysz," said the voice in a guttural Polish accent.

I had had some routine blood work done the week before, and my doctor was calling with the results.

"Everything looks normal," she said in even, modulated tones. Then an involuntary intake of breath: "Except for your cholesterol. It's a bit elevated—252."

Two hundred and fifty-two? *Two hundred and fifty-two?* That's in the danger-Will Robinson zone. It should be well under 200, she informed me.

The spoonful of hazelnut crunch hovered before my mouth. I contemplated lapping it up, but this felt too diabolical considering Dr. Rysz's pronouncement. So I just stood there dazed as it dripped onto my sandals.

Then came the death knell: "I think it's something you can get under control with diet and exercise." Diet and exercise? Didn't she know I consider Häagen-Daz's Dulce de Leche to be its own food group? How could I possibly diet?—I get paid to write about food. And exercise? Please, setting a table for eight leaves me winded.

I felt defeated. This was the middle of the summer, I was charged with writing about ice cream—the one thing people regularly (and for good reason) cite as being better than sex—and I was cut off. Verboten. Where would the inspiration for rapturous prose about silky French vanilla, pull-no-punches New York Super Fudge Chunk or exotic green-tea ice creams come from? I fell onto the couch and sulked.

This was a cruel joke. Ice cream, and all types of lusciously fatty foods, are part of who I am. Evidence: Most people mark their lives by special moments such as graduations, marriages, kids; I divvy up mine by food—especially ice cream. The summer of 1967: Sitting in the backseat of my parents' 1954 tan Buick Special eating a chocolate ice cream cone (sugar, naturally) in the parking lot at the now-demolished Milk Can in Somerset, Massachusetts. The Milk Can, a whimsical folly built during the 1930s when Somerset was a profitable stop on the summer strawhat circuit, was a 30-foot high round building with a tapering roof and an arcing green handle—a huge wooden milk jug. To a seven-year-old it was so large that it seemed to tower over the Lilliputian cars that parked around its perimeter, jutting out like so many spokes of a wheel.

High school was dominated by Friendly's giant sundaes with their gloppy toppings and neon-red maraschino cherries, until they were unceremoniously elbowed out by Newport Creamery's Awful, Awful—a ridiculously large ice-cream shake. We never knew the origin of the name, but we decided it came from the wicked ice-cream headaches we got from guzzling the monsters too quickly. Your choice of homemade ice cream was scooped into a tall metal tumbler, milk and special sauces were added and the whole concoction whirred smooth. It was then poured—in front of you—into a thick, heavy-footed parfait glass. The standing challenge: Drink two, get a third free. The only person I knew to accomplish this was Bobby Simpson. He was my hero.

In the '80s along came two men whom I'm considering including in my will: Ben and Jerry. Who else but these two eternal boys in rumpled tie-dyed shirts could have thought of folding childhood favorites into super-premium ice cream? Nearly every night during the unremitting heat waves of New York City summers I waited patiently in line on Second Avenue for my custom-made delight. First, a shimmering gob of vanilla ice cream was thwacked onto the chilled marble counter. Then the interrogation began: A little chocolate chip cookie dough? Why not. Crushed Oreo® cookies? Toss 'em in. Chunks of Heath® Bars? Don't be stingy. A few deft flicks of the wrist, and my personal lovefest was scooped into a cone. So what if it boasted one of the highest butterfat contents of any ice cream; I still had knees back then, so five or six aerobics classes a week kept me well out of harm's way. Anyway, cholesterol was something only ancient people of 40 had to worry about.

Then there was the incomprehensible amount of gelato I consumed while visiting Italy in the '90s. And what about the gallons of homemade ice cream I've foisted on my dinner guests during my bouts of Martha Stewart mania? Blueberry-peach, Leite's Double Dutch Super Chocolate, ginger, cinnamon, peanut-butter-chocolate. My motto: If it can be frozen, it can be ice cream.

No! I would not give up my raison d'être. I had no other choice: I hoisted myself up from the couch, rooted around in the bottom drawer of my bureau and pulled out my old running shorts. Tight, but serviceable. I slipped on an oversize T-shirt and my sneakers. At least I looked serious.

In Central Park, after several minutes of jogging, I decided brisk walking was a passable, though somewhat wussy, substitute. I settled upon my daily regimen: Walk for exactly one hour and consume less than 300 milligrams of cholesterol and 60 grams of fat. This, I understood, relegated me mostly to salads, fruit, veggie burgers and the occasional morsel of animal protein. But if it meant I could indulge every so often in a one-half-cup, 380-calorie, 290-milligrams-of-cholesterol bit of ecstasy, it was worth it.

Everyone doubted I would stick with my routine. Doctors before had warned me I needed to exercise, all to no avail. But now I had a valid, worthy reason. The problem now became the solution.

Every day I walked around the park, arms pumping, butt jiggling. Meals were well rounded, but a pathetic shadow of their former selves. I dutifully kept a diary listing the calories, fat grams and cholesterol milligrams of everything that passed my lips. I threw in a few sit-ups for good measure, usually when I was lying on the floor in front of the TV and had to reach up to grab another bite of my fat-free, cholesterol-free, taste-free pudding snack.

Two weeks later I was on the phone with my mother, staring down at the scale between my feet. I contemplated leaning on the door handle as I stepped up, but I decided to come clean for once. I had lost ten pounds! I said goodbye to my mother (who herself had lost five pounds; she had joined me as a show of support), headed straight for the kitchen and fished out that container of homemade pistachio gelato I had stashed away behind the meatless breakfast sausages. I doled out precisely one-half cup and grabbed a spoon. I didn't want to squander the moment, so I took my booty to the dining-room table and solemnly announced to our cat, Madame Maxine, that happy days were here again. Instead of my usual manly mouthful, I took just a dainty bit; after all, I had only a half a cup. The flavors and textures—silky sweetness mingled with the crunch and mellowness of the meaty nuts—danced in my mouth. An embarrassing groan escaped my lips. (Thankfully, my neighbors weren't at home.) The gelato tasted richer, fuller and more complex that it did just 14 days earlier. Abstinence had cleansed my palate; it was like tasting anew. I had unwittingly put my taste buds through detox.

I looked down at Max, who tossed a dispassionate glance in my direction (ice cream isn't one of her favorite people foods), and I vowed to dig in again—right after my next cholesterol test.

Delicacy

by Paul Russell

from *Gastronomica*

The old truism "you are what you eat" is truer for some people than for others. Paul Russell, certainly, in this affecting essay in the new quarterly *Gastronomica*, discovered who he was early on through what he liked to eat.

I am perusing the menu with all the sense of serious purpose a ten year old unaccustomed to restaurants can muster. It's 1966, a restaurant called The Passport in the brand new, sleekly modernist terminal of the Memphis International Airport. What catches my eye is dolphin. I have never seen dolphin on any menu, never heard of anyone eating dolphin, and I am seized by an urgent need to taste this dolphin whose allure is, like the new terminal itself, the beautiful promise of a future in which we shall all travel effortlessly to distant places, dine nightly on marvelous dishes.

When it comes my turn to order, I speak with a trembling voice, trying to sound as if it is a perfectly ordinary thing I am doing.

My words fail to slip past my mother. A cautious eater, she's inclined to instill caution in her children as well.

"Are you sure?" she asks. "Do you know what a dolphin is?"

I nod my head vigorously—a curious fifth-grader's head full of ancient Greek myths. I see graceful, leaping sea creatures, familiars of trident-brandishing Poseidon, and riding their cavorting backs, bronzed sea-sprites.

"Oh, let him try it," my father tells her. "It's good for him to be curious."

"I don't think I could bring myself to eat dolphin," my mother mentions quietly, but to no avail. Already I've slipped past the carefully guarded perimeter and am stumbling into the unknown. Already I am on my way to the future.

The dolphin, when it arrives, is a rather ordinary-looking fish fillet—redeemed, a little, by the pat of butter in the shape of a scallop shell that accompanies it. What is even more enchanting, the scallop shell of butter is itself nestled into a real scallop shell. No one else's dish comes with anything remotely like that, I note with quiet delight, and as I take my first expectant bite, I tell myself that dolphin will be the most exquisite food I have ever tasted. Like those sea-sprites, I too shall be laughingly transported.

But the dolphin is not exquisite; it's only an ordinary fish— pallid, soggy, bland. I eat slowly, trying to savor each mouthful, hoping somehow to discover a clue that will unlock dolphin's marvelous but thus far hidden essence. I close my eyes. Ancient sunlight starkly illuminates the scene. I am waiting for Achilles and Patroclus to join me at the feast. On the banquet table, dolphin has been set out on great platters. In the distance beckons the wine-dark sea, thick with the proud ships of the Greeks.

But none of this gets me anywhere at all; I can discover nothing except the dreary truth. I'm ten. I'm trapped. I will never get out of here.

"How is it?" my mother asks.

"Wonderful," I report breathlessly. At least there is the scallop shell, which I persuade her to wrap in a paper napkin and put in her purse, so I can carry it home as a souvenir of the meal that might have been.

Beyond the restaurant's grand, panoramic windows—The Passport's real attraction, I suspect, and not the food—jet planes roar down the runway, lift into the clear blue sky of early evening.

My family seldom dined out. When we did, we'd go to restaurants that more or less duplicated the fare my mother cooked at home. There was Bill and Jim's, whose most daring offerings tended toward trout almondine and liver with bacon and onions, or the family's favorite, Shoney's Big Boy, where we'd all enthusiastically order the Big Boy, a splendid double-decker hamburger and fries. Other, more suggestive restaurants I had never actually set foot in lurked at the fringes of my young imagination: Joy Young's, a Chinese restaurant downtown where my parents would sometimes go for special occasions (as a child, my only experience of Chinese food was Chicken Chow Mein from a can, poured over crunchy dry noodles); and the Luau, which served Hawaiian food and was said to feature tables set out on small islands in an indoor lagoon. There was Pappy and Jimmy's, intriguingly advertised by a neon sign showing the grinning faces of Pappy and Jimmy attached to the bodies of lobsters; and Anderson's Oyster Bar, with its green-tiled facade and large, heavily curtained windows—but my parents didn't care for seafood, so I knew nothing of what went on inside those mysterious precincts.

My mother subscribed, more or less, to the notion that cooking was something you did to kill the germs—a chore to be undertaken conscientiously, but with little enthusiasm. I remember dry meatloaf and gray pot roasts and endlessly chewy pork chops. She had evolved, in the course of raising three children, an updated, more efficient version of the foods she'd grown up with. In this suburban shorthand for the richer, deeper, older cooking her own mother daily lavished so much time and effort on, commercially canned vegetables replaced the home-grown beans and tomatoes and corn my grandmother sealed away in mason jars; toast from a toaster substituted for the flaky buttermilk biscuits my grandmother could be found rolling out before dawn each morning in her kitchen; grape jelly muscled aside homemade damson and blackberry and pear preserves. My mother refused to be a slave to the kitchen, and shook her head at the way her mother, whenever we'd visit, would persist in organizing the entire day around the production of meals whose homespun bounty—country ham and fried chicken; mustard greens, black-eyed peas, sweet potato casserole; creamed corn and mashed turnips; those heavenly buttermilk biscuits—never ceased to amaze and even confound.

"We can't eat all that food!" my mother would exclaim, confronted by memories of her childhood, when she'd been what she called a "picky eater," her appetite no doubt crippled by my grandfather's propensity to dose her with a vast variety of patent medicines, especially cod liver oil—hence her adult aversion to seafood.

The meals my mother visited on us nightly were strictly routine—ordinary food about which one never gave a second thought. The ordinary may be dependable, but it holds no mystery, not even the possibility of mystery. Everything in my family was perfectly visible in the flat glare of the ordinary, and since, early on, I saw in myself the shadow of unfathomable urges, I knew with a secret whisper of nausea that sooner or later I would have to be found out.

Into my mother's cautious cooking, I suspected, an ingredient like myself would never be allowed.

• • •

I am in the eighth grade, eating lunch in the school cafeteria; the meal on my plate resembles beef stew in the way that every meal in the school cafeteria resembles some food or another. I've been eating this stuff for years; I have no illusions (See? If I turn the bowl of so-called peach cobbler upside down, the congealed mass clings to the bowl and can't be shaken loose). Nonetheless, I am intrigued by a cube of beef lying in gummy brown sauce. A few nights earlier, I have seen on television an episode of Star Trek in which the logical and adamantly vegetarian Mr. Spock, through some accident of time travel, finds himself plunged ten thousand years into the past. Stuck in the ice ages, thrown together with a convenient cave girl, he begins to revert to the atavistic practices of his ancestors; when the cave girl offers him a succulent hunk of barely cooked woolly mammoth steak, he eats with relish, luxuriating in the forbidden taste of animal flesh. A passionately illogical kiss with the comely cook soon follows.

As a thoroughly alienated eighth grader, I fancy myself another Mr. Spock, exiled among the earthlings with all their messy emotions (which I fear as much as he). So I pretend, for the moment, staring at my cube of beef, that I too am about to taste forbidden pleasures. I glance around to see that no one is watching, and, with my fingers, pluck the meat from its viscous sauce. I raise it to my lips, imagining its tender, juicy texture, throw back my head, and drop the morsel into my mouth. But the luscious explosion of flavor I expect does not happen; the meat— its dreary simulacrum, rather—is dry and stringy, bland as anything my mother might cook. Still, in that brief moment before I actually tasted it, my imagination registered the poignant possibility of an altogether different reality.

How, though, to find that other reality I glimpsed from time to time? Often it took the form of an aimless, painful longing—for distant landscapes, people I did not yet know, musics I had discovered on my own. All my life I had been vaguely aware of the existence of what my mother called "delicacies"—foods she her-self would never eat, but that other people, inexplicably, took great pains to seek out and consume. General currency had handed me several more or less abstract instances of what she was talking about: caviar, which I could barely imagine; oysters and champagne; truffles; frog legs. For me, they were not so much actual comestibles as emblems of the lives that attached them-selves to such unholy meals.

To none of these foods, of course, had I any access. But there were other items closer to home, an eclectic and mostly accidental array of opportunities with which I proceeded to stock my imagi-nary larder: shrimp, for instance, breaded and deep-fried, which I rebelliously began to order whenever my family would eat at Shoney's Big Boy, till one day I managed to correlate those meals with nights of feeling utterly, alarmingly strange, and reluctantly concluded that I was, in fact, allergic ("I told you so," I could hear my mother say, though she never actually did; she didn't have to); the greasy canned tamales wrapped in corn husks that I bought every noon from the vending machine in the high school canteen (I remember trying to figure out how to eat them, not quite understanding for some time that the corn husks weren't meant to be eaten); kippered herring that came in a little flat tin that had to be opened with a key (anything that came in a tin rather than a can—anchovies, smoked mussels, sardines in mustard sauce—was practically guaranteed the status of delicacy). Had my mother discovered my predilections—at that point, almost entirely imaginary—she would simply have stared at me and wondered aloud, But why would you want to eat something like that? And I'm not sure I could have answered her; but I wolfed down my delicacies every chance I got, on the theory, I suppose, that if you are what you eat, then by consuming these rogue pleasures that ranged so far from the predictable orbit of my mother's cooking, I could somehow succeed at last in becoming someone other than the thwarted, unhappy creature I seemed destined to remain.

• • •

I have ordered the avocado salad. Never mind that I've never in my life tasted avocado, and have scarcely any notion even of what an avocado is.

I'm fourteen; my mother and I are visiting my aunt in Atlanta, a city, it seems to me, of enormous sophistication, unlike shabby, backwater Memphis. We are in a restaurant in a complex of shops in the glittering, modern downtown.

"Are you sure?" my mother asks, almost, at this point, by rote. "Have you ever even tasted avocado? What if you don't like it?"

I know by now there is no logic to this. Perhaps I am merely drawn to the word "avocado," which sounds foreign and humid and passionate, so unlike the unimpeachable sobriety of my family. I say the word to myself, drawing out its rich vowels. I am pretty sure I have never even seen a picture of an avocado; certainly my first encounter with guacamole lies years in the future.

"I know what I'm doing," I insist.

"You're very brave," my aunt tells me. "Trying new things like that."

"Don't encourage him," my mother says with a sigh. "It's bad enough his father does." She has not raised me to be curious like the poor proverbial cat. My curiosity seems to her, in fact, vaguely disobedient, a perverse streak running through me that will no doubt, sooner or later, land me in some kind of trouble, not so much legal as metaphysical, since in most respects I am still an extraordinarily well-behaved kid. She has tried to protect me from my riskier instincts, but is beginning to suspect that no one, not even a mother, can save another human being from himself.

The waiter places my salad before me. On a bed of romaine lettuce, in itself mildly, pleasingly exotic, lie beautiful strips of avocado, a delicate yellowish green, not unlike cantaloupe slices, I tell myself, but certain to be far more exquisite.

"Is that what you were expecting?" my mother asks. "Are you going to have enough to eat? You can have some of mine if you're still hungry." She and my aunt have ordered hamburgers, a fail-safe choice.

"This is exactly what I want," I tell her bravely. With my fork I cut off a bit of avocado, surprised by how easily the fork slides through it. I spear the piece and slide it into my mouth, prepared for a wonderful surprise.

I have never tasted anything quite so disconcerting. The texture is soft, buttery, slick. I chew warily, I force myself to swallow. To my immense relief, my mother and aunt are more interested, at the moment, in their hamburgers. My second and third bites do not make my task any easier—if anything, my disgust grows with the alarming realization that this avocado salad contains a very generous amount of avocado, every last bit of which I will have to work my way through.

"How's your salad, honey?" my mother asks, as I have known she must.

"Delicious," I tell her. "Would you like a bite?"

"Oh no, not for me," she demurs, making something of a face.

When I have successfully downed that last slimy morsel I feel vaguely sick, though the last bite, I have to admit, has not been as dreadful as the first. A subtle change has wrought itself in me. Neither my mother nor my aunt can see this; at the time I can scarcely see it myself. But I am on the way to becoming a person who will eat avocado, for whom avocado is ordinary, no longer a delicacy but the stuff of everyday. For the day will soon enough come when I forsake the south and head north to college, when I taste my first caviar and drink my first champagne, when I make love to another man. Unimaginable feats, irretrievable losses. I am beginning the journey toward that person I will one day be, the adult my mother will no longer entirely recognize anymore as her son.

Foods I never ate as a child still draw me; I delight in eel and Bulgarian feta and the dozens of varieties of olives, none cored and stuffed with pimento like those of my youth. I still long for the exotic, the unexpected, the strange, and though I no longer depend on the as-yet-untasted delicacy to transform my life, I nonetheless understand the part those foods, either real or imagined, played in provoking change of a profound and irrevocable kind. On my mother's cooking I look back with a certain melancholy fondness: all those ordinary nights of comforting sameness now utterly vanished, that quiet decent family scattered to ashes and the far ends of the earth. My father is long dead, my grandparents more recently so, the secrets of my grandmother's country recipes—her dash of this and pinch of that—irretrievably lost. My mother lives alone in our old house in Memphis. When I call her from time to time (I have not visited in years), I usually seem to catch her at dinner.

"What're you eating tonight?" I ask.

Our conversations are guarded, bland, polite. She has never forgiven me my many betrayals, I think, though she tries not to give any of it a second thought. The shadows are too dark, the mysteries too daunting. We maintain a delicate truce.

"Oh," she says. "I'm just having some cheese and crackers. A glass of milk."

She hasn't cooked in years. "I hardly even remember how anymore," she admits. "Anyway, there's no reason to these days." The supermarkets abound with frozen pizzas, microwavable dinners of every sort—though most evenings, I think, she just snacks.

I don't tell her that a handsome, interesting man I have recently met is coming to dinner tomorrow night, and that already I am contemplating what to cook that will impress him. I tell her virtually nothing of my life, and that is fine with her since the alternative is far worse, but as I grope for something to say about the weather, I am remembering some nice-looking fillets of monkfish I saw at Gadaletto's Seafood this afternoon. If they have some tomorrow, I think I'll buy a couple. I know a pretty good recipe for monkfish with mango chutney.

The Carp in the Bathtub

by Alan Deutschman
from Salon.com

Inside every epicure there's a cache of childhood cultural food memories, taken for better or worse. In this on-line essay from salon.com, Alan Deutschman takes a wry and rueful look at his own many-layered gastronomic influences.

As I was earning my reputation as a foodie in Manhattan in my 20s, when my gluttony was goaded by a ludicrously permissive Time Inc. corporate expense account and aided by the mega-burning metabolism of youth, when I was a habitué of Bernardin and Bouley, when I once shared the corner banquette at Le Cirque with the owner, Sirio, himself, I secretly harbored a deep embarrassment: While I acclimated to the delights of nine-course, wine-paired tasting menus and performed something akin to Talmudic scholarship on the Zagat's guidebooks, I suffered from a sense of guilt about my continuing passion for the comparably crude Eastern European Jewish cuisine of my childhood holidays.

It undermined my pretensions of culinary mavenhood to have such an unremitting lust for food that would be considered bad, if not awful, by the gourmand crowd. It was as if the chef at Lutece were caught pounding Ring-Dings. How could I overcome my humble roots in the Ashkenazi shtetlach and assimilate into America's ruling class of elite WASPs if, on the way to hearing a string quartet at Carnegie Hall, I swooned outside Carnegie Deli? What good were my Princeton degree and my rumpled khakis and button-down oxford broadcloths and Top-Siders if I still craved matzo balls and stuffed cabbage?

My ancestors in Poland and Russia didn't have the benefit of fresh, certified-organic produce grown by obsessive overachievers who had shed their professional careers to go back to the land. I'm not convinced that my forebears even had vegetables. They didn't have fruity, cold-pressed, extra-virgin olive oils, so they had to settle for the less mellifluous "schmaltz," aka congealed chicken fat, surely nature's purest form of cholesterol. They didn't prepare carpaccio or cook meat juicy rare or even a tolerable medium, partly because the kosher dietary laws forbid eating the blood of animals (which, after all, is what makes them taste so good), but also because their meat was so tough that you had to cook the hell out of it for countless hours to break down the sinew. The inscrutable laws of kashrut also forbid mixing dairy and meat, which is Yahweh's way of keeping the Jews from ever eating as well as the Italians (who, I'm convinced, are the real chosen people, at least from a gastronomic perspective). And in the Ukrainian outback the Yids certainly didn't have their own deep-sea divers to catch day-boat scallops especially for their kitchens (as I recall was specified on the menu at Bouley).

They didn't know from ahi tuna. For fish, they had to make do with the lowly carp and pike, which don't have the delicacy of flavor that makes a good carpaccio or the sturdier character demanded by the grill. Instead, Jewish cooks mush up the bland piscine flesh into weird otherworldly, elliptically shaped lumpen balls of cold whitish mystery meat known as gefilte fish. ("Gefilte" is from the Yiddish and German for "stuffed," since sometimes the concoction is inserted back into the fish's skin.) To my mind it's the signature dish of scrappy Ashkenazi cuisine or, better yet, our tribe's equivalent of Proust's madeleine: If as a worldly adult you still love gefilte fish, that's probably because it evokes the warm nostalgia of childhood.

For me it brings back memories of Passover in the promised land—the leafy outlying areas of the borough of Queens, N.Y.— at the home of Grandpa Julie, the Plumber to the Stars. Julie was famous in the family for his emergency calls to the leading hotels and apartment houses of Manhattan, especially the time he gallantly rode in on his Cadillac Coupe de Ville and fixed Elizabeth Taylor's toilet. Once, in a less urgent situation, he installed a washer-dryer set for Paul Newman and Joanne Woodward. But his greatest claim to fame was the time Marlene Dietrich made homemade chicken soup for him because he had a bit of a cold when he showed up for a service call.

My Grandma Pearl made a therapeutic chicken soup, too, with matzo balls that had an admirable balance between fluffy softness and structural integrity. Her Passover seders always began with an irresistible appetizer trio of the soup, gefilte fish (I liked it so much that I always insisted on a double serving) and her homemade specialty, chicken liver combined with congealed chicken fat and onions and chopped finely by hand (this was in the B.C. era, before Cuisinart) and served in mushy globular lumps that didn't resemble anything found in nature but looked much like a brownish sibling of the strange fish balls. (The dish was spectacularly inexpensive: Even today, raw chicken livers sell for only a buck a pound at upscale markets in the beaux quartiers, so imagine how cheap they were eons ago in Queens.)

Then there was roast chicken with side dishes that were generous meals in themselves. She served stuffed cabbage, which only sounds like a vegetable course but is really a carnivore's debauchery. The "stuffing" is a gargantuan meatball of ground beef and the omnipresent onions, wrapped in a thin layer of green cabbage and drenched in a spicy tomato sauce. Grandpa Julie never tired of calling it "stuffed garbage." Another favorite was kasha varnishkas: bow-tie-shaped egg noodles with buckwheat groats, also popular partly because it was cheap. (This was before Jews became hippies and discovered that whole grains had healthy fiber.)

But Grandma Pearl wasn't the real legend among the female chefs in the clan. That honor—and my favorite piece of family culinary lore—belongs to her mother, my Great-Grandma Minnie, and the story of the fish swimming in her bathtub before it was slaughtered to become gefilte fish.

Minnie's four children had it hard growing up in the Brooklyn public schools with the surname Putzer, which in Yiddish-savvy New York would have been like being known as "Dickhead" in Nebraska. But as a compensation they had a mother who brought over culinary techniques from the Old World. These traditions still thrived in the Brooklyn of the late 1940s. At the marketplace she would pick out a live chicken to be decapitated on the spot. Then she would pluck its feathers herself, which she called "flicking" the bird.

My mother, Elaine, who was a small child at the time, often accompanied Minnie and still recalls the "terrible smell" of the poultry market, but she loved it when the butchers would let her eat the raw egg yolks of the unlaid eggs taken from inside the hens, which decades later she remembers longingly as a wonderful delicacy. The chicken would still be warm when Minnie got it back to their apartment in the Williamsburg neighborhood of Brooklyn, near the ramps to the Manhattan Bridge. (This was long before Williamsburg was colonized by artists and youthful hipsters.)

Unlike roast chicken, gefilte fish had the advantage of being a dish that you could prepare well in advance, since it was served chilled and kept well in the refrigerator. But the special and undeniably strange rules about Passover made it impossible for Minnie to prepare the appetizer course ahead, which is where the live fish in the bathtub comes in. But first a bit of background about a bygone tradition so all this will begin to make sense.

Everyone, even the most goyish, knows that for the weeklong celebration of Passover—the springtime festival of the Hebrews' liberation from slavery in ancient Egypt—Jews aren't allowed to eat bread that has risen with yeast. For that matter, they can't consume any grain that isn't completely cooked within 18 minutes of contact with water. This is a way of remembering that the Jews had to flee Egypt in great haste and didn't have time to order any Chinese takeout—not even a quick stir-fry—let alone wait for their dough to rise.

Not eating real bread for a few days—such a nice symbolic gesture, no? But being Jews, we can't leave it at that. We have to overachieve in the most sensational way. So for Passover it's not enough to abstain from leavened bread or long-cooked grains, which are called "chametz." You have to systematically purge your kitchen of any of these offending foodstuffs. But that's the easy part. Next, you have to thoroughly clean any surface that has had contact with chametz; to the truly observant Jew this means taking a Q-tip or a toothpick to the tiny crevices and hidden recesses of the stove and fridge. As for the utensils that cooked chametz throughout the year—that long wooden stirring spoon, for instance—well, you have to either burn them (that's right) or sell them to someone who isn't Jewish and then buy them back after the holiday. (Today there are Web sites that facilitate this transaction.)

Needless to say, cleaning the kitchen for Passover is a real pain in the tuchis; it takes several days, and you can't get started preparing any part of the Passover feast until it's done. So Great-Grandma Minnie would have to wait until her house was completely kosher for Passover to kill the fish and chop it up. She would buy a live carp at the Williamsburg fish market and let it swim in the bathtub for several days while she purged the chametz.

That's when little Elaine, around age 4 or 5, had her fun. She would spend hours at her grandmother's apartment playing with the fish, treating it like a species of urban pet. She watched it swim and fed it lettuce. She couldn't bear it when her grandfather would swiftly chop off its head. (Decades later, she realized that her experience of love and loss was fairly common among Jewish girls of the period when she found it retold in a children's book called *The Carp in the Bathtub* by Barbara Cohen.)

But the story didn't end there. Elaine had something of a mischievous streak, and one year she fed the fish a potent Ajax-like household cleanser that she found near the bathtub, a detergent with the brand name Babbo.

As the family began consuming the first course of the seder, the gefilte fish, her Uncle Larry said to Elaine: "Look what happened to your friend."

"I fed it Babbo," she blurted out in retaliation for his cruel jibe.

"You poisoned it?!" he exclaimed, genuinely shocked.

Fortunately, the dosage wasn't deadly. Minnie lived to age 89, and her funeral was a series of tributes to the joys of her from-scratch cooking. But it would have been harder for me if I hadn't stopped for a gluttonous lunch beforehand at Pastrami King a few blocks from the mortuary in Queens.

The strange power of gefilte fish for the Jewish people has far deeper roots than my own family's escapades in New York's Outer Boroughs. Historian Claudia Rosen, author of *A Book of Jewish Food*, writes that fish has symbolized fertility ever since Jacob told his children that they should multiply like fish in the sea. As for carp in particular, the river fish was introduced to Europe in the 17th century by Jewish traders who brought it from China on the silk route. While preserved salt herring was the staple protein source of their weekday diet, carp—a fresh fish and thus more costly—became the big splurge that they saved for the special Sabbath dinner.

With the Diaspora and the newfound prosperity of Ashkenazi Jews in the West, it's hard to believe that the humble gefilte fish was once a delicacy. Today we still have a fish fetish, but it's more likely to be for smoked salmon, which is much more expensive, and highly esteemed by gentile foodies, too.

I've heard of attempts to modernize gefilte fish for gourmands adhering to the new religion of Wolfgang Puck and Alice Waters as well as the more ancient covenant of Abraham. On the Internet you can find recipes for ahi tuna gefilte fish. I've heard of Mexican Jews who make gefilte veracruzana, smothering the carp cake with a spicy tomato and pepper sauce. I've resisted these nouvelle concoctions, though. If I'm enjoying a Cal-Ital sauce, then I'm happy to have it with a Mediterranean or Pacific fish. If I'm eating white-fleshed fish mixed with matzo meal and eggs, then make it carp. Without the bland taste and the weird jelly on the side, it's not the same.

When I was a burgeoning foodie in New York, gefilte fish and chopped chicken liver were high on my shortlist of guilty gastronomy. But then, at 24, on my first culinary pilgrimage to Paris, I had an unexpected experience that changed my entire opinion of Jewish cuisine. For my very first meal in Paris I found the perfect old-school bistro on the Ile St. Louis and ordered two dishes with utterly musical-sounding names: "pâté de foie de volaille" and "quenelles de maison." In English, that's an appetizer of chopped chicken liver, much like my grandmothers made, and a weird elliptically shaped ball of bland chopped white-fleshed fish, much like gefilte. It just sounds so much more like gourmandise in French.

The Cooking Lesson

by Lisa Takeuchi Cullen

from *Bon Appetit*

This wistful gem of a personal essay by Lisa Takeuchi Cullen, a staff writer at *Money* magazine, says so much about food, about cultural heritage and family, about the threshold between life and death, and about the eternal yin-yang between mothers and daughters.

The rain beats on the roof in a steady patter. I try to match my chopping to the metronomic beating, but my hands aren't used to the motion. The pickled radish disassembles in uneven pieces, some paper-thin, some as thick as my thumb.

From the couch at the other end of the room, my mother stifles an exasperated groan. The sound of unskilled chopping grates on her nerves like a song sung out of key.

I glance up, concerned and at the same time annoyed. She has lifted her head, but she's still lying down.

"Mama, I can do it," I say. I mean to sound confident, but instead I sound peevish.

"Honto?" she says, sounding just as testy. ("Really?")

The doctor told us the chemo would bring mood swings. As I wash the mackerel, I wonder why her moods seem to swing in only one direction. Things have been rocky since I returned to my childhood home in Kobe, Japan. I thought I'd cook and manage the household in the weeks after they removed the tumor from my mother's breast. I had in mind a sort of saintly Superdaughter role, flying in to the rescue, smiling, efficient.

It's just that Supermom won't relinquish the cape. She can't seem to downshift to invalid, and it makes her crazy to watch me do her job—badly. I don't meet her standards: After all, she's a professional homemaker, and I'm a working girl with a survivalist attitude toward housekeeping. She sees dust particles where I see—well, nothing. As for my cooking skill, I am good enough with Japanese dishes to impress my American husband. But in my mother's kitchen, I will always play apprentice to the master craftsman. She lets me use her sacred tools only under supervision.

So every meal I prepare involves a cooking lesson. From the couch, she dictates directions, which I do my best to follow.

"O.K., what next?" I call out. I am determined to stay cheerful.

"Make dashi," says my mother from the couch. "You know how?"

I don't bother to answer. Of course I know how to make dashi. It's the fish stock that anchors much of Japanese cooking, and it's the first thing she taught me after explaining how to wash the rice, back when I had to stand on tiptoe to reach the sink. I plop a square of dried *konbu* seaweed into a pot of water and bring it to a boil. Then I empty a packet of dried bonito flakes into the bubbling water.

While the dashi simmers, I cut the mackerel into chunks and slice an X into each piece. I place the fish in the dashi with a few slivers of fresh ginger, as my mother instructs. "Blue fish always have smell," she says. "Ginger take smell away."

In another pot I make more dashi, which I'll use for the clear soup. I add a pinch of salt and a splash of soy sauce. A wire colander in the sink holds a burst of bright green chrysanthemum leaves. "*Kikuna* cook quickly, so you put in last," says my mother. I've already added a few morsels of *matsutake* mushroom, rare for the season and shockingly expensive. She has always loved their peaty smell.

"Too long," my mother is saying. "You boil fish too long." I feel about six years old again, dumbfounded that she knows I've only gargled when I said I brushed. Hurriedly I lower the heat and add a scoop of brown sugar, then a dollop of miso paste. Covering the stew with a sheet of aluminum foil, I fix the lid and let the food simmer.

While I wait, I find my notepad and jot it all down. I never used to record my mother's cooking lessons, preferring instead to phone her if my memory faltered. Never mind the time difference and the expense of a New Jersey-to-Japan call; my mother's voice would dance as she recounted a favorite recipe, and once again I'd be a teenage girl perched on the counter next to the stove, listening with only half an ear as she imparted the *kotsu* of a dish.

The kotsu is the secret step, the key ingredient that makes a recipe special, that takes it beyond the ordinary. *"Ginger take smell away."* Learning the kotsu was the point of every lesson. No cook parts easily with her trove of secrets; that's why they are passed down from mother to daughter, to be kept like jewels within the family.

Only I've been careless. On my twentieth birthday, my mother gave me a perfect set of pearls, her mother's before they were hers. I've locked the pearls away in a velvet-lined box, terrified at the thought of losing them. The kotsu I've always tossed in the junk drawer of my head, confident there were more where they came from. I was half right: There will always be more to learn. There will not always be someone around to teach me.

Listening for my mother's breath above the drum of rain, I

realize I am shaking with panic. I am turning my memory upside down, frantic, searching for the lessons I may have lost, grieving for the ones I may never get.

"Why you cry?" asks my mother. She has shuffled unsteadily to the stove and is lifting the lid off the mackerel. She sniffs the steam that whooshes up at her face. "You get it right."

Farewell, My Kitchen

by Deb Barshafsky
from *Augusta*

Home may or may not be where the heart is, but it's where we cook, whether we know how to or not. In this valedictory essay, *Augusta* magazine columnist Deb Barshafsky pays tribute to how a house becomes a home.

As I write this column, I'm less than two weeks away from a move across town. While I adore my old house, a tiny 60-year-old Kings Woods cottage, I'll leave most of the rooms behind without too much emotional trauma.

My bedroom, for instance, is microscopic. *Adios, adios.* And my closets? I happily bid them *adieu* due to the same spatial inadequacies.

But other features of this little home—the diamond-shaped panes in the front window, the arched entry to the dining room, my fish pond and the grand old oak in the front yard—these will be difficult good-byes. And the most difficult parting of all will be when I bid my kitchen farewell.

I haven't always loved this room. Eight years ago, this kitchen was a country fanatic's dream—country blue countertops, country blue shelves with heart-shaped cutouts, country stencils ("welcome friends") on rickety hand-hewn cabinets and country blue flowered wallpaper.

In addition to the effects of the frightful taste of the previous owners, this kitchen had other problems. The stove was a *Frigidairaus Burnitupus*—a 40-inch, four-eyed dinosaur of an appliance that had two cooking temps: off and incinerate. The door to the laundry room was hung with an inch and a half gap at the top. And you couldn't operate two small appliances simultaneously without blowing a fuse. One person's dream is another person's nightmare, I say.

But with every improvement, I grew a bit more attached to this quirky little room. I tore out the blue shelves. Installed jazzy black-and-white tile countertops. I wallpapered. Feverishly painted the fan blades. Threw in splashes of red—a telephone, a teapot, a strand of chile peppers. And, after 13 or 27 (who's counting?) batches of over-baked nutmeg cookies, I finally mastered the thermostatic idiosyncrasies of the stove.

The capstone of my kitchen bonding experience occurred just last year when I undertook a two- to three-day "minor" renovation project. (Lesson No. 1: Nothing about renovations is minor.) This really wasn't anything too industrious—just your standard cabinet refacing and construction of a basic pantry. No bells. No whistles. One carpenter, one quick job. This small project evolved into a textbook example of "renovation creep"—you know, no small home improvement ends without first leading to a half-dozen others.

It all started innocently enough. I mean, with these new cabinets, how good is that old clunker of a stove going to look? The answer to that question led to a cabinet alteration that led to another cabinet alteration that led to a tile alteration that required a chisel and hammer, removal of the sink and a little rearranging of phone and electrical lines.

The phone guy ran a new line and broke my attic stairs. No extra charge for that. (Lesson No. 2: The weight warnings on drop-down attic stairs really do mean something.) While the electrician was here, a bolt of lightning passed through my house, blue streak and all. Mother Nature fried the electrician's nerves, one lamp, one motion detector and all my phone lines, which, of course, necessitated a visit from yet another phone guy—this one well within the weight limits of the attic stairs. The proverbial icing on the cake was the inexplicable disappearance of my plumber before the reinstallation of my sink, which left me washing pots and pans in the backyard like a hillbilly for an entire weekend.

This "minor" renovation lasted more than two weeks and ended up including 11 (ELEVEN!!) different workers. I know that this "minor" inconvenience was a good investment. I did my research (see below, day job). "Minor" kitchen renovations in the Southern region garner a 92 percent return on the investment, according to *Remodeling Magazine*'s "2000—-2001 Cost vs. Value Report."

Even so, after the great outdoor pot-scrubbing adventure, I didn't possess the mental capacity or physical stamina to address any other kitchen issues, aesthetic or otherwise. Therefore, the floor remains unstripped and unrefinished. The beadboard never made it to the walls. The door to the laundry room? Still crooked. And the simultaneous toasting, microwaving and blending problem? Never resolved. Nonetheless, I love these imperfect four walls and all the memories they hold.

Perhaps my greatest attachment to this kitchen is that here, in front of that battle-ax of a stove, I learned to cook. My culinary past, pre-this kitchen, is a checkered one, consisting of one dreadful bologna noodle casserole that even the dog wouldn't eat, one visually repulsive meat loaf and a steady diet of pasta shells doused in ranch dressing. But this kitchen . . . this is where I finally learned something about cooking—that a recipe is a guide, not a dictate, that blending hot liquids is an art form, that a roux isn't all that mysterious. In this kitchen, I learned to make omelets, peel tomatoes and dice onions faster than most people can spell cat.

I've had great successes in this kitchen. I nailed lemon gelati on my first attempt; served it in lemon peels garnished with mint from my garden. I perfected upside-down pineapple parfaits. And I experimented with my mother's recipe for potato salad until I made it my very own.

But I've also had disasters of monumental proportions. And this kitchen is my witness. My orzo pudding (God rest its gooey soul), my étoufée (doomed from the very start) and my now legendary "tannies" (brownies that were neither brown nor edible).

When I look around this room, moving boxes collecting in the corners like spiders, I think of these triumphs and defeats. But I realize that this room is important to me not simply because I cooked here but because I lived here. I laughed here, cried here, cussed here.

There, through that window, I watched eight seasons of ruby-throated hummingbirds dodge and dart around the feeder. My dog, Honey, spent eight of her 14 years lazing under this table while I worked, in her estimation, to earn money for milk bones. By that sink, I stood elbow-to-elbow with good friends, washing the Fiestaware after evenings brimming with fun and fellowship. I sat right there, leaning against the fridge, as two of my buddies made a poultice out of meat tenderizer for a wasp sting on my knee (see above, cussing; see also, blue streak). I learned my aunt had cancer, talking on that red phone while chopping veggies for stir-fry. And, here, at this table, sitting on this little plank-bottomed chair, I've written every one of my columns for this magazine.

My next dispatch, dear readers, will be pecked out from new digs. "Minor" kitchen renovations are scheduled to begin the day after I close on the house. The linoleum floor? History. Those light fixtures? They, too, have to go. And the brassy cabinet hardware? It will disappear as soon as I manage to locate brushed nickel fusilli drawer pulls with three-inch centers. They'll remind me of this place.

Farewell, my kitchen. I'll miss every crazy, quirky thing about you. But I'm packing your most valuable lesson (Lesson No. 3) and taking it with me: Embrace your kitchen and your kitchen will embrace you.

acknowledgments

We gratefully acknowledge all those who gave permission for written material to appear in this book. We have made every effort to trace and contact copyright holders. If an error or omission is brought to our notice we will be pleased to remedy the situation in future editions of this book. For further information, please contact the publisher.

"Toro, Toro, Toro" by Jeffrey Steingarten. Copyright © 2000 by Jeffrey Steingarten. Originally published in *Vogue* Magazine, and reprinted by their kind permission. ✤ "The Secret Garden: Cosentino's Tiny Orchard Yields Forgotten Fruit that 'Eats Good'" by Geoffrey Tomb. Copyright © 2000 by Geoffrey Tomb. Reprinted by permission of The San Jose Mercury News. ✤ "Hadley Grass" by David Nussbaum. Copyright © 2001 by World Publications. Used by permission of *Saveur* Magazine. Appeared in *Saveur*, April 2001. ✤ "Crunch" by Dorothy Kalins. Copyright © 2000 by World Publications. Used by permission of *Saveur* Magazine. Appeared in *Saveur*, July/August 2000. ✤ "Ode on a Can of Tuna" by James Villas. Copyright © 2001 by James Villas. Reprinted by permsision of the author. *Bon Appetit* is a registered trademark of Advance Magazine Publishers, Inc., published through its division, The Conde Nast Publications Inc. Copyright © 2001 by Conde Nast Publications Inc. Reprinted with permission. ✤ "The White Album" by Allan Brown. Copyright © 2000 Conde Nast Publications. All Rights Reserved. Originally published in *Gourmet*. Reprinted by permission. ✤ "Secrets of Saffron" by Pat Willard. Copyright © 2001 by Pat Willard. Reprinted by permission of Beacon Press. ✤ "The Kitchen That Could" by Bryan Miller. Copyright © 2000 by Bryan Miller. Reprinted by permission from *Food & Wine*

sion of Penguin Putnam. ❖ "A Chef's Eye View of Dining Out" by Bill St. John. Copyright © 2001 by Bill St. John. Reprinted by permission of *The Denver Post*. ❖ "Food for the Crew" by Greg Atkinson. Copyright © 2001 by Greg Atkinson. Reprinted by permission of the author. ❖ "Another Roadside Attraction" from *A Goose in Toulouse and Other Culinary Adventures in France* by Mort Rosenblum. Copyright © 2000 by Mort Rosenblum. Reprinted by permission of Hyperion. ❖ "When the Sea Reaches for the Sky: A Favorite of France Seduces New York" by Amanda Hesser. Copyright © 2001 by The New York Times Agency. Reprinted by permission of The New York Times Agency. ❖ "Gold Plate Special" by Gael Greene. Copyright © 2000 by Gael Greene. Reprinted by permission of the author. ❖ From *Me Talk Pretty One Day* by David Sedaris. Copyright © 2000 by David Sedaris. By permission of Little, Brown and Company (Inc.). ❖ "Pocketful of Dough" by Bruce Feiler. Copyright © 2000 by Bruce Feiler. Reprinted by permission of the author. ❖ "The Döner Party" by Jeffrey Eugenides. Reprinted by permission from *Food & Wine* magazine, © December 2000. American Express Publishing. All rights reserved. Reprinted by permission from *Food & Wine* magazine and by Janklow & Nesbit. ❖ "Paris Throught Yam-Colored Glasses" by John T. Edge. Copyright © 2001 by John T. Edge. Reprinted by permission of the author. ❖ "Desperately Seeking Ceviche" by Calvin Trillin. Originally appeared in *Gourmet*. Copyright © 2000 by Calvin Trillin. Reprinted by permission of Lescher & Lescher. ❖ "A Copenhagen Christmas" by Raphael Kadushin. Copyright © 2000 by Raphael Kadushin. Reprinted with permission of *Bon Appetit* and by the author. ❖ Excerpt from *Snail Eggs and Samphire* by Derek Cooper. Copyright © 2000 by Derek Cooper. Reprinted by permission of Macmillan, London, England. ❖ "Organic? Why Has It Become a Dirty Word?" by Tamasin Day Lewis. Copyright © 2001 by Tamasin Day Lewis. Reprinted by permission of the author. Originally appeared in *The London*